T0228064

Real Sound Synthesis
for Interactive Applications

Real Sound Synthesis for Interactive Applications

Perry R. Cook

CRC Press
Taylor & Francis Group
Boca Raton London New York

CRC Press is an imprint of the
Taylor & Francis Group, an **informa** business

AN A K PETERS BOOK

Editorial, Sales, and Customer Service Office

CRC Press
Taylor & Francis Group
6000 Broken Sound Parkway NW, Suite 300
Boca Raton, FL 33487-2742

First issued in hardback 2017

CRC Press is an imprint of Taylor & Francis Group, an Informa business

No claim to original U.S. Government works

ISBN-13: 978-1-56881-168-0 (pbk)
ISBN-13: 978-1-138-42811-9 (hbk)

This book contains information obtained from authentic and highly regarded sources. Reasonable efforts have been made to publish reliable data and information, but the author and publisher cannot assume responsibility for the validity of all materials or the consequences of their use. The authors and publishers have attempted to trace the copyright holders of all material reproduced in this publication and apologize to copyright holders if permission to publish in this form has not been obtained. If any copyright material has not been acknowledged please write and let us know so we may rectify in any future reprint.

Except as permitted under U.S. Copyright Law, no part of this book may be reprinted, reproduced, transmitted, or utilized in any form by any electronic, mechanical, or other means, now known or hereafter invented, including photocopying, microfilming, and recording, or in any information storage or retrieval system, without written permission from the publishers.

For permission to photocopy or use material electronically from this work, please access www.copyright.com (http://www.copyright.com/) or contact the Copyright Clearance Center, Inc. (CCC), 222 Rosewood Drive, Danvers, MA 01923, 978-750-8400. CCC is a not-for-profit organization that provides licenses and registration for a variety of users. For organizations that have been granted a photocopy license by the CCC, a separate system of payment has been arranged.

Trademark Notice: Product or corporate names may be trademarks or registered trademarks, and are used only for identification and explanation without intent to infringe.

Library of Congress Cataloging-in-Publication Data

Cook, Perry R.
    Real sound synthesis for interactive applications / Perry R. Cook.
       p. cm.
    Includes bibliographical references and index.
    ISBN 1-56881-168-3
    1. Sound–Recording and reproducing–Digital techniques. 2. Computer sound processing.
    3. Interactive multimedia. I. Title.

    TK7881.4 .C666 2002
    621.389'3–dc21

                                      2002021546

Visit the Taylor & Francis Web site at
http://www.taylorandfrancis.com

and the CRC Press Web site at
http://www.crcpress.com

Contents

Introduction

If you're like most people, you haven't thought much about the digital synthesis of sound. If you have thought about sound, or even worked with sound on computers, you still might think that sound is something that you record, or get from a CD, or off the Web, and then manipulate to get the desired result. But there are means and methods to truly "synthesize" sound using physical models, by modeling the actual processes that make sound in nature. You might ask, "Isn't synthesizing sound from physics computationally expensive?" Actually, both old and recent theories in acoustics—combined with algorithmic advances in digital signal processing, and of course, faster processors—now allow many types of sound-producing systems to be physically modeled in real time.

It seems reasonable to ask why all of our requirements could not be satisfied by the status quo in "synthesis" based on prerecorded sounds. Also called *Pulse Code Modulation* (PCM), sampling, or wavetable synthesis, much effort has been spent on making sample-based synthesis more expressive. Using multiple recordings, filters, and various interpolation methods to traverse the space of possible sounds, the state of the art has indeed advanced to the point of absolute realism, at least for single sounds triggered only once. To have truly realistic continuously interactive sound synthesis, however, essentially infinite memory would be required to store all possible samples. The equivalent of a truly exhaustive physical model would have to be computed in order to determine which subset of the samples and parameters would be required to generate the correct output sound. Finally, the requirement that the correct samples be loaded and available to the synthesis engine would tax any foreseeable real-time sound hardware/ software systems.

As an example, imagine a "Virtual Reality Wood Shop" or a "Virtual Kitchen" controlled by *Virtual Reality* (VR) controllers such as sensor gloves and haptic (combined senses of touch, position, and movement) force feedback devices. As sound designers, our required task might be to ensure that the various tools each make realistic sounds when manipulated, such that a user cannot detect (by audition) a difference between the real and virtual worlds. A frightening number of recorded samples would be required to realistically and responsively synthesize a wood saw, hammer, wrenches, etc., or whisking, mixing, frying, cutting, and all of the other everyday devices and interactions in these environments. The act of striking an object, then restriking it while it still resonates (hammering a nail into a large board, for example) causes changes in the sound that could only be predicted by an actual physical model of the system in question.

Even without the stringent requirement of sonic perfection, it is still scientifically and artistically interesting to inspect, measure, and simulate the physics of sound-producing objects. The computer graphics and animated movie communities march bravely ahead with more elaborate and realistic models for human, dinosaur, and other motion, and though the results are still not absolutely real, large industries have been built on using graphics models for movie and commercial production.

A staple of production for movies, stage performance, television, and radio dramas is the (often last minute) addition of artificial and natural sound effects. For movies, "Foley" artists put shoes on their hands and "walk" in boxes of gravel, leaves, cornstarch (for the sound of snow), and other materials in real time, effectively acting the sounds as they watch the scenes over and over. Radio and stage sound effects performers/engineers use tape cartridges or CDs of prerecorded sounds, and physical noisemakers to add sounds in real time. For offline production and real-time dramas, these methods might indeed be the best means to add sounds. However, virtual reality, training simulations, and games are real-time computer-mediated interactive applications. The computer, not a human, is responsible for providing the sounds algorithmically, in response to external (sensors) and internal (simulations) variables. Thus, achieving the best sonic quality and responsiveness for such applications is basically impossible by simply playing back prerecorded sounds.

If we think about our interactions with sound-producing objects in the world, we note that we excite these objects with a variety of other objects, and in a wide variety of ways. Walking, preparing food, working with metal and wood tools, and riding a bicycle all create sounds. Our evolution and experience in the world has trained us to expect certain sonic responses from certain input gestures and parameters. For example, hitting something harder causes the sound not only to increase in power, but to change in sound "quality" as well. Rubbing a flat object on its edge causes different sonic results than scraping it in the center. In beginning to develop a taxonomy of interactive sounds, a list of the sound-producing interactions under our control would be helpful. These would include:

· blowing (voice, whistles, wind instruments, etc.)
· striking, plucking, etc.
· rubbing, scraping, stroking, bowing, etc.

That this is such a short list seems surprising, but it is instructive. To arrive at a more subtle classification of sounds requires looking at sound-producing mechanisms as well as the human gestures that initiate and control sound. Of course, that is exactly what this book is about: Looking at the physics of sound production and how we cause objects to make sound. Some objects exhibit strong ringing resonances (metal, glass, tubes, plates, and musical instruments). Others are characterized as noisy, but have too much structure to be modeled by just simple noise. We will develop techniques and tools for analyzing and synthesizing sounds, looking at a wide variety of methods. In the process, we will learn about *Digital Signal Processing* (DSP), *Fourier analysis*, and the general nature of sounds in the world. The goal is to come up with simple, physical (or physically motivated), and parametric models for sound synthesis. We will define a *parametric model* as one that has a few variable parameters that can be manipulated to change the interaction, object, and sound.

In the process of designing and calibrating a parametric model, we often learn a lot about the system, and we also can achieve significant compression (data reduction) over the raw sound itself. Thus, one clear benefit of parametrized sound analysis/synthesis is the possibility of significantly reducing the memory storage required for a large library of digital sound effects. Even greater benefits, however, include the ability to drive the synthesis in real time from parameters generated by sensors, game simulations, animations, and other interactive applications. The flexibility and expressiveness offered by parametric modeling makes it attractive for music composition and performance, simulation in virtual reality, computer games, interactive arts projects, human-computer interfaces, and for other real-time systems where believable sonic responses to user inputs are necessary or desired.

In this book, environmental background sounds (those produced without our own actions and interactions) could be discussed as well. Such sounds would include rain, wind, animal sounds (at least those animals that are not reacting to our presence), trucks and cars, other industrial sounds, and the sounds of humans (again, those not reacting to us). But these sounds do not respond instantly to our actions, and thus have less stringent requirements for simulation. This is not to say that we do not notice if things aren't right in the background sound, and many of the techniques we'll talk about could be directly applicable to background sounds. However, we're not going to deal directly with background sounds here, instead concentrating our focus on interactive sounds.

Thus motivated by scientific, commercial, and artistic interest, and informed by thinking a little about both physical gestures and sound production mechanisms, we will dive into the structure of the book, with some tips on reading it and using materials at http://www.akpeters.com/rss/ to supplement the reading.

Reading Strategy

Since sounds in the real world are made by physical processes, this book will take a physics-based perspective wherever possible. The book is intended for technical, semi-technical and aspiring technical people who know some physics, some programming, and some math. None of these technical skills are specifically required to understand much of what we'll talk about here.

We will present a variety of techniques, ending in Chapter 16 (Examples, Systems, and Applications) with a discussion of practical applications and scenarios. I recommend that you start by scanning Chapter 16, and then come back and start with Chapter 1. I know the world is divided into two types of readers. One type of reader reads the last chapter of any book first, to decide whether to read the book at all, and to break the tension of waiting to see how things come out. The other type of reader views it as almost immoral to learn the surprise before it is time. But for this book, I really do recommend checking out the last chapter, then reading the whole book. The final chapter will first set the stage for reading the book, and will be even more meaningful on the second reading after having learned about sound synthesis.

At the end of every chapter is a short list of recommended reference readings. These lists by no means represent complete sets of references in the various topic areas. Rather, I have tried to glean out the two or so main references on each topic, in case you want to go search and get a better understanding. Perhaps the most exhaustive and math-intensive reference on physical sound modeling is currently being written by Julius O. Smith. This very large book is not available yet, but in a wonderful move toward open publication, his book is on the web as it is being developed. The topics and techniques of Smith's web book are searchable as well, so I would recommend you check out his web book for extra in-depth reading related to many of the topics in this book.

http://www-ccrma.stanford.edu/~jos/waveguide/

Every chapter in my book also has a list of code examples that illustrate and implement the concepts and techniques that are covered. Many of the examples for the book were generated directly from this code. Some of these are simple stand-alone ANSI C programs that run in a command line and generate a sound file. Others are fairly elaborate C++ projects with real-time synthesis controlled by MIDI and/or Graphical User Interfaces. All of this code, plus much more, can be found at http://www.akpeters.com/rss/. I encourage you to check out the code while you're reading. Appendix D lists and describes the code. Appendix E is a short introductory article on the Synthesis Toolkit in C++, a large collection of classes and applications for real-time sound synthesis.

Every chapter also ends with a list of sound examples from http://www.akpeters.com/rss/. Whenever you're reading along and see an icon like this

$$(\!(\langle \# \rangle)\!)_,$$

that means that there is a sound example on the Web site that pertains to the current topic. The first segment is an audio segment. I encourage you to listen to the sound examples as you read along. Appendix D lists and describes these sound files.

Appendices A, B, and C present mathematical material not covered in the chapters. You are encouraged to refer to those appendices when they are mentioned in the text.

Chapters 1 and 2 look at PCM sampling and define some terms and fundamentals of dealing with recorded digital sound. In those chapters we will also look at problems and issues with working with prerecorded sounds, to further motivate why we want to dig deeper into the physics of sound production.

Chapter 3 dives into the heart of *Digital Signal Processing* (DSP), covering digital filters. If this chapter bores or scares you, you could skip it, but digital filter theory forms the basis of our efficient physical modeling algorithms, so

I do recommend reading as much of Chapter 3 as you can. You should at least understand the concept of linearity before moving ahead.

With Chapter 4, our development of physical modeling really gets underway. By analyzing and simulating a very simple physical mass/spring/damper system, we get our first look at oscillation and sine waves. Synthesizing sounds by adding together sinusoidal modes is introduced, as our first real parametric synthesis method.

Once we know that sine waves arise out of physical vibrations, Chapter 5 looks more at the math of sine waves, and introduces the powerful tool of Fourier analysis. We will see that the *spectrum* (energy in a sound broken up by different frequencies) is a powerful perception-related tool for analyzing and understanding sounds. Appendix A has proofs, theorems, and some other thoughts on Fourier analysis.

Chapter 6 looks further at using the Fourier analysis spectrum as a sound analysis tool. The techniques of spectral modeling are introduced, breaking up sounds into important perceptual and physical components.

Chapter 7 looks at breaking up the spectrum into fairly wide bands, extracting information (parameters) from those bands, and using those parameters to modify and "sculpt" sounds.

Chapter 8 deals with a topic that combines pure mathematics, digital filters, and physical models. Linear prediction is developed and applied to various physical systems such as the human voice, hammering a nail, and a guitar body.

Chapter 9 looks at one of the most fundamental physical vibration systems, the plucked/struck string. We develop an increasingly more realistic, yet still computationally efficient, series of models of plucked and bowed string instruments. Appendix B has derivations and proofs related to the plucked string.

Chapter 10 looks at a family of phenomena that make sonic life very lively. Nonlinearity (you'll have to read Chapter 3 and 10 to get what this really means) is investigated and modeled.

Chapter 11 looks at sounds produced by air in tubes and cavities. We develop some simple, but amazingly rich, models of a clarinet and a blown pop bottle. Appendix C has derivations and proofs related to acoustic tubes.

Chapter 12 deals with physical modeling of plates, membranes, bowls, cups, and other high-dimensional geometric structures.

Chapter 13 looks at sonic "particles" as the fundamental unit of sound production, examining wavetables, physical particle-controlled sinusoidal synthesis, and noise/filter-based statistical synthesis of noisy sounds.

Chapter 14 deals with plucking, striking, bowing, and rubbing excitations for physical models. Friction is discussed at length. MIDI and other protocols for controlling physical models are discussed. Finally, some custom-built physical modeling synthesis controllers are shown.

Chapter 15 describes a complete signal processing system for analyzing and synthesizing the sounds of walking.

Chapter 16 looks at applications for parametric sound synthesis, including user-interfaces, data sonification, digital Foley, virtual reality, augmented reality, computer music, interactive art, animation, and gaming. The chapter concludes with thoughts on the future of parametric digital sound synthesis.

Acknowledgements

There are scores of people who had major influences on this book being created in the first place, and in it coming to completion. Certainly I must credit and thank the music DSP researchers at Stanford's Center for Computer Research in Music and Acoustics (CCRMA), specifically Julius O. Smith, John Chowning, Chris Chafe, Xavier Serra, Gary Scavone, and lots of others who were around during the exciting development of DSP-based physical modeling. I am grateful for being able to teach the yearly CCRMA summer DSP courses, where I first began to sketch out the chapters and topics for this book. I also thank the students of those courses for asking great questions. I thank Paul Lansky and Ken Steiglitz for recruiting me to Princeton, and getting me to teach the wonderful undergrad Music/DSP course ("Transforming Reality Through Computers") that they had created. I thank the students of Spring 2001 Princeton COS/MUS325 for their reading and use of the preliminary chapters of this book. I thank the researchers at Interval Research for helping support some of my work, and for giving me a wonderful environment in which to hang out for short periods. Specifically I thank Bob Adams, Bill Verplank, Malcolm Slaney, Geoff Smith, Dan Levitan, and many others. For careful reading and criticisms, I thank Georg Essl, Georgos Tzanetakis, Ge Wang, Tae Hong Park, and Liz Douthitt. Thanks to Georg, Georgos, and James O'Brien for recent collaborations on sound synthesis and analysis. Thanks to Gary Scavone for his energy and persistence in pushing the Synthesis ToolKit forward. Thanks to Steve Lakatos for great collaborations on sound perception. Thanks to Dan Trueman and Curtis Bahn for founding and advancing the sensor-enhanced spherical speaker instrument cult. And thanks to many others for long conversations on the topics of digeridoos, dulcimers, and djembes, on prayer bowls, guitars, and accordions, and so many other aspects of the wonderful world of sound.

Development of this book and some of the algorithms described therein was funded in part by gifts from Intel, Interval Research, and the Arial Foundation, and by grants from the National Science Foundation (Grant # 9984087) and The New Jersey Council on Science and Technology (Grant # 01-2042-007-22).

Digital Audio Signals

1.0 Introduction

This chapter will introduce some basics of digital audio. Sampling, quantization, interpolation for sample-rate conversion and pitch shifting, and some basics of audio compression will be covered. The main purpose of this book is to derive and use techniques for generating digital audio samples directly from physical models. But in doing this we will also be analyzing and manipulating digital audio signals from recordings. Some of the models we develop will be based on the analysis of sampled sounds, and all of the models are based on digital audio fundamentals, so it is important to start out with an understanding of the basics of sampling and digital signals.

1.1 Digital Audio Signals

Typically, digital audio signals are formed by *sampling* analog (continuous in time and amplitude) signals at regular intervals in time, and then *quantizing* the amplitudes to discrete values. The time between successive samples is usually denoted as T. Sampling an analog signal requires holding the value steady for a period while a stable measurement can be made, then associating

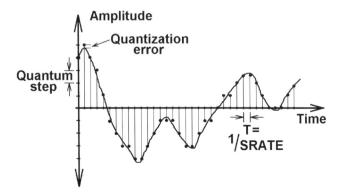

Figure 1.1. Linear sampling and quantization.

the analog value with a digital number (coding). Analog signals can have any of the infinity of real (float) amplitude values. Digital signals can only have a finite number of amplitude values. In converting from analog to digital, rounding takes place and a given analog value must be quantized to the nearest digital value. In the case of rounding down, or truncation, the analog value is quantized to the next lower digital value. The difference between quantization steps is called the quantum. Sampling and quantization is shown in Figure 1.1. Note the errors introduced in some sample values due to the quantization process.

The process of sampling a waveform, holding the value, and quantizing the value to the nearest number that can be digitally represented (as a specific integer on a finite range of integers) is called *Analog to Digital* (A to D, or A/D) conversion. A device which does A/D conversion is called an *Analog to Digital Converter* (ADC). Coding and representing waveforms in sampled digital form is called *Pulse Code Modulation* (PCM), and digital audio signals are often called PCM audio. The corresponding process of converting a sampled signal back into an analog signal is called *Digital to Analog Conversion* (D to A, or D/A), and the device is called a *Digital to Analog Converter* (DAC). Low pass filtering (smoothing the samples to remove unwanted high frequencies) is necessary to reconstruct the sampled signal back into a smooth, continuous time analog signal. This filtering is usually contained in the DAC hardware.

1.2 Sampling and Aliasing

A fundamental law of digital signal processing states that if an analog signal is bandlimited with bandwidth B Hz (Hz = Hertz = samples per second), the signal can be periodically sampled at a rate of $2B$ Hz, and exactly reconstructed from the samples. Bandlimited with bandwidth B means that no frequencies above B exist in the signal. The rate $2B$ is called the Nyquist rate, and B is called the Nyquist frequency. Intuitively, a sine wave at the highest frequency B present in a bandlimited signal can be represented using two samples per period (one sample at each of the positive and negative peaks), corresponding to a sampling frequency of $2B$. All signal components at lower frequencies can be uniquely represented and distinguished from each other using this same sampling frequency of $2B$. If there are components present in a signal at frequencies greater than half the sampling rate, these components will not be represented properly, and will "alias" as frequencies different from their true original values. To avoid aliasing, ADC hardware often includes filters that limit the bandwidth of the incoming signal before sampling takes place, automatically changing as a function of the selected sampling rate. Figure 1.2 shows aliasing in complex and simple (sinusoidal) waveforms. Note the loss of details in the complex waveform. Also note that samples at less than two times the frequency of a sine wave could also have arisen from a sine wave of much lower frequency. That is the fundamental nature of aliasing, because higher frequencies "alias" as lower frequencies.

    Humans can perceive frequencies from roughly 20 Hz to 20 kHz, thus requiring a minimum sampling rate of at least 40 kHz. Speech signals are often sampled at 8 kHz ("telephone quality") or 11.025 kHz, while music is usually sampled at 22.05 kHz, 44.1 kHz (the sampling rate used on audio Compact Disks), or 48 kHz. New and proposed formats use sampling rates of 96 kHz, and 192 kHz. I consider these ultra-high sampling rates to be generally

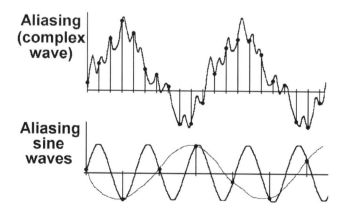

Figure 1.2. Because of inadequate sampling rate, aliasing causes important features to be lost.

quite wasteful (unless you're a dolphin). Extra bits could be much better spent to allow for more quantization levels (see next section), as in 24-bit sampling standards. Even though a roughly 96 dB *Signal-to-Noise Ratio* (see next section) enabled by 16 bits is probably sufficient perceptually, having another eight bits of "headroom" for recording, mixing, and processing is helpful in avoiding overload. For virtual reality, entertainment, and gaming applications, it seems reasonable to allocate more bits to extra channels and speakers, rather than spending them on ultra-high sample rates. In many of the examples in this book, a sampling rate of 22050 Hz is used, to provide adequate quality while conserving processor power and memory.

1.3 Quantization

In a digital system, a fixed number of *binary digits* (bits) are used to represent numbers that approximate the actual values of the samples of the analog waveform. This quantization is accomplished either by rounding to the quantum value nearest the actual analog value (see Figure 1.1), or by truncation to the nearest quantum value less than or equal to the actual analog value. With uniform sampling in time, a properly bandlimited signal can be exactly recovered provided that the sampling rate is twice the bandwidth or greater, but only if there is no quantization. When the signal values are rounded or truncated, the amplitude difference between the original signal and the quantized signal is lost forever. This can be viewed as a noise component upon reconstruction (see Figure 1.3). A common analytical technique assumes that the discarded signal component is uniformly distributed randomly at +/– half the quantum for quantization by rounding, or from zero to the quantum for quantization by truncation.

Using the additive noise assumption gives an approximate best-case *Quantization Signal-to-Noise Ratio* (SNR) of 6N dB, where N is the number

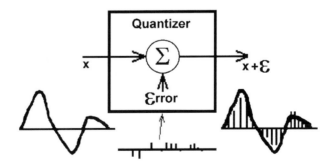

Figure 1.3. Quantization shown as an additive noise signal.

of bits. A dB is a decibel, defined as $20\log_{10}$ (highest amplitude/lowest amplitude). This SNR can be derived from assuming a square wave at maximum amplitude, which exhibits a power (power is defined as the sum of the squares of signal values) of

$$2^{N-1} \cdot 2^{N-1} = 2^{2N-2} \cong 4^N$$

and uniform random quantization noise of 1/2 bit average amplitude, which exhibits power of 1/12 (look this up in a statistics textbook as the variance of a uniform distribution). Yes, one would not find a constant amplitude square wave exhibiting random quantization noise, but play along here for the purposes of the derivation.

$$\text{SNR} = 10\log_{10}[4^N/(1/12)] = 10N\log_{10}(4) + C = N \cdot 6.0206 + C$$

Using the above approximations implies that a system using 16-bit linear quantization will exhibit an SNR of approximately 96 dB. 8-bit quantization exhibits a signal to quantization noise of approximately 48 dB. Each extra bit improves the SNR by about 6 dB.

Most computer audio systems use two or three types of audio data words. 16-bit (per channel) data is quite common, and this is the data format used in Compact Disk systems. 8-bit data is common for speech data in PC and telephone systems. There are also methods of quantization that are non linear, meaning that the quantum is not constant over the range of input signal values. In these systems, the quantum is smaller for small amplitudes, and larger for large amplitudes. This nonlinear quantization will be discussed more in Section 1.5.1.

1.4 Resampling and Interpolation

In order to synthesize music, speech, or sounds in general, accurate and flexible control of pitch is necessary. The most accurate pitch control is necessary for music synthesis. In sampling synthesis, this is accomplished by dynamic sample rate conversion (interpolation). In order to convert a sampled data signal from one sampling rate to another, three steps are required: *bandlimiting, interpolation, and resampling*.

Bandlimiting: First, it must be assured that the original signal was properly bandlimited to less than half the new sampling rate. This is always true when "upsampling" (converting from a lower sampling rate to a higher one). When "downsampling," however, the signal must be first low pass filtered to exclude frequencies greater than half the new target rate.

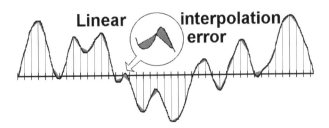

Figure 1.4. Gray regions show errors due to linear interpolation.

Interpolation: When resampling by any but trivial factors such as 2, ½, ¼, etc., the task requires computing the values of the original bandlimited analog signal at the correct points between the existing sampled points. This is called interpolation. The most common form of interpolation used is linear interpolation, where the fractional time samples needed are computed as a linear combination of the two surrounding samples. Many assume that linear interpolation is the correct means, or at least an adequate means for accomplishing audio sample rate conversion. Figure 1.4 shows resampling by linear interpolation. Note the errors shown by the shaded regions.

Some might notice that linear interpolation isn't quite adequate, so they might assume that the correct solution must lie in more elaborate curve-fitting techniques using quadratics, cubics, or higher order splines. Actually the task should be viewed and accomplished as a filtering problem, with the filter designed to meet some appropriate error criterion. As we will see in Chapter 3, linear time-invariant filtering can be accomplished by "convolution" with a filter function. If the resampling filter is defined appropriately, we can exactly reconstruct the original analog waveform from the samples.

The "correct" (ideal in a provable digital signal processing sense) way to perform interpolation is convolution with the sinc function, defined as:

$$\text{sinc}(t/T) = \sin(\pi t/T)/(\pi t/T), \text{ where } T = 1/\text{SRATE}.$$

The sinc function is the ideal low pass filter with a cutoff frequency of SRATE/2. Figure 1.5 shows reconstruction of a continuous waveform by convolution of a digital signal with the sinc function. All samples are multiplied by a corresponding continuous sinc function, and added up to arrive at the continuous reconstructed signal.

Resampling: This is usually accomplished at the same time as interpolation, because it is not necessary to reconstruct the entire continuous waveform in order to acquire new discrete samples. The resampling ratio can be time-varying, making the problem a little more difficult. However, viewing

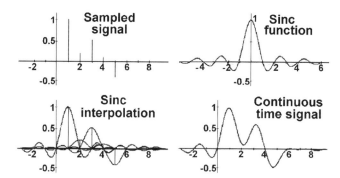

Figure 1.5. Sinc interpolation for reconstruction and resampling.

the problem as a filter-design and implementation issue allows for guaranteed tradeoffs of quality and computational complexity.

1.5 Digital Audio Compression

The data required to store or transmit CD-quality audio at a 44.1 kHz sampling rate, in stereo (two channels, left and right), and at 16 bits, is 176 kbytes per second. For storage, this means that a three minute song requires 30 megabytes of storage. For transmission, this means that an ISDN line at 128 kbits per second is over ten times too slow to carry uncompressed CD-quality audio. When using PCM to synthesize a large variety of sounds for games or virtual reality, storage and access can quickly become a consideration. Audio compression, as with any type of data compression, strives to reduce the amount of data required to store and/or transmit the audio. Compression algorithms can be either lossless (meaning that the original data can be retrieved exactly from the compressed data), as they must be for computer text and critical data files, or lossy, as they usually are for images and audio.

1.5.1 μ-Law Compression

Rather than using a linear quantization scheme, non linear quantization can be used to try to keep a more constant quantization noise, with respect to the amplitude of the signal. Figure 1.6 depicts simple non linear quantization.

The most common system for nonlinear quantization is called μ-law (mu law), which uses 8 nonlinear bits to achieve the same approximate SNR as 12-bit linear quantization. Nonlinear quantization is used in telephone systems, where 8-bit μlaw at 8 kHz is used to transmit speech over a standard US digital phone line. 8-bit μlaw decoding is easily accomplished with a

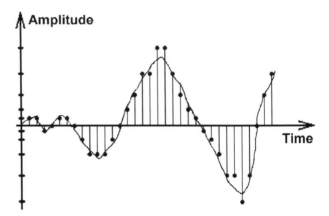

Figure 1.6. Nonlinear waveform quantization.

256 point lookup table, by storing 256 16-bit short integers for reconstruction to the standard 16-bit linear format. Since the quantization noise is related to the size of the quantum, having a small quantum ensures small quantization noise, and an improved signal-to-noise ratio for small amplitude signals. For large amplitude signals, the quantum is large, but the SNR is held relatively constant. A common metric applied to nonlinear μ-Law sampling is that N bits performs roughly as well as $N+4$ linearly quantized bits. 8-bit μ-Law is common for speech coding and transmission, providing 2:1 compression over 16-bit linear audio data with a perceptual quality roughly equal to 12-bit linear quantization.

1.5.2 Adaptive Delta Pulse Code Modulation

Adaptive Delta Pulse Code Modulation (ADPCM) endeavors to adaptively change the quantum size to best match the signal. The changes (deltas) in the signal are coded rather than the absolute signal values. For each sample, the change in the signal value versus the last value is computed, this delta is compared to the current adapted delta value, and the new adapted delta value is increased or decreased accordingly. To code ADPCM, the sign of the delta for the given step, and a 3-bit value reflecting the current quantized adapted value are stored. This allows 4 bits of information to store a 16-bit linearly quantized sample value, providing 4:1 compression over 16-bit linear audio data. ADPCM is supported by many multimedia audio systems, but the quality is generally considered too low for music and other quality-critical audio material.

1.5.3 MPEG and Other Frequency Domain (Transform) Compressors

Transform coders endeavor to use information about human perception to selectively quantize regions of the frequency spectrum in order to "hide" the quantization noise in places that the human ear will not detect it. The frequency spectrum will be defined and discussed in Chapter 5. These coders strive for what is often called "perceptual losslessness," meaning that human listeners cannot tell the difference between compressed and uncompressed data.

A transform coder performs frequency analysis using either the Fourier transform, wavelet analysis, a subband filter bank, or a combination of these. The spectral information is inspected to determine the significantly loud features, and masking threshold curves (regions under which a sound could be present and not be detected due to the loudness of a nearby spectral peak) are drawn outward in frequency from these significant peaks. Quantization noise is then "shaped" by allocating bits to sub-band regions, so that the quantization noise lies under the masking threshold curves. These curves dynamically approximate the frequency regions of human hearing where sound components would not likely be heard.

Time masking is also computed, recognizing that weaker auditory events can linger significantly in time (100 ms or so) after a loud event, and can also even precede a loud event by a short time (10 ms or so) without being heard.

Transform coding is used in multimedia standard audio formats such as *Moving Picture Experts Group* (MPEG) and Dolby's AC-2 and AC-3. Such coders can achieve perceptually lossless compression ratios of approximately four or 8:1 on some program material, and even higher compression ratios with some small acceptable degradation. MP3 (actually audio layer 3 of the MPEG-2 specification), compresses 176 kbytes/s of CD quality digital audio into 128 kbits/s, yielding an 11:1 compression ratio.

1.6 Conclusion

We've learned about PCM sampling and quantization of digital audio. A little about interpolation for resampling and sample rate conversion was introduced as well. Compression was introduced, but we won't spend any more time in this book talking about "classical" audio compression algorithms because there are plenty of great references on it. However, many of the concepts we will develop for modeling, manipulating, and synthesizing parametric audio will be directly related to those that have been important for developing compression algorithms. Further, if audio compression is to advance in the future, many people believe that it will be in the area of parametric models of audio sources. So most of the rest of the topics and techniques presented in this book will provide insights and a basis for developing possible future compression algorithms. The next chapter will look at synthesis of audio using recorded PCM waveforms, mostly to point out problems related to this type of synthesis, and to develop some ideas on why parametric audio synthesis is important.

Reading:

Ken Steiglitz. *A Digital Signal Processing Primer: With Applications to Digital Audio and Computer Music.* Menlo Park: Addison Wesley, 1996.

Ken Pohlmann. *Principles of Digital Audio.* New York: McGraw Hill, 2000.

John Watkinson. *Compression in Video and Audio.* Boston: Focal Press, 1995.

Code:

quantize.c

srconvert.c

mulaw.c

demulaw.c

adpcmcod.c

adpcmdec.c

Sounds:

[Track 1] Aliased Speech and Music.

[Track 2] Quantized Speech and Music, Various Resolutions.

[Track 3] Interpolated Speech and Music, Various Methods.

[Track 4] 8-bit MuLaw Compressed Speech and Music.

[Track 5] 4-bit ADPCM Compressed Speech and Music.

[Track 6] MP3 Compressed Speech and Music.

2 Sampling (Wavetable) Synthesis

2.0 Introduction

Chapter 1 covered background on sampling, quantization, compression, and storage of digital PCM sound waveforms. This chapter will introduce some basic aspects of reproducing and modifying PCM sounds. The majority of digital sound and music synthesis today is accomplished via the playback of stored PCM (*Pulse Code Modulation*) waveforms. Single-shot playback of entire segments of stored sounds is common for sound effects, narrations, prompts, musical segments, etc. Most high-quality modern electronic music synthesizers, speech synthesis systems, and PC software systems for sound synthesis use prestored PCM as the basic data. This data is manipulated to yield the final output sound(s). Here we'll look at some of the common manipulations and techniques. We'll also discover some of the problems with using PCM exclusively for interactive expressive audio systems.

2.1 Wavetable Synthesis

For musical sounds, it is common to store just a loop, or table, of the periodic component of a recorded sound waveform and play that loop back repeatedly.

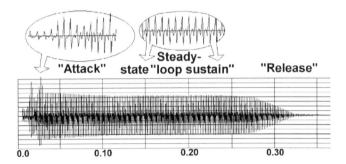

Figure 2.1. Wavetable synthesis of trumpet tone.

This is called *wavetable* synthesis. For more realism, the attack or beginning portion of the recorded sound can be stored in addition to the periodic steady state part. Figure 2.1 shows the synthesis of a trumpet tone starting with an attack segment, followed by repetition of a periodic loop, ending with an enveloped decay (or release). "Envelope" is a synthesizer/computer music term for a time-varying gain change applied to a waveform or other parameter. Envelopes are often described by four components: the *Attack Time;* the *Decay Time* ("decay" here means the initial decay down to the steady state segment); the *Sustain Level;* and the *Release Time* (final decay). Hence, envelopes are sometimes called ADSRs.

Originally called *sampling synthesis* in the music industry, any synthesis using stored PCM waveforms has now become commonly known as *wavetable synthesis.* Filters are usually added to high-quality wavetable synthesis, allowing control of spectral brightness as a function of intensity, and to achieve more variety of sounds from a given set of samples.

2.1.2 Multisampling

Pitch shifting of a PCM sample or wavetable is accomplished via interpolation as discussed in Chapter 1. A given sample can be pitch shifted only so far in either direction before it begins to sound unnatural. This can be dealt with by storing multiple recordings of the sound at different pitches, and switching or interpolating between these upon resynthesis. This is called *multisampling.* Multisampling also might include the storage of separate samples for "loud" and "soft" sounds. Linear interpolation is usually performed between these loudness multisamples as a function of the desired synthesized volume. This is necessary because loudness is not simply a matter of amplitude or power, and most sound sources exhibit spectral variations as a function of loudness. For example, there is usually more high frequency energy, or "brightness" in

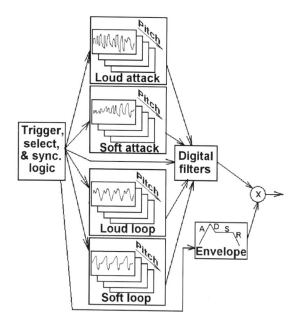

Figure 2.2. Sampling synthesis block diagram.

loud sounds than in soft sounds. Filters can also be used to add spectral control and variation. Figure 2.2 shows a block diagram of a complete sampling synthesizer.

2.2 Concatenative Speech Synthesis

For speech, the most common technique used is a form of wavetable synthesis called *concatenative synthesis*. Concatenative phoneme synthesis relies on the retrieval and concatenation of roughly 40 phonemes (for English). Examples of vowel phonemes are /i/ as in beet, /I/ as in bit, /a/ as in father, etc. Examples of nasals are /m/ as in mom, /n/ as in none, /ng/ as in sing, etc. Examples of fricative consonant phonemes are /s/ as in sit, /ʃ/ as in ship, /f/ as in fifty, etc. Examples of voiced fricative consonants are /z/, /v/, etc. Examples of plosive consonants are /t/ as in tat, /p/ as in pop, /k/ as in kick , etc. Examples of voiced plosives include d, b, g, etc. Vowels and nasals are essentially periodic pitched sounds, so a minimal required stored waveform is only one single period of each. Consonants require more storage because of their noisy nature. Figure 2.3 shows synthesis of the word "synthesize" by the concatenation of the phonemes /s/, /I/, /n/, /th/, /U/, /s/, /a/, /i/, /z/.

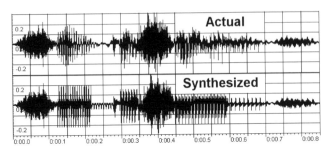

Figure 2.3. Concatenative speech synthesis of the word "synthesize" (lower). The top waveform is an actual recording of the spoken "synthesize."

The quality of concatenative phoneme synthesis is generally considered quite low, due to the simplistic assumption that all of the pitched sounds (vowels, etc.) are purely periodic. Also, simply "gluing" /s/, /I/, and /n/ together does not make for a high quality realistic synthesis of the word "sin." In actual speech, phonemes gradually blend into each other as the jaw, tongue, and other "articulators" move gradually with time (see the upper waveform of Figure 2.3).

Accurately capturing the transitions between phonemes with PCM requires recording transitions from phoneme to phoneme, called *diphones*. A *concatenative diphone synthesizer* blends together stored diphones. Examples of diphones include see, she, thee, and most of the roughly 40×40 possible combinations of phonemes. Much more storage is necessary for a diphone synthesizer, but the resulting increase in quality is significant. As with PCM music synthesis, PCM speech synthesis can be improved further by storing multisamples for different pitch ranges, genders, voice qualities, etc.

2.3 Manipulating PCM

The need and desire to manipulate PCM arises for artistic reasons (music composition, digital DJ and turntable art, sound design for movies and theater, etc.). In games and *Virtual Reality* (VR), the PCM that is available usually does not exactly match the desired application and circumstance. For example, a sound of a squeaking door stored on disk is nearly guaranteed to not be of the correct length, loudness, or character for a given event of a door opening. Even if a sound basically "works" once for the door opening, playing the same identical sound again when the door closes will cue the listener that it's the same identical sound. An even more obvious example might be the sound of a person walking up and down hills of snow, where the sound of each footstep would normally be different from all others. Timing, spectral characteristics, etc., should all be flexible in order to produce convincing, realistic, and artistic interactive sounds.

2.3.1 Pitch Shifting by Sample Rate Conversion

One way to manipulate sound is to modify the pitch by dynamic sample-rate conversion, as discussed in Chapter 1. But pitch shifting has a number of problems, one being that for a generic PCM sample, resampling not only changes the pitch, but also changes time by the same factor. This is just like turning the speed up or down on a mechanical playback device such as a turntable or tape machine. Shifting up by a factor of 20% yields a sound that plays for 20% shorter time. Shifting down by doubling the time results in a sound that has a pitch one octave lower. By the way, an "octave" is a ratio of 2.0 or 0.5 in frequency, such as the space between any two adjacent "C" notes on the piano keyboard. In fact, it's called an "oct"ave because there are a total of eight white keys, or "diatonic notes" contained in an octave.

One problem of shifting the sampling rate of a PCM sound is the intrinsic link between pitch and time. Pitch shifting upward by one octave yields a sound which plays at twice as high a pitch, and for half the time. Another problem is the so-called *munchkinification effect*. This relates to the apparent shift in the perceived sound-producing object when the pitch and time is shifted. For example, the octave-up pitch shift also yields the perception of a talker whose head sounds half the size of a normal person. This other dimension, which has to do with the quality of sounds rather than pitch, loudness, or time, is called *timbre*. Once we've learned more about the frequency domain, we'll have better tools to explain munchkinification and timbre, and we'll also have a lot more tools to avoid (or control independently) all of these dimensions.

2.3.2 Time Shifting by Overlap-Add (OLA)

To devise a way of shifting the playback time of PCM without shifting pitch, we must first resort to a little *PsychoAcoustics*. PsychoAcoustics is the study of how sound stimuli, upon reaching our ears (and possibly our other senses), becomes information that is sensible, musical, threatening, emotionally moving, etc., to our brains. An interesting aspect of perception in audio, visual, and tactile modes is what I like to call "the 30 Hz transition." This refers to the fact that events that repeat, or roughly repeat, at rates much lower than 30 Hz (cycles per second) are perceived as time events. Images flashing at a low rate; a medium speed single-stroke drum roll, or a low frequency periodic pressure on our skin, are all perceived as a series of events occurring in time if they are in the range of 1–20 Hz or so. Events that happen much faster than 30 Hz are perceived quite differently. Video and movie images are flashed every 1/60 of a second, yielding a perception of smooth and flicker-free motion.

As a vibration on the skin increases in frequency toward 100 Hz, it feels more and more like a steady constant pressure. Sound, at frequencies of 35, 60, and 100 Hz, is perceived increasingly as a pitch, and certainly not as individual repetitions of some event in time. The key as to how we might manipulate time in PCM samples without changing pitch and timbre lies in the time = 1/30 second transition.

    Overlap-Add (OLA) methods exploit the 30 Hz transition phenomenon by segmenting, repeating, overlapping, and adding an existing waveform to yield a new waveform that has the same perceived pitch characteristics, but modified time. Cutting a waveform into 1/20 second segments, moving all segments closer together by a factor of 40%, and adding them together will yield a 40% shorter file, but the same basic pitch characteristics. This is because the repetitive events beneath each 1/20 second "window" still maintain their exact frequencies, yielding the same sense of pitch. Figure 2.4 shows this process. Notice that the segments in Figure 2.4 are enveloped with triangular gain functions (called *windows*). This avoids the inevitable clicks and pops which would result if we just clipped out the audio using a so-called rectangular window. We will discuss more on windows in later chapters.

    Given this wonderfully simplistic (while still PsychoAcoustically informed) view of time shifting, we might be content to assume that we've generally solved the problem of pitch-preserving time shifting. That is at least until we begin to listen to the results. For one, we cannot simply cut up a waveform and glue it back together without suffering some artifacts. This would be similar to cutting a photo of a face into equal tiles, sliding all the tiles closer together, and blending the overlaps. We'd probably find the fuzziness and loss of important detail renders some faces unrecognizable. In the audio domain, we should expect that the overlap and add of waveforms might yield audible cancellations or reinforcements (called *destructive* and

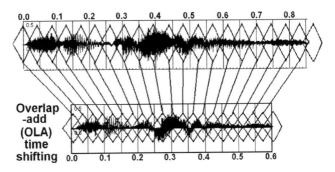

Figure 2.4. Overlap-add time shifting of a PCM waveform.

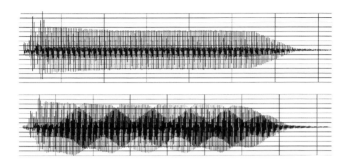

Figure 2.5. Top: Original trumpet tone. Bottom: Overlap-add timeshift shows clear modulation due to constructive and destructive interference.

constructive interference). Figure 2.5 shows examples of destructive and constructive interference due to windowed overlap-add.

2.3.3 Fixing Overlap-Add Modulation Artifacts

The modulations due to interference from overlap-add can be quite audible, and depending on the rate of artifact occurrence, can manifest as either a roughness or an actual pitch (overlap windows spaced every one hundredth of a second will cause a clear 100 Hz tone to be heard in the processed waveform). This can be fixed somewhat by randomizing the window rate. This usually results in a decrease in the "pitchiness" of the artifacts, but introduces a noisy roughness.

Another solution is to move the windows around dynamically to minimize the amount of interference. This involves deducing the pitch of a region of waveform, then setting the local window positions to be spaced apart by an integer multiple of the pitch period. This is called *Pitch Synchronous Overlap-Add* (PSOLA). For example, if the trumpet steady state is a periodic oscillation at 330 Hz, and the desired window spacing is 60 milliseconds, the window spacing would be modified from 19.8 periods of 330 Hz to 20 periods (60.60606 ms) for some windows, and 19 periods (57.5757 ms) for others, for an average of 60 ms. But how do we determine the pitch? We'll discuss that a little when we talk about autocorrelation and the *Fast Fourier Transform* (FFT) in Chapter 5.

2.3.4 Ouch!! Even More Artifacts from Overlap-Add

Another artifact that comes from overlap-add time scaling arises because certain parts of sounds are more naturally extended or shortened in time, while others are not. One example is the trumpet attack segment, which is roughly the same length independent of the length of the note played by the trumpet player. More profound examples exist in speech, where elongation of consonants causes the speech to sound slurred and drunk. Shortening of consonants can render the speech incomprehensible (shortening an /s/ sound, for example, can result in a perceived /t/ sound). Speaking slowly, or singing, involves elongating the vowels and making pauses longer, but not elongating the consonants. This argues that a good overlap-add time stretch algorithm should be intelligent enough to "figure out" when it should stretch/contract and when it should not, and do the right thing to make the average time modification come out right.

Note that multisampled wavetable synthesis, phoneme speech synthesis, and diphone speech synthesis all take into account a priori the notion of consonants and attacks, versus vowels and steady states. This allows such synthesis techniques to "do the right thing," at the expense of someone having to explicitly craft the set(s) of samples by hand ahead of time. This is not generally possible, or economically feasible, with arbitrary PCM.

Again, in later chapters we'll learn more about how we might determine vowels and consonants, or other sections of audio that should or should not be time shifted. But by that time, we will have seen that there are so many other ways to "skin the cat" of interactive parametric audio, we might not care so much about just performing blender-like manipulations on PCM audio.

2.4 Let's Pause and Think Here

The rest of this book is going to be about why we don't have to, or want to, record and play back manipulated PCM for interactive games, VR, music, and production. This chapter discussed some of the rich legacy of manipulated PCM audio, since that will be our default "fallback" if we run out of time, imagination, or algorithms to do it in more intelligent ways. We will refer back to the examples, techniques, and artifacts presented in this chapter as we continue to gain insight and tools for doing model-based parametric audio synthesis and manipulation. The motivation for doing model-based sound is, of course, the kinds of expressive controls we'll have in doing synthesis.

Reading:

Robert Bristow-Johnson. "Wavetable Synthesis 101: A Fundamental Perspective." AES 101 Conference Preprint #4400, 1996.

Perry Cook, ed. *Music, Cognition, and Computerized Sound.* Cambridge: MIT Press, 1999.

Code:

srconvrt.c

timeshif.c

Sounds:

[Track 7] Wavetable Synthesized Trumpet Passage.

[Track 8] "Synthesize," Original and Phoneme Synthesis.

[Track 9] Pitch Shifted Speech and Trumpet.

[Track 10] Time Shifted "Synthesize," Time Shifted Trumpet Passages.

Digital Filters

3.0 Introduction

This chapter introduces digital filtering, stressing intuition along with the terminology and notation used to describe digital filters. First, filtering will be discussed in general, followed by definitions and examples of *Finite Impulse Response* (FIR) and *Infinite Impulse Response* (IIR) filters. Then, the general form of a digital filter will be given and discussed. The Z transform will be introduced as a simple algebraic substitution operator, and this will be exploited to define and develop the notion of the transfer function. Zeroes and poles will be defined, and some useful filter forms will be shown. Math-averse readers could possibly skip this chapter for now, returning to it when needed in later chapters, but I'd recommend reading at least until your eyes glaze over.

3.1 Linear Systems, LTI Systems, Convolution

Linearity is a property of systems that allows us to use many powerful mathematical and signal processing techniques to analyze and predict the behavior of these systems. Linearity has two defining criteria:

Homogeneity: if $x \rightarrow y$ then $\alpha x \rightarrow \alpha y$ for any α

Superposition: if $x1 \rightarrow y1$ and $x2 \rightarrow y2$ then $x1 + x2 \rightarrow y1 + y2$

($\rightarrow$ is read "yields", and corresponds to a system operating on x to yield y).

These equations state that a mixture and/or scaling of inputs simply results in a mixture and/or scaling of the outputs. No "new" signals are created by a linear system (we'll have more rigorous means to define "new" later).

A time-invariant system obeys the property:

If $x(n) \rightarrow y(n)$ then $x(n + N) \rightarrow y(n + N)$ for any N,

which simply means that the system doesn't change its behavior with time. Here, $x(n)$ is the chain of samples put into the system, and $y(n)$ is the corresponding chain of output samples. Practically speaking, most systems actually do change over time. A reasonable assumption, however, is that many systems of interest do not change their behavior quickly, and can be treated as time-invariant over time intervals of interest. The bones of the middle ear, acoustics in rooms, a good quality stereo amplifier, and many other systems behave like *Linear Time-Invariant* (LTI) systems over much of their normal operating range. If a system is linear and time-invariant, we can characterize its behavior by measuring its impulse response as shown in Figure 3.1.

The impulse response is defined mathematically as:

$$h(n) = y(n), \text{ for } x(n) = \delta(n)$$

$$\text{where } \delta(n) = 1, n = 0,$$
$$0, \text{ otherwise.}$$

Linearity and time invariance mean that if we excite a system with an input of 1 at time zero, and 0 thereafter, we can "record" (observe) the output and use that to determine exactly what the system response would be to any arbitrary input. To prove to ourselves that this is true, all we need do is invoke

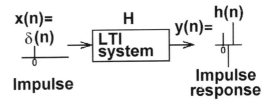

Figure 3.1. Impulse response of a Linear Time-Invariant (LTI) system.

the three properties of LTI systems: homogeneity, superposition, and time-invariance. Thus, any input can be decomposed into a time-ordered set of weighted impulses:

$$x(n) = x_0\delta(n) + x_1\delta(n-1) + x_2\delta(n-2) + x_3\delta(n-3) + \dots + x_M\delta(n-M).$$

Each input sample can be viewed as a separate weighted (x_0, x_1, etc., are the weights) impulsive input, and the outputs can be viewed as individual outputs, which are weighted versions of the impulse response $h(n)$:

$$y(n) = x_0 h(n) + x_1 h(n-1) + x_2 h(n-2) + x_3 h(n-3) + \dots + x_M h(n-M)$$
$$= \Sigma_i\, x(i)h(n-i) \qquad \text{denoted by } x(n) * h(n).$$

Figure 3.2 shows the interaction of an input signal with a linear time-invariant system as a decomposition of separate impulse responses. While

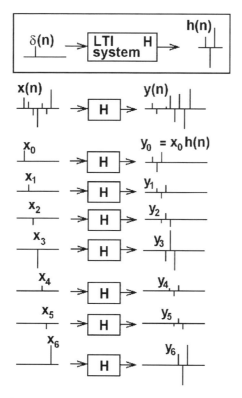

Figure 3.2. Convolution of input with impulse response of Linear Time-Invariant (LTI) system.

seeming quite tedious to calculate (which it is), this operation, called *convolution*, will be very important in that it allows us to use many mathematical tools to analyze and simulate LTI Systems.

3.2 Digital Filters

By forming linear combinations of past input and output samples, digital filters operate on streams of numbers that are uniformly sampled in time (such as samples of audio). Current and past inputs are usually denoted as

$$x(n), x(n-1), x(n-2), \ldots$$

where n is the current time, $n{-}1$ is the time one sampling period before the current one, $n{-}2$ is two sampling periods ago, etc. Current and past outputs are usually denoted as

$$y(n), y(n-1), y(n-2), \ldots$$

As discussed in Chapter 1, PCM signals are formed by sampling an analog waveform at regular intervals in time. The sampling intervals are spaced T seconds apart, where $T = 1/$sampling rate. Thus, relating the integer time indices n, $n{+}1$, etc., of a sampled signal x to actual times in seconds requires multiplying by the sampling period.

$$x(n) = x_{continuous}(nT)$$
$$x(n-1) = x_{continuous}(nT - T)$$
etc., where $T = 1/(\text{Sampling Rate})$

3.3 FIR Filters

A simple two-point moving average filter can be written as:

$$y(n) = 0.5\,(x(n) + x(n-1)). \tag{3.1}$$

Such a filter is called a FIR (*Finite Impulse Response*), because it operates only on a finite number of delayed versions of its inputs. The number of delays used is referred to as the filter "order." FIR means the filter's impulse response yields only a finite number of nonzero output samples (two successive values of one half in this case). Even though it expresses a sum, Equation 3.1 is called a *difference equation*. Figure 3.3 shows a block signal processing

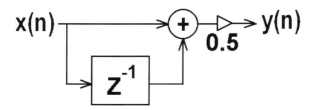

Figure 3.3. Two-point moving average digital filter.

diagram of the two-point moving average filter. The Z^{-1} block in the feedforward block represents a unit sample of delay. We'll find out more about Z and Z^{-1} later on.

Filters of the form of Equation 3.1 are also called nonrecursive, moving average, or all zero (more on that later). Figure 3.4 shows a signal processing block diagram of a general FIR filter. From the discussion of convolution in Section 3.1, note now that an arbitrary (finite length) impulse response can be stored in the coefficients of an FIR filter, and the operation of the filter would then actually perform the convolution. Thus, any LTI system with finite-length

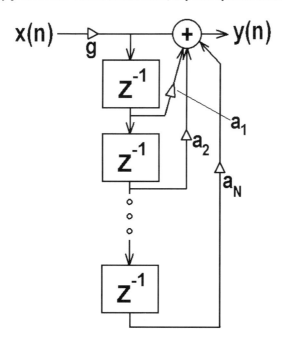

Figure 3.4. A high (Nth) order general FIR digital filter.

impulse response can be modeled by an FIR filter, provided that the impulse response of the LTI system is bandlimited to the Nyquist frequency.

3.4 IIR Filters

A simple filter that operates on past outputs can be written as

$$y(n) = (g\, x(n)) + (r\, y(n-1)) \tag{3.2}$$

It's easy to show that the impulse response of this filter for $g = 1$ is $r^n = 1.0$, r, r^*r, r^3, etc. This type of response is called an *exponential decay*. It's easy to see why filters of this form are called *Infinite Impulse Response* (IIR) filters, because for a nonzero r, the output technically never goes exactly to zero. If r is negative, the filter will oscillate positive and negative each sample, corresponding to even and odd powers of r. This is called an *exponential oscillation*. If the magnitude of r is greater than one, the filter output will grow without bound. This condition is called *instability,* and such filters are called *unstable.*

Filters of the form of Equation 3.2 are also called recursive, all pole (more on that later), and autoregressive. Figure 3.5 shows a signal processing block diagram of the simple recursive filter described in Equation 3.2. Figure 3.6 shows a higher order IIR filter block diagram.

3.5 The General Filter Form

The most general digital filter operates on both its inputs and outputs, and its difference equation is written:

$$y(n) = g(x(n) + a_1 x(n-1) + a_2 x(n-2) + \ldots + a_N x(n-N)) \tag{3.3}$$
$$-b_1 y(n-1) - b_2\, y(n-2) - \ldots - b_M\, y(n-M).$$

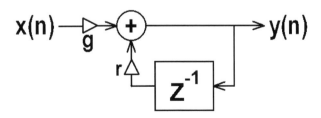

Figure 3.5. First order recursive digital filter.

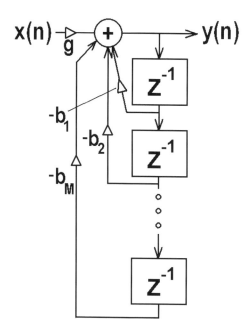

Figure 3.6. High order recursive digital filter.

Note that the length of input sample "history" is not required to be equal to the length of output sample "history," though in practice they are commonly assumed to be equal. The "order" of a filter is equal to the longest delay used in the filter; in the filter of Equation 3.3, the order would be the greater of N or M. Since general digital filters have IIR components as shown in Equation 3.3, such filters are also called IIR filters. Another term for filters with both FIR and IIR parts is *pole-zero filter* (more later). One final commonly used term is *Auto-Regressive Moving Average*, or ARMA. Figure 3.7 shows a signal processing block diagram of the general pole-zero digital filter described in Equation 3.3.

3.6 The Z Transform

A common analytical tool for digital filters is the Z transform representation. As we said before, we'll define Z^{-1} (Z to the minus 1) as a single sample of delay, and in fact, Z^{-1} is sometimes called the *Delay Operator*. To transform a filter using the Z transform, simply capitalize all variables x and y, and replace all time indices $(n-a)$ with the appropriate time delay operator Z^{-a}. Thus, the Z transformed version of Equation 3.3 would be written:

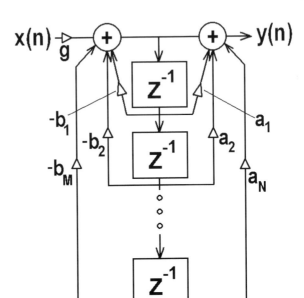

Figure 3.7. General pole-zero (IIR) filter.

$$Y = g(X + a_1 XZ^{-1} + a_2 XZ^{-2} + \ldots + a_N XZ^{-N})$$ (3.4)
$$-b_1 YZ^{-1} - b_2 YZ^{-2} - \ldots - b_M YZ^{-M}.$$

We'll see in subsequent sections and chapters how the Z transform can be used for analyzing and manipulating signals and filters.

3.7 The Transfer Function

A powerful relationship used for analyzing digital filters is the *transfer function*, which is found by solving for the ratio of output (Y) to input (X) in the Z-transformed filter expression. The transfer function for Equation 3.4 can be solved by using simple algebra:

$$Y(1 + b_1 Z^{-1} + b_2 Z^{-2} + \ldots + b_M Z^{-M})$$
$$= gX(1 + a_1 Z^{-1} + a_2 Z^{-2} + \ldots + a_N Z^{-N})$$ (3.5)

$$H = \frac{Y}{X} = \frac{g(1 + a_1 Z^{-1} + a_2 Z^{-2} + \cdots + a_N Z^{-N})}{1 + b_1 Z^{-1} + b_2 Z^{-2} + \ldots + b_M Z^{-M}}.$$ (3.6)

The transfer function is notated as H. H is the Z transform of the time-domain impulse response function $h(n)$. Transformation of x and y into the Z domain gives us a tool for talking about a function H (the Z transform of h) that takes X as input and yields Y.

3.8 Zeroes and Poles

Looking at the numerator of Equation 3.6 as a polynomial in Z^{-1}, there will be N values of Z^{-1} that make the numerator equal to zero, and the transfer function will be zero at these values. These values that make the polynomial equal to zero are potentially complex numbers: $Re + jIm$, where Re and Im are called the *real* and *imaginary* parts, and $j = \sqrt{(-1)}$. The zero values are called *zeroes of the filter* because they cause the gain of the transfer function to be zero. The two-dimensional (real and imaginary) space of possible values of Z is called the *z-plane*.

Similarly, the denominator will have M values of Z^{-1} that make it zero, and these values cause the filter gain to be infinite at those values. These M values are called *poles of the filter* (like tent poles sticking up in the transfer function, with infinite height where the denominator is zero). Poles are important because they can model resonances in physical systems (we'll see that in the next chapter). Zeroes model signal cancellations, as in the destructive interference discussed in Chapter 2.

3.9 First Order One-Zero and One-Pole Filters

The simple two-point moving average filter was defined in Equation 3.1, and shown in Figure 3.3. A more general form of the first order one-zero filter is shown in Figure 3.8, and is described by the following equations:

$$y(n) = g(x(n) + ax(n-1)) \tag{3.7}$$

$$Y/X = g(1 + aZ^{-1}). \tag{3.8}$$

This filter has a single zero at $Z = -a$, and exhibits a maximum gain of $g \cdot (1 + |a|)$. Figure 3.9 shows the gain responses versus frequency of this filter for various values of a (with g set to $1/(1 + |a|)$ to normalize the maximum gain). Such plots are called *spectral magnitude plots*, because they show the magnitude of the gain of the filter at each frequency, from zero Hz up to one half of the sampling rate (the maximum unaliased frequency). We will see a lot more on spectra and spectral plots in Chapters 5 and 6.

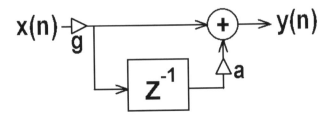

Figure 3.8. General one-zero filter.

As can be seen from Figure 3.9, positive values of a cause the filter to favor low frequencies over high. Such filters are called low pass filters. Negative values of a cause the filter to be a high pass filter, as shown in Figure 3.8. If a is set to -1 and g to T (the sampling period), the one-zero filter becomes the digital approximation to differentiation (delta in adjacent x values divided by delta time). We'll use this in later chapters.

The simple first order one-pole filter was shown in Figure 3.5 and is described by the equations below:

$$y(n) = gx(n) + ry(n-1) \tag{3.9}$$

$$Y/X = g / (1 - rZ^{-1}). \tag{3.10}$$

This filter has a single pole at $Z = r$, and exhibits a maximum gain of $g/(1 - |r|)$. Figure 3.10 shows the gain responses versus frequency of this filter for various values of r (g is set to $1 - |r|$ to normalize the filter maximum gain). As we observed before, the absolute value of r must be less than one in order for the filter to be stable. As can be seen from Figure 3.10, positive values of r cause the filter to favor low frequencies (low pass), while negative values cause the filter to favor high frequencies (high pass). If both g and r

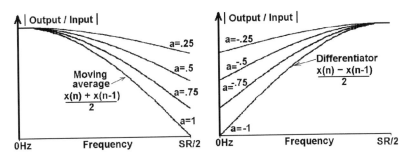

Figure 3.9. Gain versus zero location for one-zero filter.

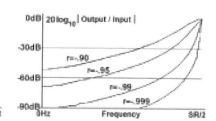

Figure 3.10. Gain versus pole location for one-pole filter.

are set to 1.0 (which is unstable), the first order one-pole filter implements the *digital integrator,* which simply sums up all prior input signals.

The plots in Figure 3.10 show amplitude mapped into a logarithmic space. This is often done in audio and for some other signal representations because the dynamic range of the signals found is often quite large. For example, our hearable range of audio signals is immense: The amplitude ratio of the quietest sound we can hear to the loudest sound we can tolerate without pain or damage is one to one million (a range of 140 dB, see Chapter 1)! Our one-pole filter, set with $r = 0.99$ can range in amplitude response from 1.0 at zero frequency, down to about 0.005 at SRATE/2. Plotting that on a simple amplitude scale wouldn't be meaningful, so we plot it on the dB scale. Each factor of ten in amplitude is equal to 20 dB change, so our gain of 0.005 would correspond to –46 dB.

3.10 The Second Order Pole/Zero (BiQuad) Filter

A special form of digital filter is the *BiQuad,* so named because the numerator and denominator of the transfer function are both second order, or quadratic polynomials in Z^{-1}. Any polynomial can be factored into first and second order polynomials with real coefficients; thus, all that's needed to factor the transfer function of Equation 3.5 or 3.6 is first and second order building blocks. The second order two-pole blocks correspond to resonators, or oscillators with exponential damping, and are very powerful building blocks for digital filter systems. The second order two-zero building blocks are antiresonators, capable of placing a pair of complex zeroes anywhere in the z-plane. A two-zero block combined with a two-pole block makes up a BiQuad.

The BiQuad in the time and Z transform domains looks like:

$$y(n) = g(x(n) + a_1 x(n-1) + a_2 x(n-2)) \qquad (3.11)$$
$$-b_1 y(n-1) - b_2 y(n-2)$$

$$\frac{Y}{X} = \frac{g(1 + a_1 Z^{-1} + a_2 Z^{-2})}{1 + b_1 Z^{-1} + b_2 Z^{-2}}. \tag{3.12}$$

This filter has two poles and two zeroes. Depending on the values of the a and b coefficients, the poles and zeroes can be placed in fairly arbitrary positions around the z-plane, but not completely arbitrary if the a and b coefficients are real numbers (not complex). Remember from quadratic equations in algebra that the roots of a second order polynomial can be found by the formula: $(-a_1 +/- (a_1{}^2 - 4a_2)^{1/2}]/2$ for the zeroes, and similarly for the poles using the b coefficients. It turns out that for complex roots, the positions will always end up as a *complex conjugate pair* of the form $Re +/- jIm$. Filters with two poles are called *resonators*, or *phasors*.

For practical use in sound processing, there is a wonderful formulation of the BiQuad that deals more directly with resonator parameters:

$$\frac{Y}{X} = \frac{g(1 - 2r_z \cos(2\pi Freq_z T)Z^{-1} + r_z^2 Z^{-2})}{1 - 2r_p \cos(2\pi Freq_p T)Z^{-1} + r_p^2 Z^{-2}} \tag{3.13}$$

$$y(n) = g(x(n) - 2r_z \cos(2\pi Freq_z T)x(n-1) + r_z^2 x(n-2))$$
$$+ 2r_p \cos(2\pi Freq_p T)y(n-1) - r_p^2 y(n-2). \tag{3.14}$$

This describes the filter coefficients in terms of an exponential damping parameter (r_z for the zeroes, r_p for the poles) and a center frequency of resonance (antiresonance for the zeroes), which is $Freq_z$ for the zeroes and $Freq_p$ for the poles. We can now control aspects of the filter more directly from these parameters, knowing that once we decide on r_z and $Freq_z$, we can convert to a_1, a_2, b_1, and b_2 directly. Figure 3.11 shows the BiQuad in block diagram form.

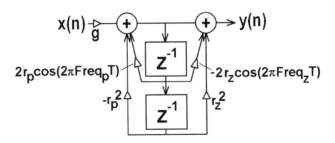

Figure 3.11. BiQuad filter block diagram.

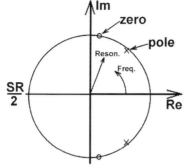

Figure 3.12. Z-plane pole/zero plot of BiQuad with zeroes at 1.0, 5000 Hz, and poles at 0.99, 3000 Hz (sampling rate is 22050).

Just as with the filter of Equation 3.2, r_p must be strictly less than one, and for the resonance formulation it is usually kept nonnegative, because we can use the frequency variable to swing the position around in an arc anywhere in the z-plane. $Freq_z$ and $Freq_p$ can take on any value from zero to one half the sampling rate (the Nyquist frequency). $Freq_z$ and $Freq_p$ can actually take on any value, but they will alias to frequencies within the Nyquist range, because of the "modulo 2π" nature of the cosine functions in Equation 3.13. Figure 3.12 shows the z-plane pole/zero plot of a Biquad filter with r_z set to 1.0; $Freq_z$ set to 5000 Hz; r_p set to 0.99; and $Freq_p$ set to 3000 Hz (sampling rate is 22050 Hz). The resonance parameters, r, are reflected by the radial distance from the origin in the z-plane. The frequency parameters determine the angle of the pole/zero locations.

Figure 3.13 shows the spectrum (top) of a random noise input to the BiQuad Filter, along with the spectrum of the filtered noise signal. *White noise* is named similarly to white light, where all frequencies are present in relatively equal amplitude, as shown in the magnitude versus frequency plot. Passing white noise through a filter results in what is called *colored noise*, in direct analogy to passing light through a color filter. Note the peak in the filtered output spectrum at 3000 Hz corresponding to the pole resonances, and the dip at 5000 Hz corresponding to the zero antiresonances.

((12))

Figure 3.14 shows some superimposed frequency responses of a Biquad with g set to 0.1; r_p set to 0.99 and 0.97; the zeroes set at special locations (+/–1 on the real axis); and $Freq_p$ swept from 0 to 4000 Hz in 500 Hz steps (sampling rate is 8000 Hz). Locating the zeroes at those locations of frequency = 0 and frequency = SRATE/2 helps to keep the total filter gain nearly constant, independent of the frequency of the resonator.

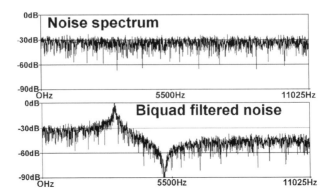

Figure 3.13. White noise input spectrum (top) versus BiQuad filtered output spectrum (bottom). The BiQuad has a resonator pole pair at 3000 Hz with $r = 0.99$, and a zero pair at 5000 Hz with $r = 1.0$ (same filter as shown in the z-plane view of Figure 3.12).

3.11 A Little on Filter Topologies

If you've had enough of digital filters, difference equations, the z-plane, and all that for now, you can skip the next sections and go on to Chapter 4. However, if you just can't get enough of this stuff, read on for some notes about implementing digital filters.

Digital filters are described by simple linear algebraic equations. As such they can be factored in a number of ways, and thus a given filter might be implemented in a wide variety of ways. As an example, we will use the filter shown in Figure 3.15 (hereafter we'll let $g = 1$ for convenience).

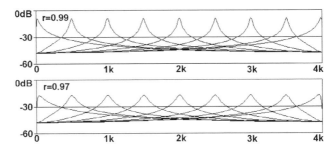

Figure 3.14. BiQuad transfer function magnitudes with zeroes set at $+/-1.0$ (one zero at DC and one at $SRATE/2$); $r = 0.99$ (top plot), and $r = 0.97$ (lower plot). Resonance frequencies are set to 0, 500, 1000, 1500, 2000, 2500, 3000, 3500, and 4000 Hz (sample rate = 8000).

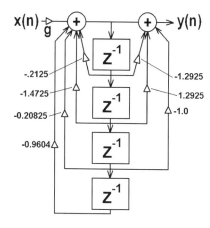

Figure 3.15. A fourth order IIR, third order FIR digital filter.

The filter of Figure 3.15 has a difference equation (for $g = 1$) of

$$y(n) = x(n) - 1.2925\,x(n-1) + 1.2925\,x(n-2) - x(n-3) - 0.2125\,y(n-1)$$
$$- 1.4725\,y(n-2) - 0.20825\,y(n-3) - 0.9604\,y(n-4).$$

We can write out the Z transform of this filter as:

$$\frac{Y}{X} = \frac{1 - 1.2925Z^{-1} + 1.2925Z^{-2} - Z^{-3}}{1 + 0.2125Z^{-1} + 1.4725Z^{-2} + 0.20825Z^{-3} + 0.9604Z^{-4}}.$$

Noting that the numerator is of third order, and the denominator is of fourth order, we can factor each into first and second order filter segments:

$$\frac{Y}{X} = \frac{(1 - 0.2925Z^{-1} + Z^{-2}) \cdot (1 - Z^{-1})}{(1 - 0.6Z^{-1} + 0.98Z^{-2}) \cdot (1 + 0.8125Z^{-1} + 0.98Z^{-2})}.$$

Now that we've factored it, we can compare the sections to our standard BiQuad forms given in Equation 3.11 and see that this filter gives us two resonances: one at $r = 0.99, f = 3/8$ SRATE; and one at $r = 0.99, f = 7/8$ SRATE. It also gives us one complex zero pair at $r = 1.0, f = 5/7$ SRATE. Finally, it implements a single zero at $f = 0$. Since the transfer function is just a product of these, we can rewrite it as a chain of simple filter segments:

$$Y/X = (1 - 0.2925\,Z^{-1} + Z^{-2}) \cdot (1 - Z^{-1}) \cdot 1/(1 - 0.6Z^{-1} + 0.98Z^{-2})$$
$$\cdot 1/(1 + 0.8125Z^{-1} + 0.98Z^{-2}).$$

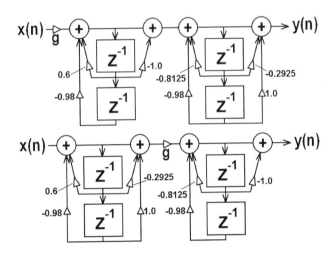

Figure 3.16. Two topological variants of the filter shown in Figure 3.15. Linearity says we can reorder the sections any way we like.

The mathematics of LTI systems tells us that these can be implemented in any order. Two of many such possibilities are shown in Figure 3.16. Note that the gain term can also go at any point in the chain.

The form shown in Figure 3.15 is called the *direct form*, and the forms shown in Figure 3.16 are all called *factored cascade forms*. There are many other forms for filters, including parallel. You might ask, "If the math says they're all the same, then why would we care about different forms?" Well, it turns out that the math is only strictly true in the pure case of infinite precision computation. For finite word sizes, even floats in computers, then rounding, truncation, quantization, etc., can all make a difference in filter implementations. Some topologies do better with finite precision computation. However, for the rest of this book we won't much care about this, because it's really not that critical of an issue for floating point computations on low order filters.

3.12 Conclusion

Digital filters operate on sampled signals by forming linear combinations of past inputs and outputs. LTI (linear time-invariant) systems are common in the acoustical world, and any LTI system can be modeled by a digital filter. Simple low order filters can be used to implement simple high and low pass functions, as well as implementing the averaging, differentiation, and integration operations. The second order pole-zero filter (called the "BiQuad") is a convenient and flexible form, allowing independent control of resonance and antiresonance. The next chapter will look at the first actual physical model in this book and relate the simulation of that physical model (and more complex systems) to digital filters.

Reading:

Ken Stieglitz. *A Digital Signal Processing Primer*. Menlo Park: Addison Wesley, 1996.

Lawrence Rabiner and Bernard Gold. *Theory and Application of Digital Signal Processing*. Englewood Cliffs: Prentice Hall, 1974.

Code:

filter.c

GUIResoLab

Sounds:

[Track 11] One-Pole Filtered Speech, r = 0.9 ,0.95, 0.99, –0.9, –0.95, –0.99.

[Track 12] BiQuad Filtered Noise.

[Track 13] Noise Filtered Through Topologies of Figures 3.15–3.16.

Modal Synthesis

4.0 Introduction

This chapter is somewhat about sine waves, but really more about physics. As such, it will be the first real parametric synthesis chapter in this book, giving us our first practical method for actually synthesizing (rather than just processing) sounds. In later chapters, we will see increasing evidence of why sine waves, or *sinusoids*, are important in mathematics, physics, and sound synthesis. In this chapter, we will first motivate the notion of sine waves, not from a purely mathematical basis, but rather from an extremely simple physical experiment. The physics will be extended to the notion of sinusoidal "modes" in many physical systems. Using modal resonant filters, a general algorithmic basis for synthesizing the sounds of many types of objects will be presented. This will be extended further to an analysis technique that allows us to take apart sounds and resynthesize them with interesting modifications.

4.1 A Simple Mechanical System

Figure 4.1 shows a mechanical system consisting of a mass attached to a spring. The mass is designated by m. An ideal spring is characterized by the force

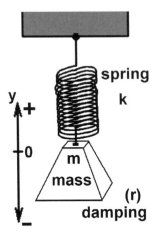

Figure 4.1. Mass/spring system.

required to displace it from rest position: This force per unit distance is designated by k. The displacement of the mass is designated by y, which is positive for upward displacement and negative for downward displacement. This choice of sign/direction is arbitrary, and could be selected to be the opposite. Any real system will have losses, such as heat lost in compressing and stretching the spring, and some wind resistance on the mass and spring as they move. The total losses are designated by r. We can write out the simple Newtonian equations for the system by accounting for all the forces on the mass and setting those equal to mass × acceleration (Newton's second law), giving:

$$\text{Force} = \text{mass} \times \text{acceleration}$$

$$-ky - mg - rv = ma. \tag{4.1}$$

Let's take a moment to understand each term in Equation 4.1. The $-ky$ term represents the spring force, acting opposite the displacement y. So if we pull down on the mass, the net force $-ky$ is positive because y is negative. This means that the spring pulls the mass upward toward the $y = 0$ position. Similarly, if we pull the mass upward, the spring pushes it downward. The $-mg$ term is gravity acting on the mass. For simplicity, we'll assume that this force is small relative to the spring restoring forces, and just remove it from our equations. If this bothers you, just take the mass and spring to a space station where there isn't any gravity. The $-rv$ term reflects loss forces that act against motion, and act proportional to velocity (v). Finally, we need to note that velocity is the rate of change of position y with time, and acceleration is the rate of change of velocity with time. Mathematical expressions for velocity and acceleration are:

$$v = dy / dt \qquad a = dv / dt = d^2y / dt^2.$$

The "d" in dy/dt stands for *difference* (also often called *delta*). So velocity is the difference in position divided by the difference in time: Consider common measures of velocity such as miles per hour, feet per second, etc. Similarly, the acceleration is the change in velocity divided by the difference in time, or the second rate of change of position with time.

Substituting our rate-of-change expressions into Equation 4.1 gives us:

$$-ky - rdy/dt = md^2y / dt^2$$

$$\text{or} \quad d^2y/dt^2 + (r/m)\, dy/dt + (k/m)y = 0. \qquad (4.2)$$

4.2 Solution of the Mass/Spring/Damper System

Equation 4.2, and thus the system of the damped[1] mass and spring, has a solution of the form

$$y(t) = y_0 e^{(-rt/2m)} \cos\left(t\sqrt{(k/m - (r/2m)^2)}\right). \qquad (4.3)$$

This is a mathematical way of saying that the mass will oscillate up and down at a single frequency that is determined by the spring constant and the amount of mass. The frequency of oscillation is affected by the damping as well. The oscillation will decay to zero according to the damping constant $r/2m$. Intuitively, we know that if we replace the mass with a smaller one (decrease m), or if we make the spring stiffer (increase k), the system will oscillate faster. This is confirmed in the frequency argument k/m in the cosine term of the solution. We also know that if we changed the damping of the system, say by allowing the mass to rub on a wall or some other surface, the oscillations would damp away much more quickly. This is equivalent to increasing r. If damping is increased beyond a certain critical point, the system will no longer oscillate, but will rather just droop back to the rest position. If we pick some values, such as $y_0 = 1$ meter, $m = 1$ gram, $k = 1000$ Newtons/meter, and $r = .002$ Newtons/meter/second, Equation 4.3 takes on a concrete form:

$$y(t) = e^{-t}\cos(1000t). \qquad (4.4)$$

---

[1] Damping is energy loss in a system. "To damp" usually involves putting material (or a thumb or finger in the case of an interactive vibrating object) on the object to introduce loss. For example, the felt pads in a piano which stop the sound when you release a key are called dampers.

The argument to the cosine function is in radians. To convert radians into frequency in Hz, we divide by 2π, meaning the oscillator frequency would be $1000/2\pi$, or 159.155 cycles per second. If we wanted to solve such a system digitally, we could just sample the solution of Equation 4.4 directly by replacing t with $n \times T$, where n is the sample number and T is the sampling interval, equal to one over the sampling rate. We could also discretize Equation 4.2 by using the approximations:

$$dy/dt = (y(n) - y(n-1)) / T$$

$$d^2y / dt^2 = dv/dt$$

$$= ((y(n) - y(n-1))/T - (y(n-1) - y(n-2))/T) / T$$

$$= (y(n) - 2y(n-1) + y(n-2)) / T^2$$

yielding:

$$(y(n) - 2y(n-1) + y(n-2)) / T^2 + r/m(y(n) - y(n-1)) / T + k/m\, y(n) = 0$$

$$\text{or } y(n) = y(n-1)(2m + Tr)/(m + Tr + T^2k) - y(n-2)m/(m + Tr + T^2k). \quad (4.5)$$

Equation 4.5 might look quite different from the continuous form in Equation 4.3, but if you run the program in Example 4.1 and compare the variables "ideal" to "approx," you will see that the two solutions are actually quite close, as shown in Figure 4.2.

The sampling rate determines the accuracy of the discrete simulation. Changing the OVERSAMP parameter in the code above will reveal that

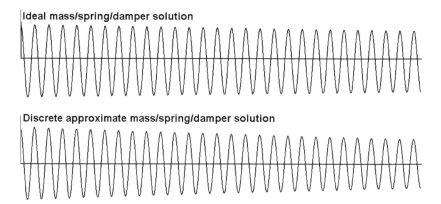

Ideal mass/spring/damper solution

Discrete approximate mass/spring/damper solution

Figure 4.2. Ideal versus approximate mass/spring/damper solutions.

```
SRATE = 8000;
m = 0.001;
k = 1000;
r = 0.002;
OVERSAMP = 50;
T = 1.0 / (SRATE * OVERSAMP);                // Oversampled rate
temp = (m + (T*r) + (T*T*k));          // Coefficient denominator
coeff1 = ((2.0*m) + (T*r)) / temp;
coeff2 = - m / temp;
Y[1] = 1.0;                       // Normalized initial condition
Y[2] = 0.0;

for (i=0;i<4*SRATE;i++)  {                // Run it for 4 seconds
    t = i / SRATE;
    ideal = exp(-t) * cos(1000.0 * t);       // Ideal solution
    for (j=0;j<OVERSAMP;j++)        {
        Y[0] = (Y[1] * coeff1) + (Y[2] * coeff2);
        Y[2] = Y[1];
        Y[1] = Y[0];
    }
    approx = Y[1] - Y[2];        // Digital approximate solution
}
```

Example 4.1. C Code—Comparison of ideal and approximate solutions of the mass/spring/damper system.

undersampling in the approximation yields errors in damping, but it doesn't affect the frequency of oscillation as much. There are other ways to discretize the differential equation, and these yield different approximations to the ideal solution. The mass/spring/damper exhibits only one "mode" (one exponentially decaying cosine at only one frequency). The combining of resonant oscillators (modes) forms the basis of modal synthesis, sinusoidal additive synthesis, and some forms of physical modeling.

4.3 Boundary Conditions and Solutions

Predictably, most systems that produce sound are more complex than the ideal mass/spring/damper system. And of course, most sounds are more complex than a simple damped exponential sinusoid. Mathematical expressions of the physical forces (thus the accelerations) can be written for nearly any system, but solving such equations is often difficult or impossible. Some systems have simple enough properties and geometries to allow an exact solution to be written out for their vibrational behavior. A string under tension is one such system, and it is evaluated in great detail in Chapter 12 and Appendix A. For

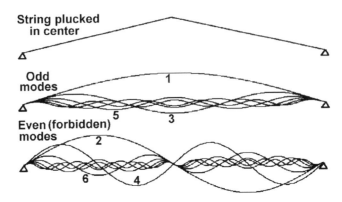

Figure 4.3. Top: Plucked string. Center: Possible sinusoidal modes of vibration of a center-plucked string. Bottom: The even modes, which would not be excited by the center-plucked condition.

our purposes, we can resort to some graphical arguments to further motivate the notion of sinusoids in real physical systems. The top of Figure 4.3 shows a string, lifted up at one point in the center (halfway along its length). Below that is a set of sinusoidal "modes" that the center-plucked string vibration could potentially have. These are spatial functions (sine as function of position along the string), but they also correspond to natural frequencies of vibration of the string. At the bottom of Figure 4.3 is another set of modes that would not be possible with the center-plucked condition, because all of these "even" modes are restricted to have no vibration in the center of the string, and thus they could not contribute to the triangular shape of the string. These conditions of no displacement, corresponding to the zero crossings of the sine functions, are called *nodes*. Note that the end points are forced nodes of the plucked string system for all possible conditions of excitation.

Physical constraints on a system, such as the pinned ends of a string and the center-plucked initial shape, are known as *boundary conditions*. Spatial sinusoidal solutions like those shown in Figure 4.3 are called *boundary solutions* (the legal sinusoidal modes of displacement and vibration). Note that if we plucked the string at a position one fourth of the way along the string length, we would excite the second mode quite strongly, but the fourth mode would not be excited at all, because of the node in that mode at the 1/4 string position. If you would plot the eighth, twelfth, etc., modes (all multiples of four), you would also find that those modes exhibit nodes at the 1/4 string position. Finally, if you were to rest your finger gently on the center of the string, and pluck with another finger located away from the center while simultaneously lifting the center damping finger, you would excite (some of) the modes shown in the lower part of Figure 4.3, but none of the odd modes. The even modes of two, four, and six are all harmonics of the note one octave higher than the fundamental mode. This is called *playing overtones* or *playing harmonics* in guitar parlance.

((‹15›))

We will learn more about the plucked string and higher-dimensional vibrating systems such as bars, plates, membranes, etc., in later chapters. The point of introducing the example of the plucked-string system here was to motivate the notion that sinusoids can occur in systems more complex than just the simple mass/spring/damper.

4.4 Sinusoidal Additive Synthesis

In later chapters we will gain more knowledge about sinusoids and modes. We'll also gain tools to allow us to determine precisely the makeup of shapes, vibrations, or waveforms as sums of sinusoidal functions. For now we will note that many sound-producing objects and systems exhibit strong sinusoidal modes. A plucked string might exhibit many modes, but all of those would be determined by the boundary conditions of the terminations, and the shape of the excitation pluck. Striking a metal plate with a hammer might excite many of the vibrational modes of the plate, but all of those can be predicted by the shape of the plate and where it is struck. The recognition of the fundamental nature of the sinusoid gives rise to a powerful model of sound synthesis based on simply summing up lots of sinusoidal modes. Figure 4.4 shows a general

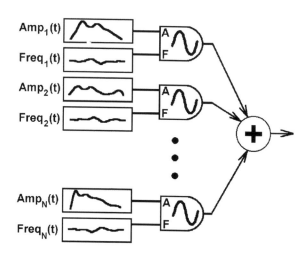

Figure 4.4. Sinusoidal additive synthesis algorithm.

Sinusoidal Additive Synthesis Model, allowing us to control the amplitudes and frequencies of a number of sinusoidal oscillators.

4.5 Filter-Based Modal Synthesis

Equation 4.5 came from a derivation that involved approximating the differential equation describing the mass/spring/damper system through the replacement of the derivatives (velocity as the derivative of position, and acceleration as the second derivative of position) with sampled time differences. But note that the equation is simply a recursion in past values of $y(n)$ with a variable position. Also note that the weight terms applied to past values of y are constant if the values of mass, damping, spring constant, and sampling rate are held constant. That is, the "weight" of the single sample delayed position variable, $(2m + Tr)/(m + Tr + T^2k)$, is constant; and the "weight" of the two sample delayed position variable, $m/(m + Tr + T^2k)$, is constant as well.

Now we should note that a standard infinite impulse response recursive filter (described in Section 3.4, and shown in Figure 3.5) can be used to implement Equation 4.5. This reinforces the fact that the second order two-pole feedback filter can be used to generate an exponentially decaying sinusoid, because the solution of the mass/spring/damper system is an exponentially decaying sinusoid as well. We can inspect the coefficients of the filter implemented in Equation 4.5 by filling in the values for m, r, k, and T, yielding:

$$b_2 = m /(m + Tr + T^2k) = 0.99998875012656 = -r^2 \rightarrow r = 0.999994375$$

$$b_1 = (2m + Tr)/(m + Tr + T^2k) = 1.9999825001969 =$$
$$2r\cos(2\pi\text{freq}/(\text{SRATE} \times \text{OVERSAMP})) \rightarrow \text{freq} = 159.1541337 \text{ Hz.}$$

If you compare these values to those from Section 4.1 ($r = 1.0$ and freq $= 159.155$ Hz), you will see once again that the digital filter approximation is actually quite close to the exact solution. More important than the accuracy of the difference equation in approximating the physical system of the mass/spring/damper system, is the connection of the second order digital filter to the physical notion of a mode of vibration. For example, we looked at the vibrating string shape as a set of sinusoidal modes. We'll see in later chapters that the vibration of any linear time-invariant system can be decomposed into sinusoidal modes. Figure 4.5 shows a general model for the modal synthesis of struck/plucked objects, in which an impulsive excitation function is used to excite a number of filters that model the modes.

The modal filter model can be improved and expanded to make it more expressive and physically meaningful. For example, we can use rules to

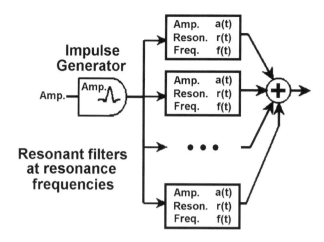

Figure 4.5. Simple modal synthesis algorithm.

excite specific modes based on boundary and excitation conditions. We could construct a modal model of a plucked string that models pluck position, automatically exciting only odd modes if we pluck in the center, exciting all but multiple-of-four modes for plucking at the ¼ string position, etc. We can also account for things like material properties, shape (boundary conditions), etc.

Figure 4.6 shows a more flexible and general model of modal synthesis. This model allows for the filter input to be arbitrary, rather than just an impulse. It also allows for that input to be processed through a simple "brightness

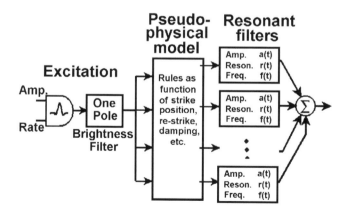

Figure 4.6. Flexible parametric modal synthesis algorithm.

filter," modeling the general trend of objects to exhibit more high frequency energy when struck harder. It also allows for arbitrary rules (tables, equations, whatever) to control the modal filter settings.

4.6 Residual Extraction and Resynthesis

Once the modes of a system (or sound) have been identified, they can be removed from the sound by various methods. Modes are associated with filter poles, so *antimodes* can be modeled by complementary zeroes. Constructing an all-zero filter and passing a modal sound through it yields a *residue,* or *residual*, which is that part of the sound left over after the modes are removed.

By removing the modes to yield a residue, we are performing an operation that is like the reverse of convolution. Taking a $y(n)$ output signal and decomposing it into two signals, a modal system filter $h(n)$, and an excitation $x(n)$ signal is called *deconvolution*. The model is called a *source-filter model*. Deconvolution is not unique, in that we could select a number of possible filters to model the spectral peaks. If the residue is kept, however, the process is invertible, meaning that convolving $x(n)$ with $h(n)$ will yield $y(n)$, the original signal. The use of deconvolution to factor a sound into a modal filter and a residual is one of a number of methods known as *identity analysis/resynthesis* techniques. The term identity refers to the fact that we can take a sound apart and then put it back together to get the original sound. Later we will see other techniques that will prove useful for identity analysis/resynthesis. We will also see other powerful synthesis techniques that do not have a known identity analysis process.

As an example of practical modal synthesis, Figure 4.7 shows a waveform and spectrum of a glass coffee mug being struck with a pencil. Figure 4.8 shows the residue waveform and spectrum after removing the six main visible modes from the struck mug sound. Note that the energy, amplitude, and time extent of the residue is much smaller compared to the original sound. This has some profound implications for modeling impulsively excited systems with a few strong modes. From a coding and compression standpoint, it means that we can often reduce the memory and precision required to represent the sound by factoring it into a residual excitation and modal filter. From an analysis and physical understanding standpoint, it means that if we are careful about selecting and removing modes, it is possible to actually factor a sound into the excitation sound and the resonant system modal behavior. If we listen to the sound of the residue, it often sounds like just the exciting object (the pencil striking a nonresonant object in the case of Figure 4.8). From a flexible synthesis standpoint, source-filter modeling means that we can often "throw away" the residue and replace it with something much simpler, like an impulse

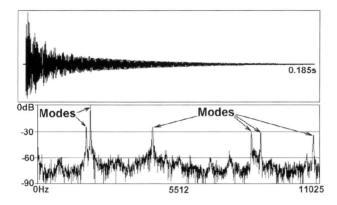

Figure 4.7. Waveform and spectrum of coffee mug struck with pencil. Note that there appear to be about six significant modes.

or a short burst of noise. We will return to some other aspects of this type of identity source-filter parametric analysis/synthesis in later chapters.

A wide variety of sounds can be synthesized using modal synthesis. Any object which exhibits a few modes and is excited by striking or plucking is a likely candidate for modal modeling. Such objects might include metal pots and pans, glasses, etc. Modal synthesis can also work well for simple wooden objects such as blocks, boards, etc.

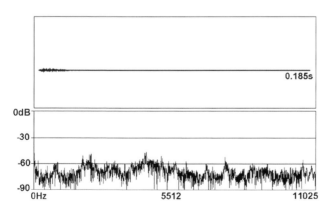

Figure 4.8. Waveform and spectrum of coffee mug residual after modes are removed (right).

4.7 Conclusion

This chapter provided our first real glimpse of the power of physical modeling, and related it to linear systems and digital filter theory. We learned that simple physical systems can exhibit sinusoidal oscillations. We also saw that more complex systems, such as a plucked string, exhibit sinusoidal modes. Some sound synthesis models were presented, including sinusoidal additive and modal filter-based synthesis. Finally, the idea of decomposing sounds into modal filters and a residual excitation signal was presented. We will gain more techniques for parametric sound decomposition in later chapters. The next chapter will move toward a deeper understanding of the frequency (sinusoidal) domain via the *Discrete Fourier Transform (DFT)*, and how sounds can be examined and modeled through its use.

Reading:

Jean Marie Adrien. "The Missing Link: Modal Synthesis." In *Representations of Musical Signals,* edited by De Poli, Piccialli, and Roads, pp. 269–297. Cambridge: MIT Press, 1991.

Perry Cook. "Physically Inspired Sonic Modeling (PhISM): Synthesis of Percussive Sounds." *Computer Music Journal* 21(3): 38–49(1997).

Kees Van den Doel and Dinesh Pai. "Synthesis of Shape Dependent Sounds with Physical Modeling." *Proceedings of the International Conference on Auditory Display*, ICAD (1996).

Code:

Masprdm.c

GUIModal

Sounds:

[Track 14] Direct and Discrete Mass/Spring/Damper Oscillations.

[Track 15] Guitar Pluck Edge versus Center, "Playing Overtones."

[Track 16] Coffee Mug Strike and Residual.

[Track 17] A Variety of Metallic/Glass Modal Sounds.

[Track 18] A Variety of Wooden Modal Sounds.

5 The Fourier Transform

5.0 Introduction

This chapter will continue the discussion of the importance of sine waves. It will introduce the *Discrete Fourier Transform* (DFT), a general and powerful tool for dealing with all types of signals and systems. The *Fast Fourier Transform* (FFT) will give us a means of computing the DFT quickly and efficiently. Properties of the DFT will show us fast and clever ways to implement and design digital filters; to identify frequencies and other parameters for modal synthesis; and new ways to look at PCM audio and synthesis. We'll present a number of properties of sound spectra, and some interesting applications of frequency domain processing.

For those who are math-averse, if you really don't want to plow through all of the math in this chapter, you should at least read Section 5.1, and Sections 5.8 through the end. The other sections (and Appendix A) present definitions, proofs, and properties intended to help you truly trust and appreciate the power of the mathematical tool of the Fourier transform. Some of the properties given in Appendix A will be important in later chapters, so at least a quick look at that appendix would be helpful.

5.1 The Frequency Domain Spectrum

In general, we live in the time domain, but perceive many aspects of objects and processes in the frequency domain. Recall that in Section 2.4.2 we discussed "the 30 Hz transition," which refers to the fact that events happening much faster than 30 times per second are perceived as spectral events in frequency, rather than gestural events in time.

Recall the importance of sinusoids in modeling physical systems like the mass/spring/damper, the plucked string, plates, membranes, and many other sound-producing objects that exhibit clear modal vibration patterns. Sine waves are also important in any type of linear time-invariant systems, because if a sine wave is passed through an LTI system, it will come out with the same frequency, but possibly with modified phase and amplitude. Passing mixtures of sine waves through LTI systems causes mixtures of those same sine waves to appear at the output (no new frequencies appear; this is an extension of the superposition property of LTI systems). You can prove this to yourself using the linear systems math we've developed and used so far.

Now we will see that sine waves are extremely important for yet one more reason. We'll learn that just as light can be passed through a prism to break it into the individual light frequencies from which it is composed, sound can be separated into individual simple frequencies (sine waves). The set of individual amplitudes and phases of the sines that make up a sound are called a *frequency spectrum*. The mathematical technique used to turn a time-domain waveform into a frequency-domain spectrum is called a *transform*. The math used to turn a frequency-domain spectrum back into a time-domain waveform is called an *inverse transform*. Using the frequency spectrum to inspect aspects of a sound is called *spectral analysis*.

5.2 The Fourier Series

We saw in Section 4.2 that the plucked string supports certain spatial vibrations, called modes. These modes have a very special relationship in the case of the plucked string (and some other limited systems) in that their frequencies are all integer multiples of one basic sinusoid, called the *fundamental*. This special series of sinusoids is called a *harmonic series*, and lies at the basis of the *Fourier series* representation of shapes, waveforms, oscillations, etc. The Fourier series solves many types of problems, including physical problems with boundary constraints, but is also applicable to any shape or function. Any periodic waveform (repeating over and over again), $F_{per,}$ can be transformed into a Fourier series, written as:

$$F_{per}(t) = a_0 + \Sigma_m \, [b_m\cos(2\pi f_0 mt) + c_m\sin(2\pi f_0 mt)]. \qquad (5.1)$$

The a_0 term is a constant offset, or the average of the waveform. The b_m and c_m coefficients are the weights of the "mth harmonic" cosine and sine terms. If the function $F_{per}(t)$ is purely even about $t = 0$ (this is a boundary condition like that discussed in Chapter 4), only cosines are required to represent it, and only the b_m terms would be nonzero. Similarly, if the function $F_{per}(t)$ is odd, only the c_m terms would be required. A general function $F_{per}(t)$ will require sinusoidal harmonics of arbitrary amplitudes and phases. The magnitude and phase of the mth harmonic in the Fourier series can be found by:

$$A_m = \sqrt{b_m^2 + c_m^2} \qquad (5.2)$$

$$\theta_m = \text{Arctan}(c_m \, / \, b_m). \qquad (5.3)$$

Phase is defined relative to the cosine, so if c_m is zero, θ_m is zero. As a brief example, Figure 5.1 shows the first few sinusoidal harmonics required to build up an approximation of a square wave. Note that due to symmetries (boundary conditions), only odd sine harmonics are required. Using more sines improves the approximation.

Being able to express periodic functions as sums of sinusoids with arbitrary magnitude and phase is a powerful thing. Being able to express any function as a sum of sinusoids is also quite profound (yes, I know we haven't yet proven this, but we do in Appendix A). But how do we arrive at the correct values of the sine and cosine coefficients? We will find this out in the next section, and we will also see that the notion of representing functions as sums of sinusoids extends to non-periodic functions as well.

5.3 The Discrete Fourier Transform

The process of solving for the sine and cosine components of a signal or waveform is called *Fourier analysis*, or the *Fourier transform*. If the frequency

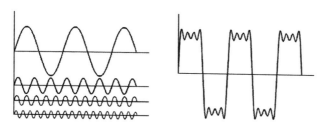

Figure 5.1. A sum of odd harmonics adds to approximate a square wave.

variable is sampled (as is the case in the Fourier series, represented by m), and the time variable t is sampled as well (as it is in PCM waveform data, represented by n), then the Fourier transform is called the *Discrete Fourier Transform*, or DFT. The DFT is given by

$$F(m) = \Sigma_{n=0 \text{ to } N-1} f(n)[\cos(2\pi mn/N) - j\sin(2\pi mn/N)], \qquad (5.4)$$

where N is the length of the signal being analyzed. The *Inverse DFT* (IDFT) is very similar to the Fourier Series:

$$f(n) = 1/N \, \Sigma_{m=0 \text{ to } N-1} F(m)[\cos(2\pi mn/N) + j\sin(2\pi mn/N)]. \qquad (5.5)$$

The complex variable j (square root of -1) is used to place the cosine and sine components in a unique arrangement where odd terms of the waveform are represented as imaginary components, and even terms are represented as real components. This gives us a means to talk about the magnitude and phase in terms of the magnitude and phase of $F(m)$ (a complex number).

There is a near-mystical expression of equality in mathematics known as Euler's Identity, which links trigonometry, exponential functions, and complex numbers in a single equation:

$$e^{j\theta} = \cos(\theta) + j\sin(\theta).$$

We can use Euler's identity to write the DFT and IDFT in shorthand:

$$F(m) = \Sigma_{n=0 \text{ to } N-1} f(n)e^{-j2\pi mn/N} \qquad (5.6)$$

$$f(n) = 1/N\Sigma_{m=0 \text{ to } N-1} F(m)e^{j2\pi mn/N}. \qquad (5.7)$$

Converting the cosine/sine form to the complex exponential form allows many manipulations that would be very difficult otherwise (for an example, see Section 2 of Appendix A: Convolution and DFT Properties). But, if you're totally uncomfortable with complex numbers and Euler's Identity (or with the identities of 18th century mathematicians in general), then you can write the DFT in real number terms as a form of the Fourier Series:

$$f(n) = 1/N\Sigma_{m=0 \text{ to } N-1} F_b(m)\cos(2\pi mn/N) + F_c(m)\sin(2\pi mn/N) \qquad (5.8)$$

where

$$F_b(m) = \Sigma_{n=0 \text{ to } N-1} f(n)\cos(2\pi mn/N)$$

$$F_c(m) = \Sigma_{n=0 \text{ to } N-1} -f(n)\sin(2\pi mn/N).$$

5.4 Orthogonality and Uniqueness of the DFT

The best way to explain the uniqueness of the Fourier transform is by exploiting the orthogonality property of sinusoids, combined with some basic linear algebra. If we assume that every signal can be composed of harmonically related sinusoids (no reason to assume such a thing, but it's proven in Appendix A, so just play along with me for now), then we can convince ourselves that the Fourier transform is a unique representation of the signal. All we need to do is invoke the *orthogonality of sinusoids* (also defined and proven in Appendix A). In simple geometric terms, *orthogonal* means that two directions lie at right angles; or there is no projection of one onto the other. Linear algebra gives us our definition of orthogonal, meaning that the inner product of two vectors is equal to zero. To state orthogonality of harmonically related sinusoids in words: Any two harmonically related sines (or cosines), when multiplied by each other and integrated (summed) over the fundamental interval, yield a zero result if the sinusoids are not of the same frequency. Further, any harmonically related sine, when multiplied by any harmonically related cosine and integrated over the fundamental interval, always yields zero. To state this mathematically, for all $0 < p, q < N/2$:

$$\Sigma_{n=0 \text{ to } N-1} \sin(2\pi pn/N)\sin(2\pi qn/N) = 0 \quad \text{if } q \neq p$$
$$= N/2 \quad \text{if } q = p;$$

$$\Sigma_{n=0 \text{ to } N-1} \cos(2\pi pn/N)\cos(2\pi qn/N) = 0 \quad \text{if } q \neq p$$
$$= N/2 \quad \text{if } q = p;$$

$$\Sigma_{n=0 \text{ to } N-1} \sin(2\pi pn/N)\cos(2\pi qn/N) = 0 \quad \text{for all } q \text{ and } p.$$

So what does orthogonality mean to us in using the Fourier transform? Well, if we know that any signal $f(n)$ can be represented by harmonically related sine and cosine components, then orthogonality means that we can extract the individual terms by multiplying $f(n)$ by each, one at a time, and get the "projection" of $f(n)$ onto each component individually. We can pull off the individual components in any order, and always come up with the same identical answer for the Fourier coefficients. This is called *uniqueness*, and is proven in Appendix A, with some nice pictures depicting orthogonality.

5.5 Convolution with the DFT and the FFT

If we visit our old pal convolution once again, a most marvelous property of the DFT emerges. I'll skip the derivation (or proof) here, which is shown in Appendix A. For here, the short story is:

$$y(n) = x(n) * h(n) \leftrightarrow Y(e^{j\omega}) = X(e^{j\omega})H(e^{j\omega}).$$

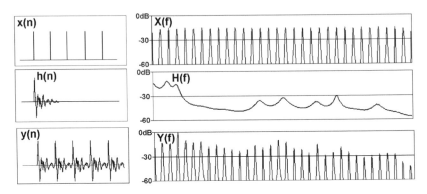

Figure 5.2. Convolution in the time (left) and frequency (right) domains.

This says that convolution (*) in the time domain transforms ($\leftrightarrow$ means "transforms to and back") to multiplication in the frequency domain. This might seem somewhat like the cascading of transfer functions that can be done in the z domain (see Figures 3.14–15), and indeed it is. In fact, we can now define z more thoroughly than just saying "it's a unit sample of delay": z is in fact equal to $e^{j\omega}$, and the unit circle in the z-plane is actually all of the values that z can take on for real values of ω. Now we've got another really good reason to believe that the impulse response of a filter characterizes what that filter will do to an input signal. We can simply form the product, pointwise for frequency samples, of the transform of the input signal x and the transform of the impulse response of the filter h, and the result is the transform of the output signal y. Figure 5.2 shows this process.

If you look at the DFT (and inverse) definition, you will see that it takes about N^2 multiplies to calculate. You have to compute one set for each frequency, of which there are N, and each of those takes N multiplies to go through the time samples. If you look at the DFT theorems in Appendix A, you will see that the data that comes out has special symmetries. That turns out to be true only if the input data consists of real numbers. (Yes, you can take the DFT of complex data, but sound isn't complex, be it Britney Spears or even Bach.) Multiplying a complex number times a real number takes two actual multiplies, but from the symmetry of the DFT for real data, we can cut the whole workload back down to exactly N^2. Except for the insights we might gain from transforming signals to the frequency domain, does it really make sense computationally why we might want to actually do convolutions in the frequency domain? Yep, read on.

The FFT is a cheap way of calculating the DFT. There are thousands of references on the FFT, and scores of implementations of it, so we won't even bother with talking much about it here, except to say that it's lots more efficient than trying to compute the DFT directly from the definition. There are some downsides, such as the fact that FFTs can only be computed for signals whose lengths are exactly powers of two, but the advantages of using it often outweigh the pesky power-of-two problems. Practically speaking, users of the FFT usually carve up signals into smaller chunks (powers of two), or *zero pad* a signal out to the next biggest power of two (see Appendix A). So what's the savings in using the FFT versus the DFT?

A well crafted FFT algorithm for real input data takes on the order of $N\log_2(N)/2$ multiply-adds to compute. Comparing this to the N^2 multiplies of the DFT, N doesn't have to be very big before the FFT is a winner. To do convolution in the frequency domain, we need to add the lengths of both signals to get the DFT length; pad both with zeroes out to the next largest power of two; transform both signals; multiply them; then inverse transform. To take an example of an input signal of 900 sample length, and an impulse response of 100 sample length, we could do the convolution using 1024 point FFTs. Direct convolution would require about 900*100 operations (multiply-adds), while FFT convolution would require about $1024*\log_2(1024) = 1024*10$ operations. So FFT convolution would be about ten times cheaper.

5.6 Some Fourier Transform Applications

As will be discussed in Chapter 6, one of the main uses of the Fourier transform is for analyzing sounds. We can pick peaks in the frequency domain and determine whether they behave like sinusoids. Those peaks can be used to calibrate an additive or modal synthesizer model like we did with the coffee mug in Chapter 4. We can look at gross spectral envelope features, and use those to control a filter-based model. We can also use frequency domain convolution to implement filters, multiplying the spectrum of an input signal by a shaping function spectrum to yield the final filtered output spectrum.

If we have a pitched sound such as a singing voice or trumpet, we can use the FFT to do pitch detection. The term *pitch* is actually a perceptual quantity, meaning that it describes what a human would say or judge about the pitch height of a tone. The FFT can be used to measure frequency, which is a fairly strong correlate of the perception of pitch. There are many methods to estimate pitch, but they generally fall into two classes: time-domain methods and frequency-domain methods. A common time-domain pitch estimation method involves simply inspecting the waveform to determine the period of repetition. This is easily possible with some waveforms such as $x(n)$ and $y(n)$, as shown in Figure 5.2. Many sounds, however, evoke a strong perception of pitch but do not show a clear time-domain periodicity.

Phase corruptions, such as those caused by echoes in rooms, can change the shape of a waveform quite radically, but the pitch of the source is still quite evident to human listeners. The frequency domain provides us with much more robust methods of pitch estimation.

Recall that pitched sounds exhibit a special pattern of sinusoidal modes, called harmonics, which are related by integer ratios. This means that a singing voice at 220 Hz would exhibit a spectrum with sinusoidal peaks at 220, 440, 660, 880, etc. The pitch perception of this sound would be a musical A3 (the A below Middle C on the piano keyboard). To do pitch detection in the frequency domain, all we need to do is to find the peaks and determine what the fundamental is. If we are absolutely sure that the sound is a pitched sound with a strong fundamental, we would simply need to find the fundamental peak. But, if we are sure of that, we can probably do the pitch estimation in the time domain. In reality, even very pitched sounds are noisy; not strictly periodic; or do not exhibit a strong fundamental peak. A fairly simple algorithm for estimating the pitch of a sound consists of finding the significant peaks in the spectrum, sorting them, and finding the most likely fundamental (greatest common divisor) of the peaks.

There are various ways of estimating the "pitchiness" of a sound. One common measure is *harmonicity*, which is how close the first few peaks are to being true integer multiples of the fundamental. Perception research tells us that usually the first five–seven harmonics play the most important role in pitch perception. Another measure of pitchiness is the *Harmonic-to-Noise Ratio* (HNR). This is estimated by computing the power in the harmonics (the sum of the squares of magnitudes of the peaks), computing the power in the remaining (nonpeak, noise) part of the spectrum, and dividing those two numbers. Often HNR is given in dB, which requires computing $10*\log_{10}$(Peak power/noise power). Figure 5.3 shows the process of frequency domain pitch estimation and HNR calculation. The five highest peaks are used to do the calculations, and the HNR is computed up to the frequency of the fifth (highest frequency) peak. An "ahh" vowel is compared to an sss consonant.

The frequencies of the five strongest detected peaks of the sss consonant are 5970, 7816, 8236, 8279, and 8435 Hz. The HNR was computed to be –7 dB, reflecting the fact that the sound is really noise. The frequencies of the five strongest detected peaks of the "ahh" vowel are 1325, 2450, 3412, 3980, and 4730 Hz. These have a common divisor of about 670 Hz (it's a baby saying ahh, thus the high pitch). The HNR was computed to be 8.7 dB.

Another method of estimating the pitch of a signal uses a special form of convolution called *autocorrelation* defined as:

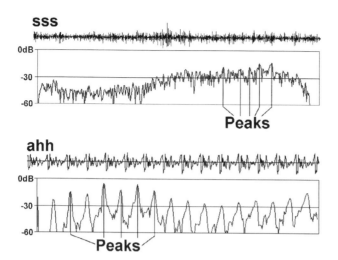

Figure 5.3. Pitch estimation in the frequency domain.

$$x \blacklozenge x(n) = \Sigma_{i = 0 \text{ to } N - 1} x(i)x(i + n). \qquad (5.9)$$

This is a time (lag) domain function that expresses the similarity of a signal to lagged versions of itself. It can also be viewed as the convolution of a signal with the time-reversed version of itself. Pure periodic signals exhibit periodic peaks in the autocorrelation function. Autocorrelations of white noise sequences exhibit only one clear peak at the zero lag position, and are small (zero for infinite length sequences) for all other lags.

The autocorrelation signal can be used to estimate pitch by inspecting for the significant peaks within the expected range of interest. For example, male speaking voice typically ranges from 60 to 200 Hz, while the female singing voice can commonly range up to 2 kHz. The ratio of peak height (periodicity power) to the zero lag peak height (signal power) can be used as an estimate of pitchiness. Figure 5.4 shows the process of pitch estimation on the "ahh" vowel and the "sss" consonant using autocorrelation. The "sss" autocorrelation signal shows no clear peak in the pitch range of interest. The "ahh" autocorrelation signal shows periodic peaks at the lag = 66, 134, etc., sample locations, as well as peaks at 33, 100, etc. The true pitch peak is the lag = 66 location, indicating a pitch of 44100/66 = 668 Hz. The other peaks could potentially yield a false pitch estimate one octave above or below the actual pitch. The lag = 33 peak is due to a pronounced second harmonic component in the "ahh" sound.

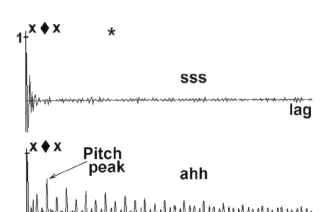

Figure 5.4. Autocorrelation pitch estimation in the lag domain.

5.7 The Short-Time Fourier Transform

Overlap-add time shifting was introduced in Chapter 2, and shown in Figure 2.4. The motivation was to segment the sound into perceptually meaningful slices, then manipulate those. The *Short-Time Fourier Transform* (STFT) breaks up the signal and applies the Fourier transform to each segment individually. By selecting the window size (length of the segments), and hop size (how far the window is advanced along the signal) to be perceptually relevant, the STFT can be used as an approximation of human audio perception. Figure 5.5 shows the "synthesize" waveform and some STFT spectra corresponding to particular points in time.

In addition to audio analysis, there are many other applications of the STFT. Time-varying filtering can be accomplished by STFT in the frequency domain by changing the filter with each window hop. Additive synthesis can be accomplished by "painting" the components into frequency domain frames, then inverse transforming those to form the synthesized signal. The parameter choices of window shape, window size, and hop size are important design decisions that greatly affect the STFT results, behavior, and appearance. In a way, those parameters can be viewed as the lens through which we zoom into our signal and inspect the relevant details. Appendix A talks a little about windowing and the effect on spectral analysis, and we'll talk more about selecting windows and hop sizes in Chapter 7.

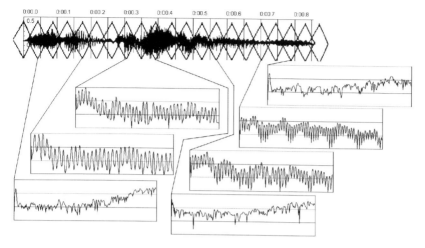

Figure 5.5. Some STFT frames of the word "synthesize."

5.8   Conclusions

Fourier analysis has been called the most important mathematical tool in the history of engineering. The Fast Fourier Transform makes Fourier Analysis economical and much more useful. In the next chapter, we'll look at the spectra of different kinds of signals, and some tools for better analyzing, displaying, and modeling the spectra of sound source objects and systems.

Reading:

Ronald Bracewell. *The Fourier Transform and its Applications.* Boston: McGraw Hill, 2000.

Code:

fft.c

peaksfft.c

pitch.c

colvolve.c

reverse.c

Sounds:

[Track 19] Building a Square Wave from Sine Waves (Bottom Up/Top Down).

[Track 20] Convolving an "ahh" Impulse with a Pulse Train to Make "ahh."

[Track 21] Spoken "Synthesize" and Individual Frames.

Spectral Modeling and Additive Synthesis

6.0 Introduction

In prior chapters we discovered (over and again) how important sine waves are for modeling physical systems (Chapter 4; modes), and for mathematically representing signals and shapes (Chapter 5; Fourier analysis). We finished in Chapter 5 with the notion of a frequency spectrum, computed from a signal by means of the Fourier transform. In this chapter we will look at different types of spectra, noting certain properties and perceptual attributes. We will then revisit the additive synthesis algorithm with an eye toward improving the representation and parametric flexibility for synthesis.

6.1 Types of Spectra

6.1.1 Harmonic

In Chapter 5 we motivated the notion of the Fourier series for representing periodic signals. We saw that periodic (or quasi-periodic) signals exhibit a harmonic spectrum. In general, periodic signals with harmonic spectra are perceived with a strong sense of pitch (at least between 100 and 4000 Hz fundamental frequency). When we think of sounds that give us a strong perception of pitch, we often think of musical tones. The sounds produced by

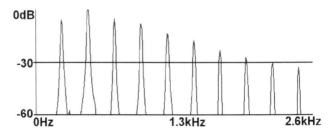

Figure 6.1. Spectrum of trumpet tone steady-state (same tone as shown in Figure 2.1).

trumpets, violins, clarinets, etc., are examples of such harmonic spectra. Figure 6.1 shows the steady-state spectrum of a trumpet tone (from the trumpet tone of Figure 2.1).

Another important set of periodic sounds that have harmonic spectra are the voiced sounds of speech. Figure 6.2 shows the spectrum of the voiced vowel sound "ahh" (as in father), and Figure 6.3 shows the spectrum of the voiced vowel sound "eee" (as in beet).

(((22)))

Speech spectra have important features called *formants* which are the three–five gross peaks in the spectral shape located between 200 and 4000 Hz. These correspond to the resonances of the acoustic tube of the vocal tract. We will discuss formants further in Chapter 8 (Subtractive Synthesis). For now, we will note that the formant locations for the "ahh" vowel are radically different from those for the "eee" vowel, even though the harmonic spacing (and thus, the perceived pitch) is the same for the two vowels. We know this, because a singer can sing the same pitch on many vowels (different spectral shapes, but same harmonic spacings), or the same vowel on many pitches (same spectral shape and formant locations, but different harmonic spacings).

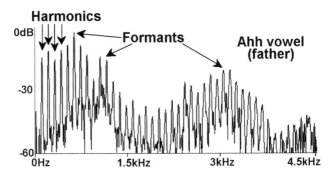

Figure 6.2. Spectrum of voiced vowel sound "ahh" (as in father).

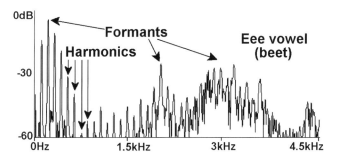

Figure 6.3. Spectrum of voiced vowel "eee" (as in beet).

The property of audio related to spectral shape is called *timbre*. Timbre is often defined as *those properties that allow us to differentiate two sounds which have the same pitch and loudness*. So an "ahh" versus an "eee" sound at the same pitch and loudness would be said to have different timbres. There are other properties related to timbre, such as the attack time of a sound, whether it is sustained or not, harmonicity versus inharmonicity, and the amount of noise contained in the signal. In the next sections, we will look at these components, and how they evolve in time.

6.1.2 Inharmonic

Many systems exhibit strong sinusoidal modes, but these modes are not restricted to any specific harmonic series. Such systems include even relatively simple shapes such as circular drum heads, square plates, and cylindrical water glasses. For example, a square metal plate would exhibit modes that are spaced related to the roots of integers (irrational numbers, so clearly inharmonic),

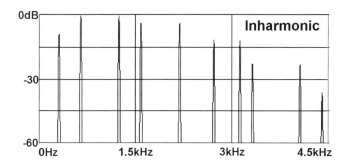

Figure 6.4. The inharmonic spectrum of a metal chime.

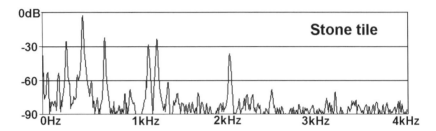

Figure 6.5. Spectrum of a struck square stone tile.

while a circular drum head would exhibit modes related to the roots of Bessel functions (also irrational, and clearly inharmonic). Figure 6.4 shows the inharmonic spectrum of a metal chime tone.

Figure 6.5 shows the spectrum of a struck square stone tile, and Figure 6.6 shows the spectrum of a struck circular drum (an African djembe). All of these spectra show clear sinusoidal modes, but the modes are not harmonically related.

6.1.3 Noise

There are many sounds that do not exhibit any clear sinusoidal modes. Whispered speech, wind blowing through trees, the crunches of our feet on gravel as we walk, and the sound of an airplane taking off are all examples of sounds that do not have clear sinusoidal modes. We can still represent these sounds using sums of sinusoids via the Discrete Fourier Transform, although it might not be a particularly efficient or revealing representation. Such sounds are generally classified as *noise*. Figure 6.7 shows the spectrum of a *white* (flat spectrum) noise signal. Another type of *pure* noise is called *pink* noise, which has a spectrum that rolls off linearly with log frequency.

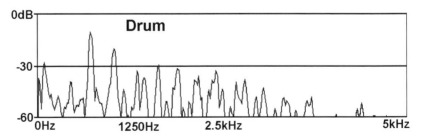

Figure 6.6. Spectrum of a circular drum head.

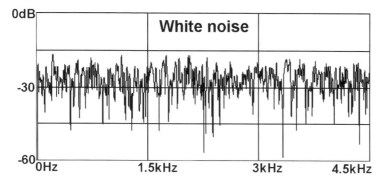

Figure 6.7. Spectrum of white noise signal.

Since we know we can whisper speech as well as voice it, we might get some clues as to what is going on perceptually from looking at the spectra of whispered vowels. We can whisper an "ahh" or "eee," and there will be no particular pitch to the sound, but the perception of each vowel remains. Figure 6.8 shows the spectrum of a whispered ahh, and Figure 6.9 shows the spectrum of a whispered eee. Note that the spectrum has no clear sinusoids (at least not spaced widely enough to be perceived or seen as individual sinusoidal modes), but still exhibits the formant peaks that are characteristic of those vowels.

((‹24›))

6.1.4 Mixtures

Of course, most of the sounds we hear in day-to-day life are mixtures of other sounds. Even isolated single-source sounds will usually exhibit a mixture of spectral properties. For example, even our voiced speech vowels still have

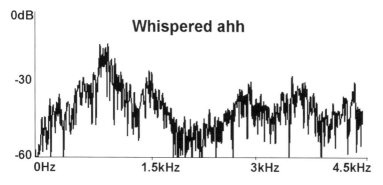

Figure 6.8. Spectrum of a whispered "ahh" sound.

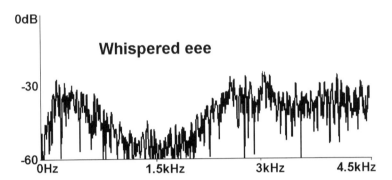

Figure 6.9. Spectrum of a whispered "eee" sound.

some noise components mixed in. A close inspection of Figures 6.2 and 6.3 will reveal that there is some amount of "fuzz" between the harmonics, corresponding to a breathy component in the voice. Another example can be found in percussive sounds, which might display clear sinusoidal modes, but also have lots of noise during the excitation segment of the sound. Figure 6.10 shows the spectrum of a struck wooden bar. Note that there are only three clear modes. The other spectral information is better described as noise.

6.2 Spectral Modeling

The notion that some components of sounds are well-modeled by sinusoids, while other components are better modeled by spectrally shaped noise, further motivates the residual-excited refinement to the purely sinusoidal additive synthesis model presented in Chapter 4 (Figure 4.4). Using the Fourier transform, we can inspect the spectrum of a sound and determine which

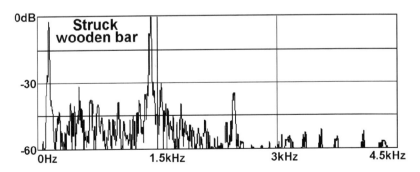

Figure 6.10. Spectrum of a struck wooden bar.

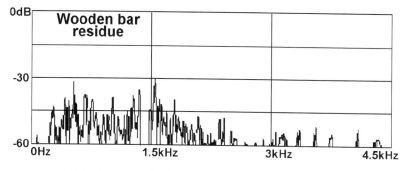

Figure 6.11. Spectrum of noise-only component of wooden bar strike.

components would be well-modeled by sinusoids. With careful signal processing, we can then subtract those components from the original signal. Ideally, what is left after subtracting the sinusoids will have no sinusoidal components remaining, and will thus be only noise component. Figure 6.11 shows the spectrum of the noise residual of the wooden bar strike after removing the sinusoidal modes.

((‹25›))

The notion of "sines plus noise" modeling was posed and implemented by Xavier Serra and Julius Smith in the *Spectral Modeling Synthesis* (SMS) system. They called the sinusoidal components the *deterministic* component of the signal, and the leftover noise part the *residual* or *stochastic* component. Figure 6.12 shows the decomposition of a sung "ahh" sound into deterministic (harmonic sinusoidal) and stochastic (noise residue) components.

6.2.1 Spectral Modeling to Improve Additive Synthesis

Informed by the technique of sines plus noise spectral modeling, we can now improve our sinusoidal additive synthesis model significantly by simply adding a filtered noise source as shown in Figure 6.13.

The beauty of this type of model is that it recognizes the dominant sinusoidal nature of many sounds while still recognizing the noisy components that might be also present. More efficient and parametric representations— and many interesting modifications—can be made to the signal on resynthesis. For example, removing the harmonics from voiced speech, followed by resynthesizing with a scaled version of the noise residual, can result in the synthesis of whispered speech. Pitch and time shifting can be accomplished, but extra information is available to do the shifts more intelligently. For example, if the signal is speech and a segment seems to have no sinusoidal components, it is likely a consonant. Time or pitch shifting might be performed differently, or not at all, in such segments.

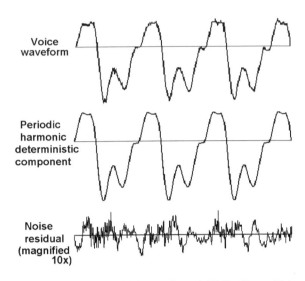

Figure 6.12. Top: Original sung "ahh" waveform. Middle: Sinusoidal components. Bottom: Residual components.

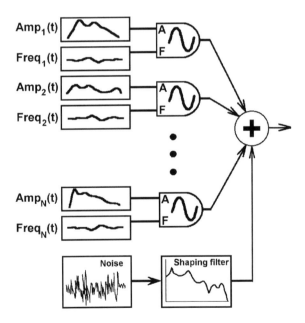

Figure 6.13. Sinusoidal additive model with filtered noise added for spectral modeling synthesis.

6.3 Sines Plus Noise Plus Transients

One further improvement to spectral modeling is the recognition (by Verma and Meng) that there are often brief (impulsive) moments in sounds that are really too short in time to be adequately analyzed by spectrum analysis. Further, such moments in the signal usually corrupt the sinusoidal/noise analysis process. Such events, called transients, can be modeled in other ways (often by simply keeping the stored PCM for that segment). Figure 6.14 shows the process of decomposing a signal into a transient, then sinusoidal components, then a noise residual.

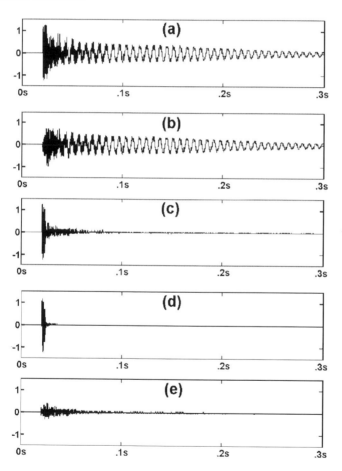

Figure 6.14. a) Original signal; b) without transient; c) transient with noise (sines removed); d) transient alone; e) noise alone (see *Verma and Meng*).

6.4 Spectra in Time

Of course, one of the most important aspects of sound is that it takes place in, and evolves over time. The basis of many of our time-domain manipulations in Chapter 2, and of short-time Fourier analysis as discussed in Chapter 5, is the breaking up of long sounds into shorter windows to more closely match our perception of frequency-domain aspects (relatively constant within a window) versus time-domain aspects (things that change slowly—remember the 30 Hz shift). Thus, it is often useful to plot spectra as they evolve in time. The two most common ways to do that are called the *spectrogram* (or *sonogram*), and the *waterfall plot*. In the spectrogram (sonogram), time runs left to right on the abcissa (*x*-axis), frequency runs bottom to top, and intensity is plotted as grayscale or color. In the waterfall plot, frequency runs left to right, intensity is plotted as height, and time runs diagonally upward plotted as a pseudo-three-dimensional depth. Each waterfall time "slice" shown is a traditional frequency spectrum.

Figure 6.15 shows a spectrogram plot of a plucked string tone, and Figure 6.16 shows a waterfall plot of the same plucked string tone. Note the harmonics and the way that high frequencies decay faster than the low frequencies. Also note that the first and second modes are strong, the third is weaker, and the fourth is nearly absent. The fifth is strong, and the sixth and seventh are weak. The eighth and ninth are stronger, and the tenth–twelfth are weak. These observations, combined with the plucked string boundary condition discussion in Chapter 4, indicate that the string was plucked at somewhere between the 1/3 and 1/4 position along the string.

To present an additional example of the usefulness of the sonogram, Figure 6.17 shows a sonogram of the "synthesize" utterance introduced in

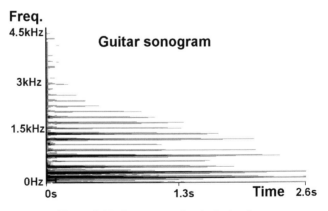

Figure 6.15. Sonogram of a plucked string.

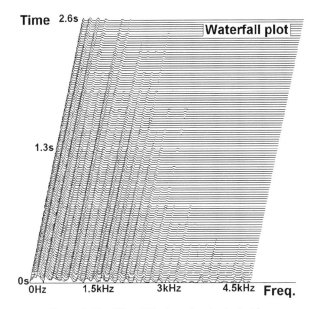

Figure 6.16. Waterfall plot of a plucked string.

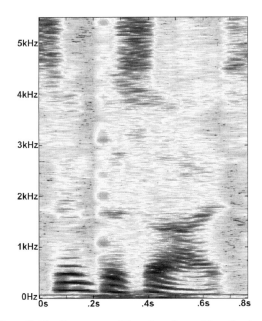

Figure 6.17. Sonogram of the uttered word "synthesize."

Chapter 2. Inspecting the spectrogram allows us to see the individual phonemes. Vowels /I/, /U/, /a/, etc., exhibit harmonics (parallel horizontal stripes), while consonants /s/, /th/, and /z/ show as vertical clouds of high-frequency fuzz.

6.5 Conclusion

In this chapter (and in the prior chapter on the Fourier transform) we've seen that lots of interesting information can be gleaned by transforming waveforms into the frequency domain. The appearance of a spectral plot can often be directly related to the sonic quality of the auditory experience of hearing that sound. In future chapters, we will return to the spectrum often to observe characteristics of sounds and the vibrations of physical systems.

Reading:

Robert J. McAulay and Thomas Quatieri. "Speech Analysis/Synthesis Based on a Sinusoidal Representation." *IEEE Transactions Acoustics, Speech, and Signal Processing ASSP* (34): 744–754 (August 1986).

Xavier Serra and Julius O. Smith. "Spectral Modeling Synthesis: A Sound Analysis/Synthesis System Based on a Deterministic Plus Stochastic Decomposition." *Computer Music Journal* 14(4):12–24 (1990).

Tony Verma and Teresa Meng. "An Analysis/Synthesis Tool for Transient Signals that Allows a Flexible Sines + Transients + Noise Model for Audio." IEEE ICASSP-98. (1998).

Code:

```
fft.c

peaksfft.c

notchfft.c
```

Sounds:

[Track 22] Harmonic Sounds: Trumpet, "ahh," and "eee."

[Track 23] Inharmonic Sounds: Synth Bell, Stone Tile, Djembe Drum.

[Track 24] White Noise, Pink Noise, Whispered "ahh" and "eee."

[Track 25] Marimba Strike and Residue, Voice Original, Periodic, Residue.

[Track 26] Transient Extraction/Modeling (from *Verma and Meng*).

Subband Vocoders
and Filterbanks

7.0 Introduction

This chapter will look at the powerful signal processing techniques known collectively as spectral subband *vocoders* (VOice CODERs). Vocoders came from the early legacy of speech signal processing. In the *channel vocoder* and *phase vocoder*, the spectrum is broken into sections called *subbands*, and the information in each subband is analyzed. The analyzed parameters are then stored or transmitted (potentially compressed) for reconstruction at another time or physical site. The parametric data representing the information in each subband can be manipulated in various ways, yielding transformations such as pitch or time shifting, spectral shaping, cross synthesis, and other effects.

7.1 Subband Decomposition of Audio

Based (somewhat) on the frequency analysis properties of the human ear and auditory system, a common signal processing technique involves splitting sound into separate frequency bands. A common decomposition is based on octaves, successively dividing the spectrum by two. Ten bands are required

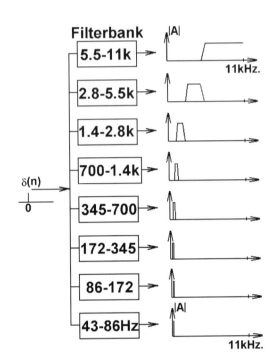

Figure 7.1. An eight-band octave filterbank.

to cover the entire audible range: 10–20 k; 5–10 k; 2.5–5 k; 1.25–2.5 k; 600–1.25 k; 300–600; 150–300; 75–150; 37–75; and 18–37 Hz. A bank of filters is used to perform the subband decomposition. An eight-band octave filterbank is shown in Figure 7.1.

Sometimes 30 bands are used on a logarithmic scale to cover the audible range in 1/3 octave steps. These steps correspond roughly to an important resolution attribute of the human auditory system called the *Critical Band*. Sound intensity within a critical band can be manipulated in fairly extreme ways without changing the perceptual result, as shown in Figure 7.2.

Figure 7.3 shows an eight–octave filterbank decomposition of the utterance of the word "synthesize." Note the high frequency energy in the "s" and "z" sounds (0.05, 0.35, and 0.75 seconds) in comparison with the vowels "ih" (0.15 s), "uh" (0.35 s), etc. Also note how the energy shifts in the lower bands during the diphthong "ai," from "aah" to "eeh" (0.45 to 0.55 s).

Those of you who have shopped for stereo or recording equipment might remember that graphic equalizers often come in flavors of five–seven bands (car radios), ten bands, and 30 bands (for professional recording). Many

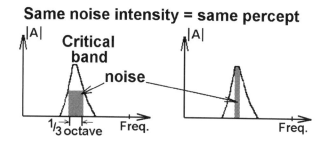

Figure 7.2. A critical band is roughly 1/3 octave. Equal noise intensity within a critical band sounds the same.

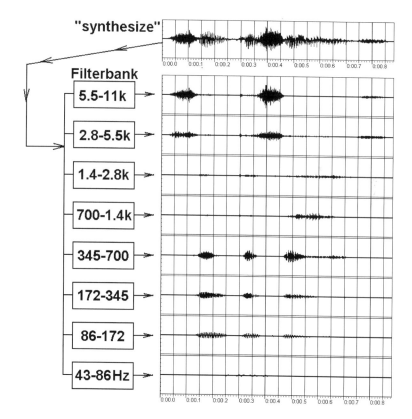

Figure 7.3. Eight-octave decomposition of "synthesize."

computer audio player programs provide a real-time spectrum display, often as a set of 10 or 30 bars whose heights display the energy in each frequency band. This is further indication that splitting the spectrum into roughly equal width bands in log frequency space allows for interesting spectral analysis and manipulation.

7.2 The Channel Vocoder

The *channel vocoder* captures the time-varying sound energy within each frequency subband, typically using eight to 30 subbands to cover the entire audible spectrum. We've seen how a filterbank can split a signal into separate frequency bands. To build a channel vocoder, we need a method of measuring the energy in each subband. If we look at the separate audio bands in Figure 7.3, we can easily see places where the energy increases and decreases. We'd like to measure how this energy changes with time, sampling the energy in small windows (10–50 ms based on our 30 millisecond rule introduced in Chapter 1). The signal energy (square root of the power) over a window of length N is defined as:

$$E(x) = 1/N \sqrt{\Sigma_{i=1 \ to \ N} \ x(i)^2}. \qquad (7.1)$$

One way to approximately estimate energy without actually computing Equation 7.1 is to sum the magnitude of the samples:

$$\hat{E}(x) = 1/N \Sigma_{i=1-N} |x(i)|. \qquad (7.2)$$

For either of Equation 7.1 or 7.2, the length-N window would be "hopped" along in the same way the STFT is computed (discussed in Chapter 5). Additional simplifications can be introduced. A common method of computing a running estimate, called *envelope following*, is shown in Figure 7.4.

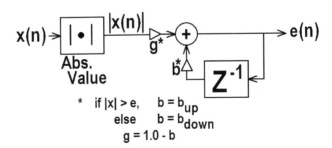

Figure 7.4. Nonlinear digital envelope follower.

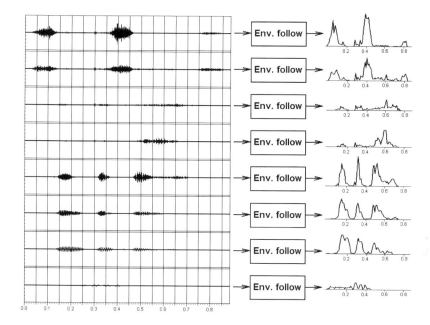

Figure 7.5. Envelope follower outputs of "synthesize" subbands.

The absolute value stage serves to turn negative valleys into positive peaks (rectification). The peaks are then integrated using a special nonlinear one-pole filter. The one-pole filter has one time constant (pole position = b_{up}) for rising signals and another, (b_{down}), for falling signals. The rising time constant is set to be faster (less low pass filtering) than the fall time (more filtering). The result is a signal that is a smoothed envelope of the peak amplitude of the signal. Figure 7.5 shows the result of processing each of the eight subbands of "synthesize" (from Figure 7.3) through an envelope follower. The smoothed envelope signals have much lower bandwidth (due to low pass filtering) than the subband output signals, and can be sampled at a much lower rate than the audio signals. Typical envelope sampling rates range from 20–200 Hz.

Figure 7.6 shows a block diagram of a channel vocoder. The detected envelopes serve as *control signals* for a bank of bandpass *synthesis filters* (identical to the *analysis filters* used to extract the subband envelopes). The synthesis filters have gain inputs that are fed by the control signals.

When used to encode and process speech, the channel vocoder explicitly makes an assumption that the signal being modeled is a single human voice. The *source analysis* block extracts some parameters about the fine spectral detail, such as whether the sound is pitched (vowel) or noisy (consonant or

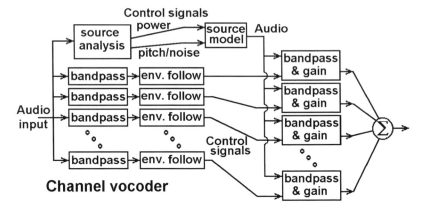

Figure 7.6. Channel vocoder block diagram.

whispered). If the sound is pitched, the pitch is estimated. The overall energy in the signal is also estimated. These parameters become additional low-bandwidth control signals for the synthesizer. Intelligible speech can be synthesized using only a few hundred numbers per second. An example coding scheme might use eight channel gains, plus pitch and power per frame, at 40 frames per second; yielding a total of only 400 numbers per second.

The channel vocoder, as designed for speech coding, does not generalize to arbitrary sounds, and fails horribly when the source parameters deviate from expected harmonicity, reasonable pitch range, etc. But the ideas of subband decomposition, envelope detection, and driving a synthesis filterbank with control signals give rise to many other interesting applications and implementations of the vocoder concept.

7.3 The Cross-Synthesizing Channel Vocoder

Bandpass filterbanks and envelope followers can be implemented using analog circuitry. The control signals can be fed to voltage-controlled amplifiers in the synthesis stage. A number of analog hardware devices were produced and sold as musical instrument processing devices in the 1970-80s. These were called simply vocoders, but had a different purpose than speech coding. Figure 7.7 shows the block diagram of a *cross-synthesizing vocoder*. The main difference is that the parametric source has been replaced by an arbitrary audio signal.

The cross-synthesizer can be used to make nonspeech sounds talk or sing. A typical example would be feeding a voice into the analysis filterbank,

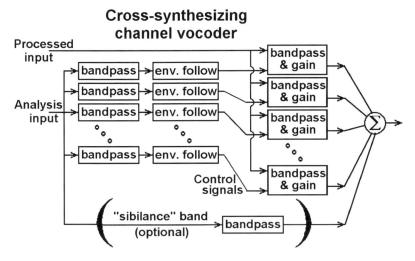

Figure 7.7. Cross-synthesizing vocoder block diagram.

and an electric guitar sound into the synthesis bank audio inputs. To be effective, the synthesis audio input should have suitably rich spectral content (distorted electric guitar for instance works better than nondistorted). Some vocoders allowed an additional direct *sibilance band* (like the one or two highest bands shown in Figure 7.3) pass-through of the analyzed sound. This would allow consonants to pass through directly, creating a more intelligible speech-like effect.

((28))

7.4. The Phase Vocoder

The channel vocoder uses only information about the time-varying energy within each band, and no attempt is made to retain the actual waveshape or fine detail of the original signal. Using the Fast Fourier Transform (FFT), the *phase vocoder* processes sound by calculating and maintaining both magnitude and phase. The frequency bins (basis sinusoids) of the Discrete Fourier Transform (DFT) can be viewed as narrowband filters; thus the Fourier transform of the input signal can be viewed as passing it through a bank of narrow bandpass filters. This means that hundreds to thousands of subbands are used. Unlike the speech channel vocoder, the phase vocoder does not perform an explicit source/filter decomposition, and there is no parametric model of the source. The phase vocoder does not strictly assume that the signal is speech, and thus can generalize to other sounds. For this reason, the phase vocoder has found extensive use in computer music composition.

Cross-synthesis can be accomplished using the phase vocoder in much the same way as the channel vocoder. Assuming one signal is the analysis signal, the time-varying magnitude spectrum of that signal (usually smoothed in the frequency domain) is multiplied by the spectral frames of the input signal (sometimes brightened first by high frequency emphasis pre-filtering), yielding a composite signal that has the attributes of both. Many effects can be accomplished using the phase vocoder, including nearly artifact-free time and pitch shifting; and also cross-synthesis, including talking cows, "morphs" between people and cats, trumpet/flute hybrids, etc.

The FFT-based phase vocoder processes the signal in blocks of many samples and analyzes it into an equal number of subbands. As such it does little by itself to make sounds meaningfully parametric. Analysis systems that make the data parametric in some way allow manipulation of a relative few parameters rather than thousands of numbers per second. For anything other than simple time shifting, spectrum stretching, and cross-synthesis, more processing must be done on the raw spectral data yielded by the phase vocoder to make it useful for composition, sound effects processing, or production sound design.

7.5 Conclusions

Much in the same way as our auditory systems, subband decomposition allows us to inspect sound in terms of energy in different regions of the frequency spectrum as it evolves in time. For some types of sounds, this kind of model can be a natural and efficient parameterization of the signal. Because of the natural match to the source-filter model of the human vocal system, spectral subband vocoders have found success in coding and compressing speech. By analyzing speech sounds and applying the extracted parameters to other types of sounds, cross-synthesis allows us to create talking guitars, singing cows, etc. The Fourier Transform can be used as a high-precision phase vocoder, but takes more processing and software to use it effectively as a sonic manipulation tool. The next chapter will look at more flexible source-filter decomposition methods.

Reading:

Homer Dudley. "The Vocoder." Bell Laboratories Record, December, 1939. Reprinted in *IEEE Transactions on Acoustics, Speech and Signal Processing ASSP* 29(3):347–351(1981).

James Andy Moorer. "The Use of the Phase Vocoder in Computer Music Applications." *Journal of the Audio Engineering Society* 26 (1/2): 42–45(1978).

Mark Dolson. "The Phase Vocoder: A Tutorial." *Computer Music Journal* 10 (4): 14–27(1986).

Code:

fft.c

subband.c

vocod.c

Sounds:

[Track 27] Original "Synthesize" and Separate Octave Subbands.

[Track 28] Cross Synthesis Examples.

[Track 29] Phase Vocoder Pitch and Time Shifting Examples.

Subtractive Synthesis and LPC

8.0 Introduction

In prior chapters we found that spectral shape is important to our perception of sounds, such as vowel/consonant distinctions, the different timbres of the vowels "eee" and "ahh," etc. We also discovered that sinusoids are not the only way to look at modeling the spectra of sounds (or sound components), and that sometimes just capturing the spectral shape is the most important thing in parametric sound modeling. Chapters 5 and 6 both centered on the notion of additive synthesis, where sinusoids and other components are added to form a final wave that exhibits the desired spectral properties. In this chapter we will develop and refine the notion of subtractive synthesis and discuss techniques and tools for calibrating the parameters of subtractive synthesis to real sounds. The main technique we will use is called *Linear Predictive Coding* (LPC), which will allow us to automatically fit a low-order resonant filter to the spectral shape of a sound.

8.1 Subtractive Synthesis

The basic idea of subtractive synthesis is to use a complex sound source to excite resonant filters. Certain types of spectrally rich sounds are simple to

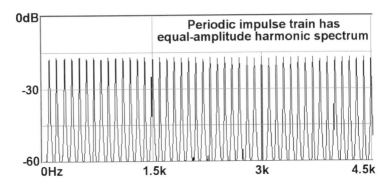

Figure 8.1. Flat spectrum of periodic impulse train.

create: Examples include an impulse, a chain of periodic impulses, and a series of random numbers (noise). From our experience in Chapter 6, we found that fine features of the spectrum (individual sine peaks, harmonicity, inharmonicity, noise, etc.) are important for some aspects of perception, and that coarse features such as overall spectral tilt and peaks (formants) are also important for perception. From earlier chapters on filters, convolution, and the Fourier transform, we know that filters can be used to shape the spectrum in fairly arbitrary ways. If we start with a chain of periodic impulses, exhibiting a harmonic spectrum of equal-amplitude sinusoids as shown in Figure 8.1, and process it with a filter whose magnitude transfer function has the spectrum shown in Figure 8.2, the result is the product of the two spectra (convolution in the time domain is point-wise multiplication in the frequency domain— from Chapter 3 and Appendix A) as shown in Figure 8.3. The filter is used to shape the sound to the desired spectrum, or subtract away the unwanted parts.

《‹30›》

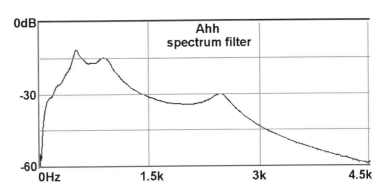

Figure 8.2. Magnitude transfer function of "ahh" filter.

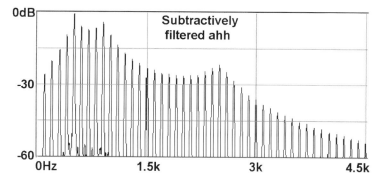

Figure 8.3. Result of filtering impulse train by "ahh" filter.

8.2 Resonance-Factored (Formant) Synthesis

In Chapter 4, we developed the notion that individual resonant filters can be used to model each vibrational mode of a system excited by an impulse. Thus, modal synthesis is a form of subtractive synthesis. For modeling the gross peaks in a spectrum, which could correspond to resonances (although these resonances are weaker than the sinusoidal modes we talked about in Chapter 4), we can exploit the resonance-factored form of a filter to perform our subtractive synthesis. The benefits of this are that we can control the resonances (and thus, spectral shape) independently. The filter can be implemented in series or cascade (chain of convolutions) as shown in Figure 8.4. The filter can also be implemented in parallel (separate subband sections of the spectrum added together), as shown in Figure 8.5.

But how do we know how to set the filter parameters (coefficients and gains) for subtractive synthesis? If we have control over the input and access

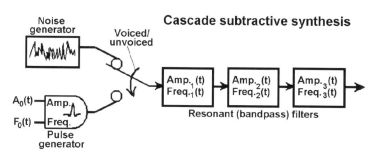

Figure 8.4. Cascade-factored formant subtractive synthesizer.

Parallel subtractive synthesis

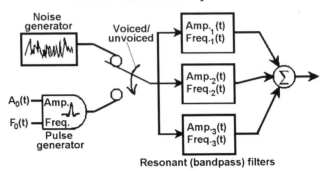

Resonant (bandpass) filters

Figure 8.5. Parallel-factored formant subtractive synthesizer.

to the output of the system we're trying to model, we can put an impulse into the input, and the output will be the impulse response of our desired filter (if the system is linear and time-invariant). But what if we just have a recording of a sound? We would like a technique that could automatically extract the gross spectral features, design a filter to match those, and give us a "source" that we could then use to drive the filter. We could try to do this by looking at the spectrum, noting the gross shape and the fine features. The next section will discuss a mathematical technique that does this same kind of decomposition automatically.

8.3 Linear Prediction

Time series prediction is the task of estimating future samples from prior samples. It has origins and applications in many disciplines. For example, what if you could predict the prices of stocks by observing their past behavior, or imagine how life would change if we could accurately predict rainfall and temperature? Linear prediction is the task of estimating a future sample (usually the next in the time series) by forming a linear combination of some number of prior samples. Figure 8.6 shows linear prediction in block diagram form. The difference equation for a linear predictor is:

$$y(n) = \hat{x}(n + 1) = \Sigma_{i = 0 \text{ to } m} a_i x(n - i). \tag{8.1}$$

Note that this is the standard FIR form as discussed in Chapter 3, but the output is an estimate of the next sample in time. The task of linear prediction is to select the vector of predictor coefficients:

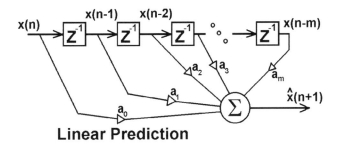

Linear Prediction

Figure 8.6. A linear prediction filter.

$$A = [a_0, a_1, a_2 \ldots, a_m],$$

such that $\hat{x}(n + 1)$ (the estimate) is as close as possible to $x(n + 1)$ (the real sample) over a set of samples (often called a frame) $x(0)$ to $x(N - 1)$.

Usually "as close as possible" is defined by minimizing the *Mean Square Error* (MSE) citerion, which minimizes:

$$\text{MSE} = 1/N \, \Sigma_{i=0 \text{ to } N-1} [\hat{x}(n + 1) - x(n + 1)]^2. \qquad (8.2)$$

Many methods exist for arriving at the set of predictor coefficients a_i which yield a minimum MSE: One will be discussed in the next section.

Once a set of predictor coefficients has been computed, the error signal can be computed as:

$$\varepsilon(n + 1) = \hat{x}(n + 1) - x(n + 1). \qquad (8.3)$$

You should recognize this signal as the one that is being squared and summed over the frame to form the MSE. This signal is also sometimes called the *innovations signal,* because it represents all that is new about the signal that the linear prediction cannot capture.

8.3.1 Autocorrelation Method for LPC Coefficients

One commonly used method of computing the linear prediction coefficients uses the "autocorrelation" function, defined as:

$$x \blacklozenge x(n) = \Sigma_{i=0 \text{ to } N-1} x(i) \, x(i + n). \qquad (8.4)$$

Remember, we used autocorrelation as a means to do pitch estimation in Chapter 5. Autocorrelation computes a time (lag) domain function that expresses the similarity of a signal to lagged versions of itself. It can also be viewed as the convolution of a signal with the time-reversed version of itself. Pure periodic signals exhibit periodic peaks in the autocorrelation function. Autocorrelations of white noise sequences exhibit only one clear peak at the zero lag position, and are small (zero for infinite length sequences) for all other lags. Since the autocorrelation function contains useful information about a signal's similarity to itself at various delays, we might suspect it could help us arrive at the linear prediction coefficients. Indeed it does. If we form the autocorrelation matrix, denoted here as R,

$$R = \begin{bmatrix} x \blacklozenge x(0) & x \blacklozenge x(1) & x \blacklozenge x(2) & \cdots & x \blacklozenge x(m) \\ x \blacklozenge x(1) & x \blacklozenge x(0) & x \blacklozenge x(1) & \cdots & x \blacklozenge x(m-1) \\ x \blacklozenge x(2) & x \blacklozenge x(1) & x \blacklozenge x(0) & \cdots & x \blacklozenge x(m-2) \\ x \blacklozenge x(3) & x \blacklozenge x(2) & x \blacklozenge x(1) & \cdots & x \blacklozenge x(m-3) \\ \cdot & \cdot & \cdot & \cdots & \cdot \\ x \blacklozenge x(m) & x \blacklozenge x(m-1) & x \blacklozenge x(m-2) & \cdots & x \blacklozenge x(0) \end{bmatrix}$$

(8.5)

we can get the least-squares predictor coefficients by forming:

$$A = [a_0, a_1, a_2, a_3 \ldots a_m] = PR^{-1} \qquad (8.6)$$

where P is the vector of prediction correlation coefficients:

$$P = [x \blacklozenge x(1) \ x \blacklozenge x(2) \ x \blacklozenge x(3) \ldots x \blacklozenge x(m+1)]. \qquad (8.7)$$

8.4 LPC Speech Examples

A common and popular use of LPC is for speech analysis, synthesis, and compression. The reason for this is that the voice can be viewed as a source-filter model, where a spectrally rich input (pulses from the vocal folds or noise from turbulence) excites a filter (the resonances of the vocal tract). LPC is another form of vocoder (voice coder) as discussed in Chapter 7, but since LPC filters are not fixed in frequency or shape, fewer bands are needed to dynamically model the changing speech spectral shape.

LPC speech analysis/coding involves processing the signal in blocks and computing a set of filter coefficients for each block. Based on the slowly varying nature of speech sounds (the speech articulators can only move so fast), the coefficients are relatively stable for milliseconds at a time (typically

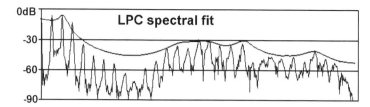

Figure 8.7. Tenth order LPC filter fit to a voiced "ooo" spectrum.

5–20 ms is used in speech coders). If we store the coefficients and information about the residual signal for each block, we will have captured the essential aspects of the signal. Figure 8.7 shows an LPC fit to a speech spectrum. Note that the fit is better at the peak locations than at the valleys. This is due to the least-squares minimization criterion. Missing the mark on low amplitude parts of the spectrum is not as important as missing it on high amplitude parts. This is fortunate for audio signal modeling, in that the human auditory system is more sensitive to spectral peaks (formants, poles, resonances) than valleys (zeroes, antiresonances).

Once we've performed LPC on speech, if we inspect the residual we might note that that it is often a stream of pulses for voiced speech, or white noise for unvoiced speech. Thus, if we store parameters about the residual— such as whether it is periodic pulses or noise, the frequency of the pulse, and the energy in the residual—then we can get back a signal that is very close to the original. This is the basis of much of modern speech compression. Figure 8.8 shows the waveform and spectral slices of the diphthong /ai/ (from "synthesize"), and the residual after linear prediction. Note how the residue spectrum has been "whitened," making it essentially flat. The filters model all the peaks and valleys in the spectrum, leaving a pulse stream (with some noise) as the residue.

If a signal is entirely predictable using a linear combination of prior samples, and if the FIR predictor filter is doing its job perfectly, we should be able to hook the output back to the input and let the filter predict the rest of the signal automatically. Any deviation of the predicted signal from the actual original signal will show up in the error signal, so if we excite the IIR LPC filter (the FIR predictor with output connected to input) with the residual signal itself, we can get back the original signal exactly. Performing deconvolution to separate the source from the filter and using the residue to excite the filter to arrive at the original signal is another form of identity analysis/resynthesis.

LPC can be used for cross-synthesis, as described in Chapter 7, by keeping the time-varying filter coefficients and replacing the residual with some other

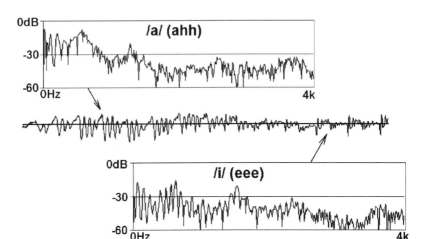

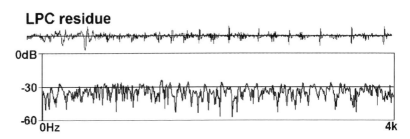

Figure 8.8. Top: Original /ai/ diphthong. Lower: Residual and spectrum of entire diphthong after linear prediction.

sound source. Singing cows, talking door squeaks, etc., are all easy to synthesize using LPC cross-synthesis. Using the parametric source model also allows for flexible time and pitch shifting, without modifying the basic timbre. The voiced pulse period and the frame rate update of the filter can be modified independently. Thus, it is easy to speed up a speech sound while making the pitch lower, still retaining the basic spectral shapes of all vowels and consonants.

8.5 LPC for Nonspeech and Real-World Sounds

There are sounds other than speech that can be decomposed using the source/filter model. Recall our struck coffee cup example from Chapter 4, where we

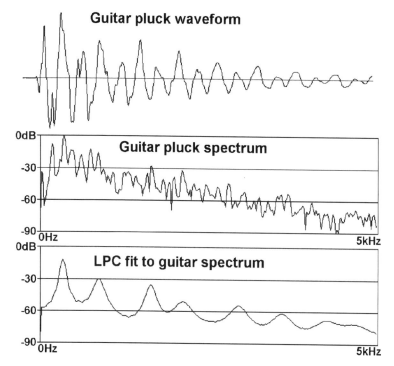

Figure 8.9. Top: Time waveform of guitar pluck. Center: Spectrum of guitar pluck. Lower: Spectrum of LPC fit to guitar pluck.

removed the main resonances of the cup (our filter), yielding a residue that was just the sound of the pen hitting (our source). LPC can be used to design filters whenever there is an interesting spectral resonant structure. It is also useful when there is significant time variation in the timbral content of a sound.

As a musical example, Figure 8.9 shows the time domain waveform and frequency spectrum of a guitar pluck, and the LPC filter fit to the guitar sound. If everything worked perfectly in decomposing the sound into a source and a filter, the filter would model the gross resonances related to the body of the guitar, and the residual would contain the raw string sound.

As a final example, let's take a common real-world interaction—hammering a nail—and investigate the use of LPC to model it. The left side of Figure 8.10 shows a spectrogram of 12 strikes of a hammer on a nail, driving it into a wooden 2 × 4 board. Note the characteristic nail resonance sweeping upward from 200 Hz as the steel nail shortens going into the wood. The sound was analyzed and parametrically resynthesized (using only pulse/

((‹32›))

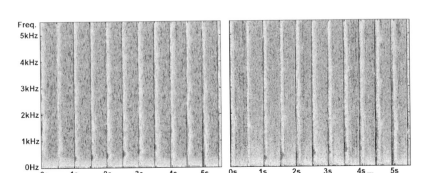

Figure 8.10. Left: Hammering a nail. Right: LPC resynthesis.

noise excitation, no residue) with tenth order LPC, a frame size of 12 ms, and a hop size of 6 ms. The right side of Figure 8.10 is the spectrogram of the parametric LPC resynthesis.

While the original and resynthesized hammer/nail spectrograms differ somewhat, the perceptual quality of the resynthesis is quite good. Once analyzed and parameterized, the sound can be resynthesized with time scaling, pitch scaling, modifications on the filter parameters, etc. Finally, there is an approximate 30:1 compression ratio in coding the sound using LPC (the silence between the hammer strikes helps a lot).

((‹**33**›))

8.6 LPC and Physics

In decomposing signals into a source and a filter, LPC can be a marvelous aid in analyzing and understanding some sound producing systems. The all-pole LPC reconstruction filter can be implemented in a ladder filter structure (just another IIR filter topology), which carries with it a notion of one-dimensional spatial propagation as well. Figure 8.11 shows a ladder filter realization of a tenth order IIR filter. We will refer to this type of filter when we investigate some one-dimensional physical models in the next chapters.

8.7 Conclusions

Subtractive synthesis uses a complex source wave—such as an impulse, a periodic train of impulses, or white noise—to excite a spectral-shaping filter. Linear prediction, or linear predictive coding (LPC), gives us a mathematical technique for automatically decomposing a sound into a source and a filter. For low order LPC (6–20 poles or so), the filter is fit to the coarse spectral

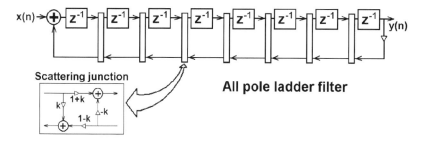

Figure 8.11. Ladder filter implementation of all-pole LPC filter.

features, and the residue contains the remaining part of the sound that cannot be linearly predicted. LPC works well for speech, because of the source-filter nature of the human vocal tract. It can also be a useful tool for analyzing and modeling other types of sounds.

Reading:

L. Rabiner. "Digital Formant Synthesizer." *Journal of the Acoustical Society of America* 43(4): 822–828 (1968).

Dennis Klatt. "Software for a Cascade/Parallel Formant Synthesizer." *Journal of the Acoustical Society of America* 67(3): 971–995 (1980).

Bishnu Atal. "Speech Analysis and Synthesis by Linear Prediction of the Speech Wave." *Journal of the Acoustical Society of America* 47.65(Abstract) (1970).

J. Markel and A. Gray. *Linear Prediction of Speech.* New York: Springer, 1976.

James Moorer. "The Use of Linear Prediction of Speech in Computer Music Applications." *Journal of the Audio Engineering Society* 27(3): 134–140 (1979).

Code:

fitlpc.c

lpcresyn.c

Sounds:

[Track 30] Impulse Train Filtered through "ahh" Filter Yields Subtractive "ahh."

[Track 31] Speech Original, LPC Residual, Resynthesis, Pulse Resynthesis.

[Track 32] Guitar Pluck, LPC Residual, Resynthesis, Pulse Resynthesis.

[Track 33] Hammer Nail, LPC Parametric Resynthesis

Strings and Bars

9.0 Introduction

Physical modeling synthesis endeavors to model and solve the physics of sound-producing systems in order to synthesize sound. Unlike sinusoidal additive and modal synthesis (Chapter 4), or PCM sampling synthesis (Chapter 2), both of which can use one powerful generic model for any sound, physical modeling requires a different model for each family of sound producing object. LPC (Chapter 8) is a spectral modeling technique, but also has physical interpretations in the one-dimensional ladder implementation.

This chapter will focus on one-dimensional physical models, and on the techniques known as *waveguide filters* for constructing very simple models that yield expressive sound synthesis. First we'll look at the simple ideal string, and then refine the model to make it more realistic and flexible. At the end we will have developed models that are capable of simulating an interesting variety of one-dimensional vibrating objects, including stiff structures such as bars and beams.

9.1 The Ideal String

One way to model a vibrating string would be to build it as a chain of coupled masses and springs, as shown in Figure 9.1.

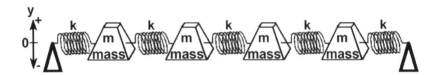

Figure 9.1. A "string" made of masses and springs.

We could solve this using a separate *force = mass * acceleration* term for each mass. There are some problems with Figure 9.1 as drawn, however. One problem is that the masses are free to move side-to-side as well as up and down. This is called *longitudinal motion,* and it doesn't usually happen with actual strings under tension. If it does, it isn't nearly as important as the up and down *transverse motion.* We could restrict the mass-spring system as shown in Figure 9.2, placing each mass on a frictionless *guide rod* so that the masses could only move up and down.

If we force the masses to move only up and down and restrict them to small displacements, we don't actually have to solve the acceleration of each mass as a function of the spring forces pushing them up and down. There is a simple differential equation that completely describes the motions of the ideal string. Appendix B gives the derivation of this equation describing the ideal string, which is

$$d^2y/dx^2 = (1/c^2)\,d^2y/dt^2. \tag{9.1}$$

This equation means that the acceleration (up and down) of any point on the string is equal to a constant times the curvature of the string at that point. The constant c is the speed of wave motion on the string, which is proportional to the square root of the string tension, and inversely proportional to the square root of the mass per unit length. This equation could be solved numerically by sampling it in both time and space, and using the difference approximations for acceleration and curvature (much like we did with the mass/spring/damper

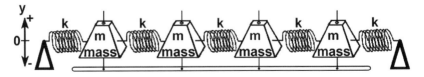

Figure 9.2. Mass-spring string network with frictionless guide rods to restrict motion to one dimension.

system in Chapter 4). However, there is a wonderfully simple solution to Equation 9.1, given by:

$$y(x,t) = y_L(t + x/c) + y_r(t - x/c). \tag{9.2}$$

This equation is proven in Appendix B, and says that any vibration of the string can be expressed as a combination of two separate traveling waves, one going leftward (y_L) and one going rightward (y_r). They travel at the rate c, which is the speed of sound propagation on the string. This left/right decomposition might not be so intuitive, but the math doesn't lie. You can do a simple experiment with a rope to convince yourself that waves do indeed travel left and right along a stretched string. Tie one end of the rope to a solid object such as a door knob or a pole, hold the other end, stretch the rope tight, and give it a hard tap downward near your hand. You'll see a pulse propagate along the rope, hit the other end, and reflect back with an inversion, traveling back to your hand. If you hold it tight enough, you'll see the reflected wave reflect once again, with another inversion. For an ideal rope (no damping) and ideally rigid boundaries at the ends, the wave would travel back and forth indefinitely.

This view of two traveling waves summing to make a displacement wave gives rise to the *waveguide filter* technique of modeling the vibrating string. Figure 9.3 shows a waveguide filter model of the ideal string. The two delay lines model the propagation of left- and right-going traveling waves. The conditions at the ends model the reflection of the traveling waves at the ends. The −1 in the left reflection models the reflection with the inversion of a displacement wave when it hits an ideally rigid termination (like a fret on a guitar neck, or your experimental rope tied to a pole or doorknob). The −0.99 on the right reflection models the slight amount of loss that happens when the wave hits your handheld end of the experimental rope (or the bridge of the guitar which couples the string motion to the body), and models all other losses the wave might experience (internal damping in the string, viscous losses as the string cuts the air, etc.) in making its round-trip path around the string.

Figure 9.4 shows the waveguide string as a digital filter block diagram. Initial conditions would be injected into the string via the input $x(n)$. The

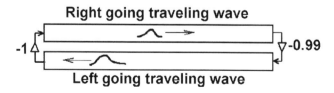

Right going traveling wave

−1   −0.99

Left going traveling wave

Figure 9.3. Waveguide string.

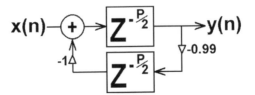

Figure 9.4. Filter view of waveguide string.

((·34·))

output $y(n)$ would yield the right-going traveling wave component. Of course, neither of these conditions is actually physical in terms of the way a real string is plucked and listened to, but feeding the correct signal into x is identical to loading the delay lines with a predetermined shape.

The impulse response and spectrum of the filter shown in Figure 9.4 is shown in Figure 9.5. As would be expected, the impulse response is an exponentially decaying train of pulses spaced $T = P/\text{SRATE}$ seconds apart, and the spectrum is a set of harmonics spaced $F_0 = 1/T$ Hz apart. This type of filter response and spectrum is called a *comb filter*, named for the comb-like appearance of the time domain impulse response and of the frequency domain harmonics.

The two delay lines taken together are called a waveguide filter. The sum of the contents of the two delay lines is the displacement of the string, ' and the difference of the contents of the two delay lines is the velocity of the string (check this yourself using the methods and equations given in Appendix B). If we wish to pluck the string, we simply need to load one-half

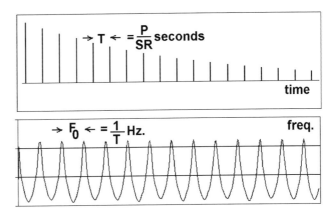

Figure 9.5. Impulse response and spectrum of comb (string) filter.

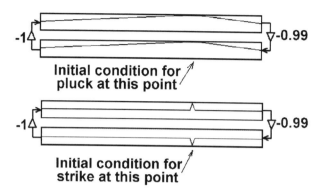

Figure 9.6. Waveguide pluck and strike initial conditions.

of the initial shape magnitude into each of the upper and lower delay lines. If we wish to strike the string, we would load in an initial velocity by entering a positive pulse into one delay line and a negative pulse into the other (difference = initial velocity; sum = initial position = 0). These conditions are shown in Figure 9.6.

9.2 Refining the Ideal String

We can make the ideal string simulation more efficient by noting that the two delay lines (per waveguide) can be combined into one. It could be made even more efficient by calculating the delay lines as circular buffers (modulo pointers, read chases write) rather than "bucket-brigade" arrays (each cell passes sample to next one). Karplus and Strong discovered that a delay line initialized with random numbers makes for a pleasant and bright plucked-string tone. They also added a simple moving average low pass filter to model high frequency losses. This filter is commonly called the *loop filter*.

More refinements to the basic string model are possible, and needed, to bring the model to reality. A multipole resonant filter can be added to model the body of the instrument. This *radiation filter* can be derived by analyzing the sound of tapping an actual instrument body to measure its impulse response; inspecting the spectrum of guitar tones for the gross shape; or performing source/filter decomposition using LPC as discussed in Chapter 8.

As discussed in Chapter 4 (Section 4.2), the position of the excitation (pick) causes certain modes of the string to be emphasized, and others to be cancelled entirely. For example, picking in the center causes even harmonics to be absent in the spectrum. Picking 1/3 of the way along the string causes harmonics 3, 6, 9, etc., to be missing. In general, picking at a point located at

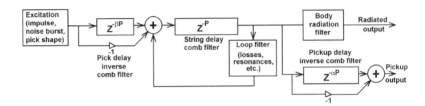

Figure 9.7. Fairly complete digital filter simulation of plucked-string system.

βL (beta is a number between 0 and 1.0, and L is the total length of the string) causes notches to appear in the spectrum at multiples of f_0 / β. This can be modeled explicitly by feeding in the appropriate initial condition. We can also cleverly get the same effect by placing an inverse comb filter (all zero, harmonically spaced notches) in the excitation path, and adjusting the length to cause the correct nulls in the spectrum.

To model a pickup on the string, we observe that any mode of vibration that exhibits a node at the pickup position will not be seen at that point. So modeling a pickup position is exactly like modeling a picking position. This can be accomplished explicitly by summing the left- and right-going delay lines at that point, or by putting another inverse comb filter on the output of the string filter.

Figure 9.7 shows a relatively complete model of a plucked-string simulation system using digital filters. Output channels for pickup position and body radiation are provided separately. A solid-body electric guitar would have no direct radiation and only pickup output(s), while a purely acoustic guitar would have no pickup output, but possibly a family of directional filters to model body radiation in different directions.

Noting that everything in the block diagram of Figure 9.7 is linear and time-invariant, we can commute (swap the orders) of any of the blocks. For example, we could put the pick position filter at the end, or move the body radiation filter to the beginning. Since the body radiation filter is just the impulse response of the instrument body, we can actually record the impulse response with the strings damped, and use that as the input to the string model. This is called *commuted synthesis*. Figure 9.8 shows a commuted synthesis plucked-string model.

Adding a model of bowing friction allows the string model to be used for the violin and other bowed strings. This focused nonlinearity is what is responsible for turning the steady linear motion of a bow into an oscillation of the string. The bow sticks to the string for a while, pulling it along, then the forces become too great and the string breaks away, flying back toward rest

((35))

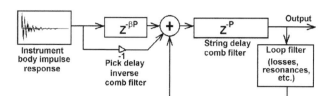

Figure 9.8. Commuted plucked-string model.

position. This process repeats, yielding a periodic oscillation. Figure 9.9 shows a simple bowed-string model, in which string velocity is compared to bow velocity, and then put through a nonlinear friction function controlled by bow force. The output of the nonlinear function is the velocity input back into the string. We'll return to this interaction in depth in Chapter 14.

$((\cdot 36 \cdot))$

9.3 Weak Stiffness

When we derived the ideal string equation in Appendix B, we assumed that the restoring force on the string was caused only by the tension component acting to move the string back to rest position. But we know that if we bend a stiff string, even one under no tension, it wants to return back to straightness even when there is no tension on the string. Cloth string or thread has almost no stiffness. Nylon and gut strings have some stiffness, but not as much as steel strings. Larger diameter strings have more stiffness than thin ones. In the musical world, piano strings exhibit the most stiffness. The traveling wave solution is still true in stiff systems, but a frequency-dependent propagation speed is needed:

$((\cdot 37 \cdot))$

$$y(x,t) = y_l(t + x/c(f)) + y_r(t - x/c(f)) \qquad (9.3)$$

and the waveguide filter must be modified to simulate frequency dependent delay, as shown in Figure 9.10.

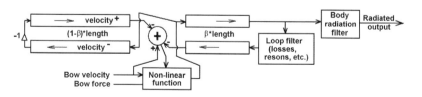

Figure 9.9. Bowed string model.

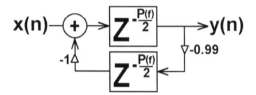

Figure 9.10. Stiffness-modified waveguide string filter.

Unfortunately, implementing the $Z^{-P(f)/2}$ frequency-dependent delay function is not simple, especially for arbitrary functions of frequency. For basic stiff strings, a function that predicts the frequencies of the partials has a form like

$$f_n = nf_0(1 + Bn^2)^{\frac{1}{2}},$$

where B is a number slightly greater than zero, equal to zero for perfect harmonicity, and increasing for increasing stiffness. Typical values of B are 0.00001 for guitar strings, and 0.004 or so for piano strings. This means that $P(f)$ should modify P by the inverse of the $(1 + Bn^2)^{\frac{1}{2}}$ factor.

One way to implement the $P(f)$ function is by replacing each of the Z^{-1} with a first order all-pass (phase) filter, as shown in Figure 9.11. The first order all-pass has one pole and one zero, controlled by one coefficient. The all-pass implements a frequency-dependent phase delay, but exhibits a gain of 1.0 for all frequencies; α can take on values between -1.0 and 1.0. For $\alpha = 0$, the filter behaves as a standard unit delay. For $\alpha > 0.0$, the filter exhibits delays longer than one sample, increasingly long for higher frequencies. For $\alpha < 0.0$, the filter exhibits delays shorter than one sample, decreasingly so for high frequencies.

It is much less efficient to implement a chain of all-pass filters than a simple delay line. But for weak stiffness it is possible that only a few all-pass sections will provide a good frequency-dependent delay. Another option is to implement a higher order all-pass filter (designed to give the correct stretching

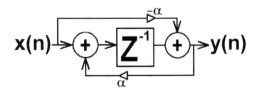

Figure 9.11. First order all-pass filter.

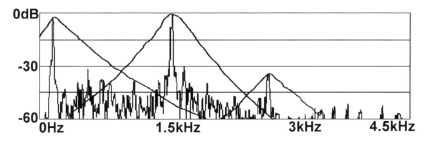

Figure 9.12. Banded decomposition of struck bar spectrum.

of the upper frequencies) added to simple delay lines to give the correct longest bulk delay required.

9.4 Really Stiff Structures: Bars

For very stiff systems such as rigid bars, a single waveguide with all-pass filters is not adequate, or far too inefficient to calculate. A technique called *banded waveguides* employs sampling in time, space, and frequency to model stiff one-dimensional systems. This can be viewed as a hybrid of modal and waveguide synthesis, in that each waveguide models the speed of sound in the region around each significant mode of the system. As an example, Figure 9.12 shows the spectrum of the struck marimba bar (from Figure 6.10), with additional bandpass filters superimposed on the spectrum, centered at the three main modes. In the banded waveguide technique, each mode is modeled by a bandpass filter and a delay line to impose the correct round trip delay, as shown in Figure 9.13.

((38))

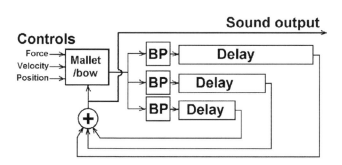

Figure 9.13. Banded waveguide model.

9.5 Conclusions

For the special one-dimensional geometry of a stretched string under tension, digital waveguide filters provide a cheap, but exact computational simulation method. Waveguide filters use delay lines to model the traveling wave components on the string. Adding the left and right-going components yields the displacement wave function, and subtracting them yields the velocity function. For weakly stiff systems, all-pass filters can be used to model frequency-dependent delay. For highly rigid systems exhibiting lots of stiffness, banded waveguides factor the spectrum into separate modal regions, and explicitly model the delay in each modal region.

Reading:

K. Karplus and A. Strong. "Digital Synthesis of Plucked-String and Drum Timbres." *Computer Music Journal* 7(2):43–55 (1983).

D. A. Jaffe and J. O. Smith. "Extensions of the Karplus-Strong plucked string algorithm." *Computer Music Journal* 7(2):56–69 (1983).

J. O. Smith. "Acoustic Modeling Using Digital Waveguides." In *Musical Signal Processing*, edited by Roads et al. Netherlands: Swets and Zeitlinger, 1997.

J. O. Smith and S. A. Van Duyne. " Overview of the Commuted Piano Synthesis Technique." In *Proceedings of the IEEE Workshop on Applications of Signal Processing to Audio and Acoustics, New Paltz, NY*. New York: IEEE Press, 1995b.

Perry Cook and D. Trueman. "Spherical Radiation from Stringed Instruments: Measured, Modeled, and Reproduced." *Journal of the Catgut Acoustical Society:* 3–15(November 1999).

George Essl and Perry Cook. "Banded waveguides: Towards Physical Modeling of Bar Percussion Instruments." In *Proc. 1999 Int. Computer Music Conf., Beijing, China*. Computer Music Association, 1999.

Code:

Plucked.cpp

Mandolin.cpp

Bowed.cpp

Stiff.cpp

StifKarp.cpp

BowedBar.cpp

GUIPluckedStruk

GUIBowedBar

Sounds:

[Track 34] Simple Plucked String.

[Track 35] More Complete Plucked String.

[Track 36] Bowed-String Model.

[Track 37] Weak All-Pass Stiffness in a String Model.

[Track 38] Banded Waveguide Bar.

Nonlinearity, Waveshaping, FM

10.0 Introduction

Most of the concepts and techniques presented so far in this book have rested on a few simple notions such as linearity, time-invariance, convolution, and sinusoids. In this chapter we're going to look at things that break the linearity assumption, first by examining some common and important physical nonlinear mechanisms in sound production. Some efficient techniques for simulating acoustical nonlinearity will be presented. Finally we will look at some techniques of nonlinear waveform synthesis, in which a simple waveform (and spectrum) is distorted to yield a more complex sound. By removing the linearity condition, we will no longer be able to use some of our tools like convolution and the FFT. But the richness we can gain from nonlinearity, coupled with the fact that nearly everything in real life behaves with some (or lots of) nonlinearity, means we must check it out.

10.1 Simple Physical Nonlinearity

If we look back at our simple mass/spring/damper model from Chapter 4, we note that we assumed that the spring exerted a restoring force that was linearly related to the displacement. This is true for ideal springs or small displacements of real springs. But actual springs exert more force for larger displacements.

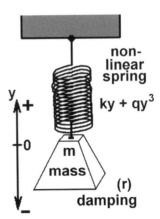

Figure 10.1. Nonlinear mass/spring/damper system.

A simple mathematical model of the nonlinearity in a spring might assume an extra cubic term, as shown in Figure 10.1.

The new equations governing the nonlinear system would be:

$$-ky - qy^3 - r\, dy/dt = m\, d^2y / dt^2$$

$$\text{or} \quad d^2y/dt^2 + (r/m)\, dy/dt + (k/m)\, y + (q/m)y^3 = 0. \tag{10.1}$$

We now have an interesting new situation, because the linear differential equations folks don't have a closed form solution to Equation 10.1. But we know how to solve this system (and they do too) by discrete approximation. We replace the velocity and acceleration derivatives by their difference equation versions, yielding:

$$(y(n) - 2y(n-1) + y(n-2)) / T^2 + r/m\, (y(n) - y(n-1)) / T$$
$$+ k/m\, y(n) + q/m\, y(n)^3 = 0. \tag{10.2}$$

By substituting the cubic term $y(n)^3$ with $y(n-1)^3$ (so the system can actually be solved), the new nonlinear difference equation is:

$$y(n) = \frac{[(2 + Tr/m)y(n-1) - y(n-2) - T^2q/m\, y(n-1)^3]}{(1 + Tr/m + T^2k/m)}. \tag{10.3}$$

For small values of y, the spring will behave as a linear spring exerting a force equal to ky. But for larger values of y, even for a very small value of the constant q, the cubic term will begin to change the system behavior.

Figure 10.2. Nonlinear mass/spring/damper system response. Initial displacements are 0.1 (left); 1.0 (center); and 10.0 (right).

Figure 10.2 shows sonograms resulting from running simulations of a nonlinear mass/spring/damper model with mass = 0.001, k = 1000, damping = 0.002, q = 1, and initial displacement conditions of 0.1, 1.0, and 10.0. For a displacement of 0.1, the system response is essentially a decaying sinusoid. For a displacement of 1.0, however, extra harmonics show in the response. For an initial displacement of 10.0, the extra harmonics show up clearly. The extra harmonics are odd (this comes from the cubic nonlinearity), and the extra nonlinear restoring force acts to raise the fundamental oscillation frequency significantly. As the system damps toward zero displacement, the fundamental frequency goes steadily down. This can even be seen, but not as strongly, in the 1.0 displacement case.

((**39**))

10.1.1 Continuous Nonlinearity in Strings and Membranes

Another real-world physical nonlinearity can be explored by looking at the plucked string. In Chapter 9 and Appendix B, our equation derivation and solution was based on uniform tension, and small displacements ($\sin(\theta) \approx \theta$) from rest position. If we were to displace the string farther from rest position, however, we would note that the string would experience an increase in tension. This increase in tension would cause the pitch of the string to be higher than in the low displacement case, because the speed of sound on the string is a function of the square root of tension. Just as in the case of the nonlinear spring in the previous section, the increase in string tension should cause the pitch to begin high and go lower as the string displacement damps out. Further, as the string oscillates up and down in the large displacement case, the tension increases twice each cycle. This could cause extra even harmonics to appear in the spectrum, even in the center-plucked case. Figure 10.3 shows a sonogram of a plucked string with high initial displacement. Note the bending downward of the harmonics.

Mode bending due to displacement-dependent tension modulation also occurs in membranes and thin plates. Figure 10.4 shows a sonogram comparing

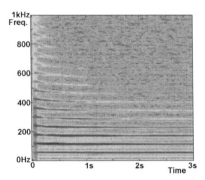

Figure 10.3. Plucked string with high initial displacement shows pitch bending due to displacement-dependent tension.

a drum struck softly versus loudly. Again, note the slight bending downward of the modes as the amplitude decays, especially in the first 0.1 seconds.

10.1.2 Discontinuous Physical Nonlinearity

The nonlinearities discussed in Sections 10.1 and 10.1.1 are of a continuous (smooth) nature. That is, the nonlinear addition to spring force, or string tension, is a continuous function of displacement. A more extreme type of nonlinearity—*discontinuous nonlinearity*—tends to have a more profound effect on the system and spectrum.

Figure 10.5 shows a vibrating string system with a discontinuous nonlinear interaction. As the string vibrates, it "chatters" against the secondary bridge

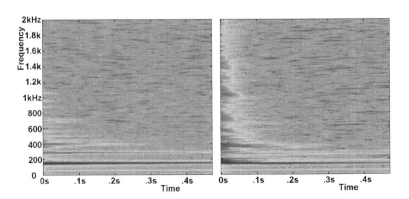

Figure 10.4. When struck hard (right), a drum shows more downward mode bending than when struck softly (left).

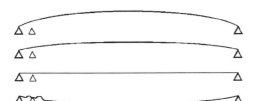

Figure 10.5. Plucked-string system with a discontinuous nonlinearity. High frequency components are introduced as the string comes into contact with the secondary termination.

(which could be a fret in a guitar) whenever negative excursions exceed a particular displacement. This serves to instantaneously shorten the string for those contacts, causing high frequency distortions in the string shape. It also causes the string to bounce rapidly away from the temporary boundary. This discontinuous nonlinearity causes extra high frequency energy to be introduced into the system because of the rapid modulations. Figure 10.6 compares a guitar tone with nonlinear chatter to one without nonlinear chatter. Even though the guitar is used here as an example, many forms of everyday nonlinear chatter interactions are common (that rattling noise in your car dashboard or engine that drives you crazy, for instance).

((‹41›))

10.2 Simulating Physical Nonlinearity

The bending of pitch as a function of amplitude can be modeled explicitly in additive and modal models, by controlling the modal frequencies with a time-

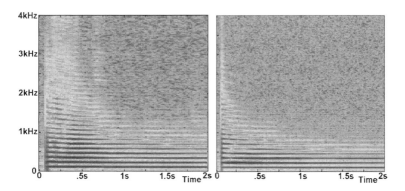

Figure 10.6. Guitar tone with nonlinear chatter (left) and without (right).

varying control envelope. In physical models like the plucked string, the change in simulated string tension can be calculated and used to control the loop delay length. Total string displacement, maximum string displacement, or other means of determining the approximate increase in tension can be computed. The nonlinear spring shown in Figure 9.1 is passive, but care must be taken when introducing nonlinearity into digital simulation models, because instabilities can occur. A simple mathematical nonlinearity (such as squaring or cubing the signal) is, in general, not a passive operation (energy may be added to the system, rather than conserved or lost). Passivity is a property of actual physical systems that contain no energy-producing components. Filters that are otherwise stable can become unstable in the time-varying case. In simulations, weak nonlinearity that is not strictly passive can often be offset by damping losses in the system. To simulate strong nonlinearity, especially in systems that have low damping, extra design considerations must be taken into account to ensure stability of the simulated system.

As a simulation example, let's extend our plucked string model to simulate nonlinearities like those discussed in Sections 10.1.1 and 10.1.2 (the spectral effects are shown in Figures 10.3, 10.5 and 10.6). These are found commonly in some stringed instruments like the dobro (a folk instrument) or the Indian sitar. Figure 10.7 shows a model of a waveguide plucked string with added nonlinearities. A nonlinear *scattering bridge* computes the displacement at one point on the string, and depending on the value of that displacement, either passes the left and right-going traveling waves along normally (the "No" conditions shown in the block diagram of Figure 10.7), or reflects those components directly back into the two string segments left and right of the chattering bridge (the "Yes" conditions). This is similar to a displacement-dependent nonlinear spring model based on a signal-dependent all-pass filter invented by Pierce and VanDuyne. The other nonlinearity added to the diagram of Figure 10.7 models the displacement-dependent (tension) speed of sound (pitch bend). This is accomplished by computing the summary absolute value string displacement, and using that value to modify the net string length.

((‹42›))

Both the nonlinear chattering bridge and the tension-modulated pitch bend could be modeled using lookup tables as well. The next sections will look at modeling nonlinearity, or arbitrary waveshapes, using tables.

10.3 Nonlinear Wave Synthesis by Lookup Table

In Chapter 2 we looked at concatenative (wavetable) synthesis of music and speech. The idea there was to store pieces of waveforms and join them together in the time domain to make sound. The idea of a loop for periodic sounds (steady state of a trumpet, vowels of speech, etc.) was introduced. One way to

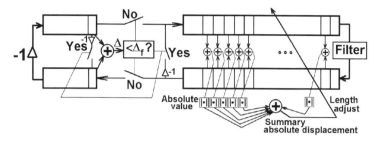

Figure 10.7. Simple nonlinear waveguide string model.

think about the synthesis of a loop is as a sawtooth (ramp wave) address lookup into a wavetable. That is, if the samples of a periodic loop are stored in a table q of length L, then the function $q(n{+}{+} \bmod L)$ will yield a periodic output of the wavetable. The function $n{+}{+} \bmod L$ is the sawtooth input address (linear rise, an immediate fall back to zero, rising again, etc.) to the wavetable. Figure 10.8 shows this process.

We could use something other than a sawtooth wave as our pointer function into the wavetable. For example, we could use an inverse sawtooth, yielding a time-reversed version of the waveform stored in the table. The perception of a time-reversed version of a steady-state waveform would not likely differ from the forward version, however, because the power spectra are identical (time reversal is just the phase conjugate of the spectrum, with the same magnitudes; see Appendix A). Using a sawtooth of a higher frequency results in the output being pitch shifted upward (interpolation should be used for noninteger values of the input to a wavetable). If we distort the sawtooth somewhat, the output waveform becomes distorted from the original. Figure 10.9 shows a few possible deviations of the basic sawtooth pointer function, and the changes in the resulting output waveform.

10.3.1 Wave Shaping Synthesis

As an exercise, let's switch the roles of the wavetable and the sawtooth. Storing a linear ramp in the table results in the input simply being passed through to

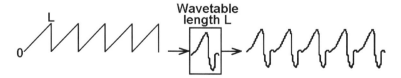

Figure 10.8. Periodic synthesis by sawtooth-addressed lookup table.

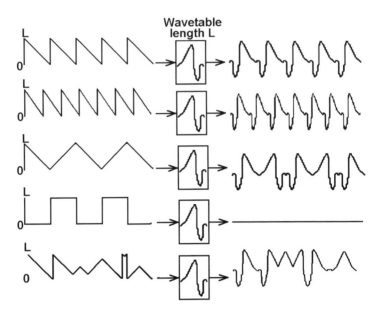

Figure 10.9. Distorting a lookup table by modifying the input address pointer.

the output, with a gain modification corresponding to the slope of the ramp (See Figure 10.10). For convenience later on, we've modified the ramp slightly to allow for negative inputs as well as positive.

Distorting the ramp a little would result in a distortion of the output wave. We can store any shape in the wavetable, resulting in a wide variety of possible outputs. Accessing a wavetable (often a simple waveform) with another (usually simple) waveform is called *waveshaping synthesis.*

10.3.2 Frequency Modulation Synthesis

One common form of waveshaping synthesis, called *Frequency Modulation* (FM), uses sine waves for both input address and wavetable waveforms.

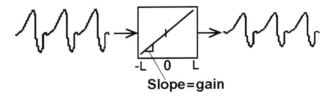

Figure 10.10. Waveform passed through linear gain wavetable.

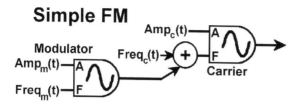

Figure 10.11. Simple FM (one carrier and one modulator sine wave) synthesis.

Frequency modulation relies on modulating the frequency of a simple periodic waveform with another simple periodic waveform. When the frequency of a sine wave of average frequency f_c (called the carrier) is modulated by another sine wave of frequency f_m (called the modulator), sinusoidal sidebands are created at frequencies equal to the carrier frequency plus and minus integer multiples of the modulator frequency. FM is expressed as:

$$y(t) = \sin(2\pi t f_c + \Delta f_c \cos(2\pi t f_m)). \qquad (10.4)$$

Figure 10.11 shows a block diagram for simple FM synthesis (one sinusoidal carrier and one sinusoidal modulator).

The index of modulation, I, is defined as $\Delta f_c / f_c$. Carson's rule (a rule of thumb) states that the number of significant bands on each side of the carrier frequency (sidebands) is roughly equal to $I + 2$. For example, a carrier sinusoid of frequency 600 Hz, a modulator sinusoid of frequency 100 Hz, and a modulation index of three would produce sinusoidal components of frequencies 600, 700, 500, 800, 400, 900, 300, 1000, 200, 1100, and 100 Hz. Inspecting these components reveals that a harmonic spectrum with 11 significant harmonics, based on a fundamental frequency of 100 Hz, can be produced by using only two sinusoidal generating functions. Figure 10.12 shows the spectrum of this synthesis.

Selecting carrier and modulator frequencies that are not related by simple integer ratios yields an inharmonic spectrum. For example, a carrier of 500 Hz, a modulator of 273 Hz, and an index of five yields frequencies of: 500 (carrier), 227, 46, 319, 592, 865, 1138, 1411 (negative sidebands); and 773, 1046, 1319, 1592, 1865, 2138, 2411 (positive sidebands). Figure 10.13 shows a spectrogram of this FM tone, as the index of modulation is ramped from zero to five. The synthesized waveforms at $I = 0$ and $I = 5$ are shown as well.

By setting the modulation index high enough, huge numbers of sidebands are generated, and the aliasing and addition of these (in most cases) results in noise. Figure 10.14 shows the synthesized waveform and spectrum of an FM

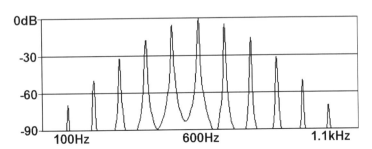

Figure 10.12. Simple FM with 600 Hz carrier, 100 Hz modulator, and index of modulation of three.

tone using a 10,000 Hz carrier, a 373 Hz modulator, and an index of 200 (sampling rate is 22,050 Hz).

By careful selection of the component frequencies and index of modulation, and by combining multiple carrier/modulator pairs, many spectra can be approximated using FM. The amplitudes and phases (described by Bessel functions) of the individual components cannot be independently controlled, however, so FM is not a truly generic waveform or spectral synthesis method. Since the very definition of FM is a nonlinear function transformation,

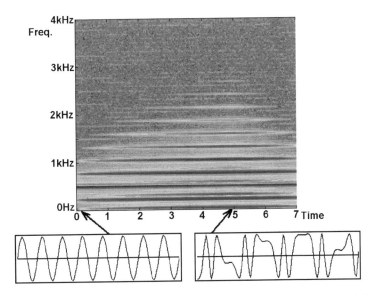

Figure 10.13. Inharmonic simple FM with a 500 Hz carrier and 273 Hz modulator. The index of modulation is ramped from zero to five, then back to zero.

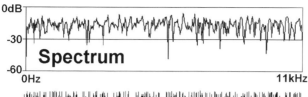

Time domain

Figure 10.14. Synthesis of noise using FM with high index of modulation.

the system does not extend additively for complex waveforms (or sums of modulator or carrier sine functions). Using multiple carriers and modulators, connection topologies (algorithms) have been designed for the synthesis of complex sounds such as human voices, violins, brass instruments, percussion, etc. Because of the extreme computation/memory efficiency of FM, in the 1980's FM was the algorithm used in of the most popular music synthesizers. Later FM found use in early PC sound cards.

10.4 Conclusions

Nonlinearity occurs in most real-world systems, but often doesn't show up except in large-displacement cases. When it does appear, it serves to extend and add bandwidth to even simple vibrational systems. Nonlinearity can be exploited as a pure signal processing technique for creating rich waveforms and spectra from simple building blocks. In later chapters we will see that with some caution in evaluating nonlinear physical systems, we can use linear models for most of the systems, but add some focused nonlinear modeling to build up interesting sound-synthesis algorithms.

Reading:

J. Chowning. "The Synthesis of Complex Audio Spectra by Means of Frequency Modulation." *Journal of the Audio Engineering Society* 21(7): 1973. Reprinted in *Computer Music Journal* 1(2): 1977. Reprinted in *Foundations of Computer Music*, edited by C. Roads and J. Strawn. Cambridge: MIT Press, 1985.

J. R. Pierce and S. A. VanDuyne. "A Passive Nonlinear Digital Filter Design Which Facilitates Physics-Based Sound Synthesis of Highly Nonlinear Musical Instruments." *Journal of the Acoustical Society of America*, 101(2):1120–1126(1997).

Code:

NLMassSpringDamper.c

Sitar.cpp

GUIPluckStruck

Sounds:

[Track 39] Nonlinear Mass/Spring/Damper System.

[Track 40] Plucked String and Drum Displacement-Modulated Pitch.

[Track 41] Guitar Chatter Nonlinearity.

[Track 42] Simulated Sitar/Dobro model.

[Track 43] Various FM Sounds.

11 Tubes and Air Cavities

11.0 Introduction

This chapter extends our modeling techniques from solids to tubes and chambers of air (or other gasses). First we will look at the simple ideal acoustic tube. Next, we will enhance the model to create musical instruments like a clarinet. Then we'll look at our first three-dimensional acoustical systems—air cavities—but we'll discover that many such systems can be treated as simpler (essentially lumped resonance) models.

11.1 The Ideal Acoustic Tube

Figure 11.1 shows a simple cylindrical acoustic tube of cross-sectional area a. The force acts to move air in the x direction along the tube.

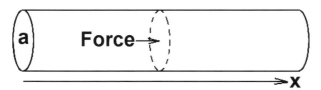

Figure 11.1. Acoustic tube.

As derived in Appendix C, the physical equation for the air pressure P in an ideal cylindrical tube, with length much greater than its width, is:

$$d^2P \, / \, dx^2 = (1 \, / \, c^2)(d^2P \, / \, dt^2) \tag{11.1}$$

"But wait," you might say, "That's just string Equation 10.1 with string displacement y replaced by air pressure P!!!" And I would reply, "BINGO!!!" It's the same wave equation, and the solution has the same form:

$$P(x,t) = P_l(t + x/c) + P_r(t - x/c) \tag{11.2}$$

In fact, if you find a nice long piece of pipe and slap the end, you'll get a sound very much like a simple damped plucked string.

11.2 Building a Simple Clarinet

A very important paper in the history of physical modeling by McIntyre, Schumacher, and Woodhouse noted that many musical instruments can be characterized as linear resonators, modeled by filters such as all-pole resonators or waveguides, and a single nonlinear oscillator like the reed of the clarinet, the lips of the brass player, the jet of the flute, or the bow-string friction of the violin. If we'd like to do something interesting with a tube, we could use it to build a flute or clarinet. Our simple clarinet model might look like the block diagram shown in Figure 11.2.

All we need is a model of the reed to build a clarinet. A simple model of a clarinet reed is shown in Figure 11.3. We can assume that the reed is nearly massless, that is, the mass is so small that the only thing that must be considered is the instantaneous force on the reed (spring). The pressure inside the bore, P_b, is the calculated pressure in our waveguide model; the mouth pressure, P_m, is an external control parameter representing the breath pressure inside the

Simple clarinet model

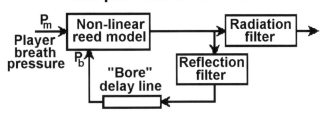

Figure 11.2. Simple clarinet model.

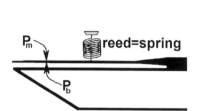

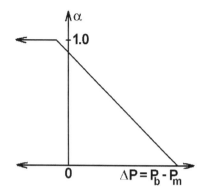

Figure 11.3. Simple reed model.   **Figure 11.4.** Reed reflection table.

mouth of the player. The net force acting on the reed/spring can be calculated
as the difference between the two pressures, multiplied by the area of the reed
(pressure is force per unit area). This can be used to calculate a reed opening
position from the spring constant of the reed. From the reed opening, we can
compute the amount of pressure that is allowed to leak into the bore from the
player's mouth.

If bore pressure is much greater than mouth pressure, the reed opens far.
If mouth pressure is much greater than bore pressure, the reed slams shut.
These two extreme conditions represent an asymmetric nonlinearity in the
reed response. Even a grossly simplified model of this nonlinear spring action
results in a pretty good model of a clarinet. Figure 11.4 shows a plot of a
simple reed reflection function (as seen from within the bore) as a function of
differential pressure. Once this nonlinear, signal-dependent reflection
coefficient is calculated (or looked up in a table), the right-going pressure
injected into the bore can be calculated as $P_b^+ = \alpha P_b^- + (1 - \alpha)P_m$. This can be
seen as computing only two terms of the general scattering junction as shown
in Appendix C, Section C.5, Figure C.3.

The clarinet is open at the bell end, and essentially closed at the reed end.
This results in a reflection with inversion at the bell and a reflection without
inversion (plus any added pressure from the mouth through the reed opening)
at the reed end. These odd boundary conditions cause odd-harmonics to
dominate in the clarinet spectrum.

((‹44›))

We noted that the ideal string equation and the ideal acoustic tube equation
are essentially identical. Just as there are many refinements possible to the
plucked-string model to make it more realistic, there are many possible
improvements for the clarinet model. Replacing the simple reed model with a
variable mass/spring/damper allows the modeling of a lip reed as is found in

brass instruments. Replacing the reed model with an air jet model (see next section) allows the modeling of flute and recorder-like instruments. With all wind-excited resonant systems, adding a little noise in the reed/jet region adds greatly to the quality (and behavior) of the synthesized sound.

11.3 Resonance in Air Cavities

We know that containers of air can exhibit strong resonances. Glass bottles, plastic bottles, large jugs, or any large cavity with a small opening all produce a satisfying "thunk" when excited by slapping the open end. The larger the bottle, the lower the resonance. If we blow across the top of one of these bottles in the right way, it will resonate continuously giving us a pleasing simple flute-like tone. As we might expect, there is a nice mathematical model that predicts the acoustical behavior of such systems quite accurately. Figure 11.5 shows a large air cavity of volume V, with an opening of radius r, coupled to the outside air through a pipe of length L.

As a mental (and physics/math development) exercise, we can view the air in the pipe opening as a small elliptical piston in a cylinder as shown in Figure 11.6. Pulling this piston outward causes a negative pressure inside the cavity. The negative cavity pressure acts to pull the piston back inward to rest position. Pushing the piston inward causes the cavity pressure to rise, acting to push the piston outward toward rest position. Since the pipe and piston are cylindrical, the amount of volume change and pressure change is proportional

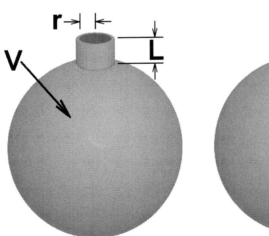

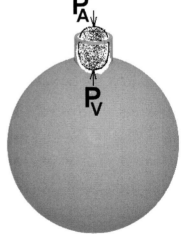

Figure 11.5. Cavity resonator.   **Figure 11.6.** Pressures on air "piston."

to the displacement of the piston in the cylinder. The change in force on the piston is proportional to the displacement. Sound familiar? This is just like the mass/spring/damper system presented in Chapter 4, where a displacement of the mass results in a spring restoring force that is linearly proportional to the displacement.

To make our model work, we assume that the wavelength of the frequency of oscillation will be much longer than the dimensions of the resonator. This means that the pressure inside the resonator will be roughly the same at any location, but will change with time. If this is not the case, we'd be obliged to model propagation within the cavity. In our air cavity case, the *spring constant* is the pressure change multiplied by the cross-sectional area of the mass (pressure = force per unit area). Our mass is a small piston of air, roughly equal to $\rho \pi r^2 L$ (air density times the volume of the cylinder). Finally, we have to include a little thermodynamics related to heat transfer when the air is compressed and rarified. This introduces an extra constant γ into our equation. We'll denote P as the undisturbed rest pressure inside and outside the chamber. Putting this all together into Newton's $F = ma$ equation, the expression for the oscillation of the cavity resonator is:

$$\frac{d^2 x}{dt^2} + \frac{\gamma \pi r^2 P x}{\rho V L} = 0, \qquad (11.3)$$

which is just like our expression for the mass/spring/damper system. Cavity resonators are also called "Helmholtz Resonators," named after the 19th century physician/scientist, who was one of the most important figures in the history of acoustics. The frequency of oscillation of the cavity resonator is:

$$f = \frac{cr}{2\pi} \sqrt{\frac{\pi}{V L}} \qquad (11.4)$$

Note that decreasing the radius of the opening, increasing the volume of the cavity, or increasing the length of the neck opening all cause the resonant frequency to go down. To check this, let's plug in some numbers measured from real bottles. We'll check it with a large three gallon water bottle and a little airline drink bottle. A simple geometric rendering of the large bottle is shown in Figure 11.7.

The large bottle is composed of a main cylinder that is 8.75" in diameter and 12" tall (we're using inches here because the fluid volume is expressed in gallons; normally we'd try to use meters and liters). A cone atop the cylinder rises for about 3," then joins a small cylindrical neck which is 2" tall and 1.5" in diameter. The little bottle is a cylinder 2.375" tall and 1.125" in diameter,

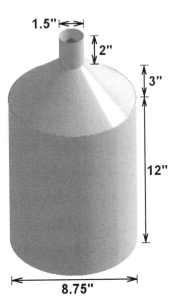

Figure 11.7. Three gallon water bottle model.

with a short .25" shoulder tapering to a neck that is 1.2" tall and 0.625" in diameter. Crunching through the numbers for these yields $V = 722 + 70 = 790$ cubic inches; $L = 2$" and $r = 0.75$" for the large bottle, and $V = 2.5$ cubic inches; $L = 1.2$ and $r = 0.3125$ for the small one. This would predict oscillation frequencies of 70 Hz for the large bottle and 672 Hz for the small bottle (remember to express the speed of sound in inches per second if inches are the unit of measurement for your resonator).

Blowing on the actual bottles shows their oscillation frequencies to be 61 Hz for the large bottle and 480 Hz for the small one. It turns out that we have to adjust L to get a more accurate answer. This is because the piston of air is not really a perfect cylindrical piston, but more like an egg that extends slightly out from the neck both inside and outside. The *end correction factor* usually applied is between 1.0 and 1.5 times the radius of the opening. The new correct L values would be $2 + 0.75 = 2.75$"; and $1.2 + 0.3125 = 1.5125$", yielding corrected frequencies of 59 Hz and 595 Hz. This agrees well for the big bottle, and not so good for the little one. The error in the small bottle is probably due to size measurement errors, and the closeness in radius of the bottle and the neck, which could make it behave more like a pipe than a resonator (a ¼ wave cylindrical pipe resonator of length equal to the small bottle would exhibit a fundamental resonance of about 780 Hz, and other odd harmonic resonances).

The end correction factor means that we wouldn't really need a pipe attached to the volume cavity to make a resonator. Just drilling a hole in the wall of a cavity will cause it to behave like a resonator. One big low resonance of an acoustic guitar is a Helmholtz resonance due to the cavity of the body and the sound hole.

11.3.1 Building and Blowing a Bottle Model

As a final wind modeling exercise, we'll build an efficient and blowable model of a bottle. We know the pressure inside the volume cavity acts like a mass/spring/damper system. As with the clarinet reed, and shown in Figure 11.6, there are two pressures acting on our little piston/lozenge of air in the neck. One pressure is the internal pressure in the chamber (P_V); and the other pressure is the outside air pressure (P_A), which is usually constant, or varies so slowly or so little that it isn't acoustically significant. However, when we blow across the opening of the neck of the bottle, we change the pressure. Blowing into the neck raises the pressure, but blowing across the neck actually lowers the pressure because of *Bernoulli force*. Bernoulli force is an expression of conservation of energy in fluids, and says that for a constant density, if the velocity of air goes up (kinetic energy), the pressure must go down (potential energy). So when we blow across the bottle, the increased velocity of air causes the pressure to drop, pulling our piston up out of the neck, and causing the pressure to go down inside the chamber. The top of the prior piston joins the flowing air. At this point the whole system could be at equilibrium, with the rarified air in the chamber pulling down on the piston, and the rarified air in our blowing jet pulling equally up. However, our blowing has lots of little perturbations in it, and the fact that we had to begin blowing at some point means that we probably put energy into the mass/spring/damper system in a non-gradual way. These perturbations allow the piston to move back down, restoring some of the rarified air back into the chamber, and pulling some of our blowing air into the neck of the bottle. But the now further rarified air in our blowing jet pulls the piston back up, and this process continues until it has built up a steady-state oscillation at the natural frequency of the bottle. Thus, the Helmholtz bottle resonator system will oscillate, convolving our input blowing fluctuations with the exponentially decaying sinusoidal function of the resonator. The jet reflection function also serves to draw extra energy from our blowing, and converts that (nonlinearly) into what can become a strong oscillation at the natural bottle frequency.

Figure 11.8 shows the signal-processing model of the blown bottle. The funny shaped function in the middle models the tendency of air to flow into or out of the bottle as a function of the differential pressure on the piston. It is similar to the reed reflection coefficient table shown in Figure 11.4, but the

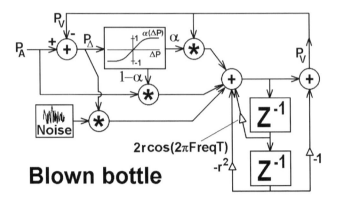

Figure 11.8. Computational model of a blown bottle.

jet table is symmetric because air can flow in or out of the bottle pretty much equally. Of course, all of this is a simplistic view of the fluid dynamics around the neck of a bottle, because there is actually complex three-dimensional flow going on in all directions. But even this simple one-dimensional model oscillates in basically the right way. To fake many of the effects of complex fluid dynamics in the region around the bottle neck, we can add noise, modulated by the differential neck pressure fluctuations.

$((45))$

11.4 Conclusions

Although extremely simple, the low dimensional models of air-based resonators presented in this chapter capture remarkable amounts of the behavior of such systems. More refinements can be made if needed, but much open research remains to be done in the area of the effects and computation of fluid dynamics in wind-based sound producers. In the next chapter, we will turn back to solid resonators, looking at higher dimensional systems.

Reading:

M. E. McIntyre, R. T. Schumacher, and J. Woodhouse. "On the Oscillations of Musical Instruments." *Journal of the Acoustic Society of America* 74(5): 1325–1345 (1983).

Julius O. Smith. "Efficient Simulation of the Reed-Bore and Bow-String Mechanisms." *Proceedings of the International Computer Music Conference.* 275–280 (1986).

C. Chafe. "Adding Vortex Noise to Wind Instrument Physical Models," *Proceedings of the International Computer Music Conference.* 57–60 (1985).

Matti Karjalainen, Unto K. Laine, Timo I. Laakso, and Vesa Välimäki. "Transmission-Line Modeling and Real-Time Synthesis of String and Wind Instruments." *Proceedings of the International Computer Music Conference:* 293–296 (1991).

Perry Cook, "A Meta-Wind Instrument Physical Model, and a Meta-Controller for Real-Time Performance Control." *Proceedings of the International Computer Music Conference:* 273–276 (1992).

Code:

Clarinet.cpp

BotlBlow.cpp

GUIPhysical

Sounds:

[Track 44] Synthesized Clarinet.

[Track 45] Real and Synthesized Blown Bottles.

Two and Three Dimensions

12.0 Introduction

This chapter extends our physically based sound synthesis techniques from low dimensional models to higher dimensions. Our models of waveguide strings and tubes were based on one-dimensional propagation or flow. Our other models based on modal resonators, sinusoids, and modal filters were basically zero-dimensional, taking into account only the important frequency components and ignoring the spatial aspects of sound in the synthesis. In this chapter, we will look at some simple two-dimensional structures such as membranes and plates. We will then branch out to three dimensions. Finally, motivated by the banded waveguide concept presented in Chapter 9, we'll reduce the computational complexity by looking at higher-dimensional structures as simplified networks of one-dimensional waveguide paths.

12.1 Membranes and Plates, Mass/Spring Models

Just as we looked at the string as a chain of masses and springs (Figure 4.1), we could model a plate or membrane as a "mesh" of masses and springs as shown in Figure 12.1. The mathematical setup and equations for this physical system are not simple, and of course the computation of the whole mesh can become quite expensive, especially for fine sampling and/or large structures.

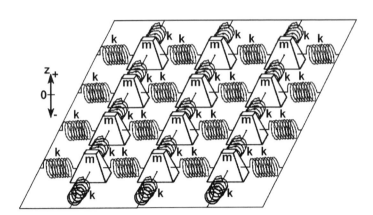

Figure 12.1. Membrane modeled as a mesh of masses and springs.

The computational expense could be worth it, if the masses and springs all have different coefficient values (this is called an *inhomogeneous* medium), or, if we need lots of spatial resolution for a simulation. Imposing arbitrary boundary conditions (such as a strange boundary shape like a small star or jagged edge of broken glass, for instance) might require a high spatial resolution. Note that we might not need all the resolution for the final sound output, because of the natural bandwidth limitation of our hearing. But remember that our simple one mode mass/spring/damper system had to be calculated at higher than the audio rate in order to behave realistically. So we might expect that the spatial resolution of a two- or higher-dimensional simulation might need to be quite high to make the system behave correctly, and to make the actual computations stable and realistic.

12.1.2 Fourier Boundary Solutions

Just as we used Fourier boundary methods (Chapter 4, Section 4.2) to solve one-dimensional string and tube systems, we can also extend boundary methods to two dimensions. Figure 12.2 shows the first few modes of vibration of a homogeneous square membrane. A homogeneous membrane/plate has the property that the density (mass per unit area), tension, thickness, etc., are the same at all points. The little boxes at the lower left corners of each modal shape diagram in Figure 12.2 depict the modes in a purely two-dimensional way, showing lines corresponding to the spatial sinusoidal nodes (regions of no displacement vibration).

The square membrane acts much like a two-dimensional string, exhibiting vibrations which are sums of sinusoidal components in both x and y directions. It might not seem like these simple shapes could take care of any possible

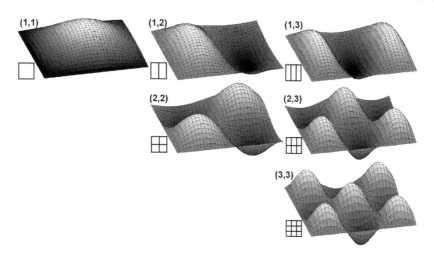

Figure 12.2. Vibrational modes of a square membrane.

shape and excitation, but that's the power of Fourier. Of course the natural modes must obey the two-dimensional boundary conditions at the edges, but unlike the string, the square membrane modes are not integer-related harmonic frequencies. In fact, they obey the relationship

$$f_{mn} = f_{11} \sqrt{((m^2 + n^2)/2)}, \tag{12.1}$$

where m and n range from 1 to (potentially) infinity, and f_{11} is $c/2L$ (the speed of sound on the membrane divided by the diagonal lengths). As with the ideal string, c is the square root of tension/density (mass per unit area). Note that there are multiple (called degenerate) modes with the same frequency. For example, the (1,2) and (2,1) modes are identical. If the membrane were rectangular, the modal shapes would be spatially stretched, and the frequencies would change also. If the ratio of the rectangular dimensions cannot be expressed as a ratio of integers, all modal frequencies are unique.

$(\!(46)\!)$

Figure 12.3 shows the two-dimensional nodal lines for a circular membrane. The labeling convention for the circular membrane modes numbers the diameter nodes first, then the circular nodes. Unfortunately, circles, rectangles, and other simple geometries turn out to be the only ones for which the boundary conditions yield a closed-form solution in terms of spatial and temporal sinusoidal terms. Also, only extremely simple excitations (initial shapes for plucking, initial velocities for striking) have known boundary solutions. Of course, all linear time invariant systems do have solutions in terms of spatial and temporal sine components, but we can't guess and prove

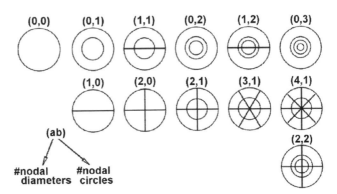

Figure 12.3. Circular membrane modes (modified from Essl).

closed-form solutions except for very simple geometries and excitations. So the Fourier boundary solution method is mostly of academic interest, especially when we think about the wide variety of objects and interactions we might find in the world of real sounds.

12.1.3   2D Waveguide Meshes

If the stiffness is negligible, then the simple delay-based waveguide techniques can be extended to two dimensions as shown in Figure 12.4. As discussed in

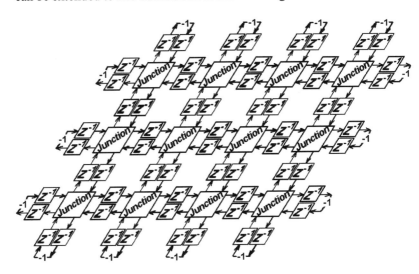

Figure 12.4. Two-dimensional waveguide mesh model.

Chapter 9, all-pass filters can replace the unit delays in the mesh to model the frequency-dependent dispersion due to stiffness.

If the mesh structure is based on square samples, then the computation is simplified in that no multiplications are required (in integer arithmetic, multiplication by 0.5 is accomplished by a simple arithmetic bit shift). Note that the overall shape doesn't have to be square, just the relationship between adjacent spatial samples. The calculations required at each junction of four waveguides in a square mesh is:

$$z_J = 0.5 \, (z_{inU} + z_{inD} + z_{inL} + z_{inR}) \tag{12.2}$$

$$z_{outU} = z_J - z_{inU} \qquad z_{outD} = z_J - z_{inD} \tag{12.3, 12.4}$$

$$z_{outL} = z_J - z_{inL} \qquad z_{outR} = z_J - z_{inR} \, , \tag{12.5, 12.6}$$

z is the signed transverse membrane displacement. U and D are the incoming displacements from neighbors above and below in the y direction, and L and R are the incoming displacements from the left and right neighbors in the x direction. The junction calculation is shown in block diagram form in Figure 12.5. To implement a mesh, one buffer is required to store the current states of each unit delay cell, and another buffer is used to store the junction displacements. One computation pass is done to calculate the junction sums from the input displacements, and another pass computes the output displacements and propagates the delays. Boundary conditions are imposed at the edges, and could include simple reflections, nonlinear springs, etc.

Aside from the large amount of computation and memory required to calculate every junction in the mesh, there are other downsides to waveguide

$((\cdot 47 \cdot))$

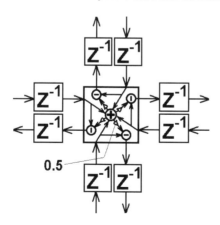

Figure 12.5. Two-dimensional waveguide mesh junction calculation.

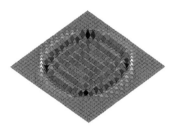

Figure 12.6. A 32 × 32 rectangular mesh shape 17 time steps after impulse at center, showing dispersion problems(deviations from circle).

meshes. Essentially any discretization or meshing structure introduces nonrealistic dispersion into the simulation. This is most easily seen by looking at the rectangular mesh, where a disturbance at one point will be felt by its nearest x and y neighbors on the next time step, but it must travel around a right angle, taking two time steps to be felt by any nearest diagonal point. This means that the speed of sound on the mesh is shorter by a factor of $\sqrt{2}$ in the up/down directions versus the diagonal directions. An impulsive input at any point should yield a wavefront that propagates outward in a circle, but the $\sqrt{2}$ speed distortion causes the circular wavefront to be distorted (held back) along the diagonals. Figure 12.6 shows a propagating waveform after 17 time steps on a 32 × 32 rectangular mesh in response to an impulsive displacement in the center, pointing out the obvious difference from the ideal circular wavefront. Other meshing schemes involving diamonds, triangles, etc. can improve the dispersion error, but still don't fix it completely. Nonrectangular meshing schemes require giving up the no-multiply integer computation capability.

12.2 Three-Dimensional Structures

Coupled masses/springs/dampers, waveguide meshes, and Fourier boundary solution methods can all be applied to three-dimensional structures. The methods and issues are similar and straightforward, usually just extending the methods from two to three dimensions. Unfortunately, the computational burdens go up significantly.

12.2.1 Three-Dimensional Waveguide Meshes

Waveguide meshes are being investigated more and more as a simulation technique. As an example, let's look at what it would take to use a three-dimensional waveguide mesh to model the large three gallon water bottle resonator that we studied in Chapter 11. A *critically sampled mesh* sets the

Figure 12.7. Air in three gallon water bottle as three-dimensional waveguide mesh.

internodal distance to be the distance traveled by a sound wave in the time of one audio sample. At 44,100 samples per second, and a speed of sound of 1100 feet per second, critical spatial sampling requires a grid of 0.3 inch resolution. Thus the approximately 800 cubic inch volume of the bottle would require a whopping 30,000 three-dimensional waveguide junctions to model! Figure 12.7 shows the bottle with a cutaway showing the mesh inside. Each junction would require 12 add/subtract operations and one multiply per time step.

The basic setup for the waveguide mesh assumes that the material being modeled is homogeneous. This isn't strictly necessary, but makes the math and computations cleaner. For the air inside the water bottle, this is true, but not true or applicable for modeling solid deformable objects with arbitrary shapes and possibly made up of different materials.

12.2.2 Solving the Wave Equation on an Arbitrary Three-Dimensional Mesh

At significant computational cost, we can return to the first principles of physics to solve meshes in three dimensions. In fact, this turns out to be the only guaranteed solution for arbitrary shapes made up of inhomogeneous materials with the twists and turns we might find in real-world objects. Figure 12.8 shows a bowl modeled with two different multiresolution meshes. *Multiresolution* means that regions of high feature detail (edges, corners, etc.) have more mesh points per unit volume than smoother regions. The higher average resolution mesh is in general more accurate, but more expensive to compute. Selecting the right resolution is a tradeoff between computational complexity, stability, and accuracy.

Figure 12.8. Low resolution(left) and high resolution (right) bowl meshes. *(Image courtesy James O'Brien.)*

If we assume the object represented by the mesh can be deformed (otherwise it wouldn't vibrate, and thus wouldn't make any sound), then the physical equation describing the pressure waves in the object is

$$\frac{\partial^2 p}{\partial t^2} = c^2 \nabla^2 p \qquad (12.7)$$

the three-dimensional equivalent of the second order Newtonian equations we've seen so many times before. The $\nabla^2 p$ term is the three-dimensional spatial *curvature*, which is the sum of the second spatial pressure derivatives in the x, y, and z directions. Just as we discretized the one-dimensional mass/spring/ damper version of Equation 12.7, we can do the same in three dimensions and solve it explicitly. Oversampling in space and time is required to ensure stability and accuracy, but the multiresolution meshing helps by doing the spatial oversampling in regions of higher detail where it matters the most.

Collisions of the mesh with other objects can be computed providing a suitable energy/penalty method is used to ensure passivity. The benefit of this method is that it can be used both for animation and sound computation. Figure 12.9 shows an animation of the bowl bouncing from a rigid floor surface, and the resulting synthesized waveform and spectrogram. All were computed from the same simulation.

12.2.3 Ray Propagation Paths in Three Dimensions

Another approach to modeling vibration looks at individual propagation paths. This can work well, especially in large contained spaces such as rooms. Figure 12.10 shows a singer and a listener in a simple room. Only the first few wave paths from the singer's mouth to the listener's ears are shown.

The direct sound and the first order reflections (bouncing off of only one surface) are shown in Figure 12.10, but there would be many second, third, and higher order reflections as well. These individual paths can be modeled as simple delay lines, with attenuation due to the spherical sound waves

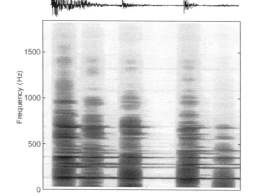

Figure 12.9. Bouncing bowl animation, waveform and spectrogram. *(Image courtesy of James O'Brien.)*

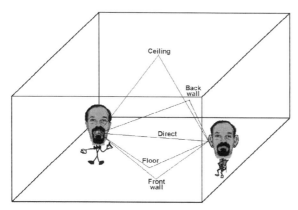

Figure 12.10. Direct and first order reflected sound paths from singer to listener in a simple room.

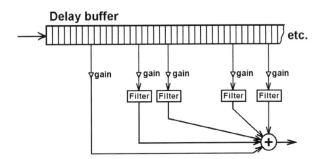

Figure 12.11. Signal processing diagram of direct and first order reflected sound paths in room of Figure 12.10.

spreading linearly with distance (1/distance amplitude attenuation), and other losses (possibly with filtering) due to reflections from the walls. Note that this view of sound space is similar to graphical ray tracing, but since the speed of sound is low compared to light speed, it is necessary to add all the individual path signals at their correct delays and attenuations. Of course, this weighted addition of delayed and filtered inputs corresponds to an FIR digital filter. Figure 12.11 shows a signal processing model of the direct and first order reflections in a room.

This book focuses on how sounds are created and doesn't cover room acoustics and propagation, so we won't deal more with wavepaths in three dimensions here. But the waveguide wavepath notion will combine with boundary methods in the next section to give us a simplified computational model of many higher dimensional systems.

12.3 Banded Waveguides in Higher Dimensions

Let's look again at the modes of the square membrane shown in Figure 12.2. Table 12.1 shows some of the modes computed according to Equation 12.1. The frequencies of these modes are clearly not harmonic, but they do have the regularly symmetric spatial behaviors shown in Figure 12.2.

If we were to hit a square membrane, record the sound, and inspect the spectrum, we would be able to (depending, of course, on how and where we hit it) observe these modes. We could use additive exponentially decaying sinusoids, or modal filters, to model the observed modes. But neither of these methods takes into account the spatial aspects of the boundaries: excitation and vibration.

If we remember our development and use of banded waveguides (Section 9.4), we added delay lines to model the frequency dependent

M	n	f_{mn}
1	1	f_{11}
1	2	$f_{11}\sqrt{(5/2)} = 1.58f_{11}$
1	3	$\sqrt{5}f_{11} = 2.24f_{11}$
1	4	$f_{11}\sqrt{(17/2)} = 2.92f_{11}$
2	2	$2f_{11}$
2	3	$f_{11}\sqrt{(13/2)} = 2.55f_{11}$
2	4	$f_{11}\sqrt{10} = 3.16f_{11}$
3	3	$3f_{11}$
3	4	$5f_{11}/\sqrt{2} = 3.54f_{11}$

Table 12.1. Modal frequencies for square membrane.

propagation speed, breaking the spectrum into bands centered around the modes of the bar. Could we treat the struck membrane spectrum in the same way, attaching the appropriate delays corresponding to traveling wavepaths around the membrane? All that is needed is the assurance that each mode actually corresponds to a closed wavepath, and the knowledge of the geometry of that wavepath. Neither of these is necessarily easy. It turns out that for each given resonant mode of a system, there exists one or more closed wavepaths which give rise to the mode. This makes sense in an intuitive physical sense, in that if the wave travels around the path and doesn't meet itself at the starting point in the proper phase, there would be no standing wave resonance, and the mode wouldn't exist. This is easily seen in strings and bars where the wave simply travels down and back in exactly the time corresponding to one or more periods of the spatial frequency of the standing wave. But higher-dimensional structures are more difficult to visualize.

From their individual shapes, there are quite a lot of things we do know about the modes of the square membrane. All modes have nodes at the edges (the basic boundary conditions) as well as other nodal lines, as shown in Figure 12.2. For example, if we strike the membrane in the center, we should expect to excite modes (1, 1), (1, 3), (3, 1), (3, 3), and all (odd n, odd m) modes. In fact, striking the membrane with an ideal impulse at any point should excite each mode with a gain equal to the corresponding mode shape value at that point. That is, striking a unit (1 × 1) square membrane at an arbitrary point (x, y) will excite each mode with gain:

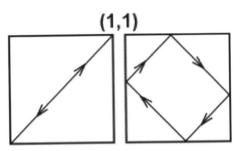

Figure 12.12. Wavepaths for f_{11} mode on square membrane.

$$gain_{nm} = \sin(n\pi x)\sin(m\pi y) \tag{12.8}$$

The speed of sound on a 1 × 1 membrane is $c = 2\sqrt{2}f_{11}$. Wavelength λ is the speed of sound divided by the frequency, so we should be able to determine, for each mode, the wavelength λ_{nm}. The wavelength for f_{11} is $\lambda_{11} = c / f_{11} = 2\sqrt{2}$. This corresponds to a wave trip to the corner, a reflection, travelling back through the center, reflecting off the opposite edge, then home again, as shown in the left-hand side of Figure 12.12. There are many (an infinity) of such paths, one shown in the right-hand side of Figure 12.12. Each path bounces identically once off of each edge, and they all have the same $\lambda_{11} = 2\sqrt{2}$. Adding all of these up gives the shape of the (1, 1) mode shown in Figure 12.2.

Note that harmonics of f_{11} are also supported by the (1,1) spatial mode. This includes (2, 2), (3, 3), and all such (I, I) modes as shown in Table 12.1. There are many more nonharmonic modes than harmonic ones however. The wavelength λ_{12} for mode (1, 2)—or (2, 1)—is $2\sqrt{(2/5)}$. Figure 12.13 shows the wavepath corresponding to the basic (1, 2) mode. Note that this path, and all of the infinite (1, 2) paths, bounce exactly twice off each of two edges, and once each off the other two edges (hence the (2, 1) or (1, 2) relationship). The

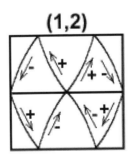

Figure 12.13. Base wavepath for f_{12} mode on square membrane.

paths are shown slightly bent to emphasize the +/− transitions at reflections and nodal lines.

Working all of these paths out gets more and more difficult for higher order modes (except for the simple (N, N) harmonics). The important thing to realize here is that each mode has a unique path length, which could be modeled by a delay line in a banded waveguide network.

12.4 Spatial Modes in Complex Geometries

Given how difficult it is to plot banded waveguide paths for a geometry as simple as the square membrane, could we have any hope of using the concept on more complex geometries? We know that for an arbitrary object, we cannot write simple closed form expressions for the spatial modal patterns. We also know that we can always degenerate to the pure modal model for our synthesis if we can't figure out the closed waveguide paths. One simple method would be to attach a waveguide delay of length corresponding to one wavelength of any given mode, as we did in the bar case. But the actual closed wave path of interest might consist of more than one spatial period of the mode we're trying to model.

There are experimental *modal analysis* methods that allow us to measure, record, or even "see" the modal patterns of a vibrating object. One classic, but messy, method is to sprinkle powder or sand on the object. As the object vibrates, the fine particles gravitate to the nodal lines, showing the lines of no vibration. Unfortunately, this method works best on flat plates or membranes. Another method is to place microphones or acceleration sensors on the object surface, reading the output levels of the individual sensors and building up a map of the vibration. Another method is to strike the object at many points, observing which modes are excited, and at what amplitude for each point. This also allows us to build up a map of the modal patterns. One more method involves bouncing a laser off the surface, and picking up the reflected wave with a sensor. The laser can be scanned rapidly over the object, allowing the entire surface vibration to be scanned and graphed.

Some real object geometries are symmetric enough, or simple enough, to allow us to infer the modes of interest, especially for bowing interactions (we'll see this later). Figure 12.14 shows a computer graphics model of a Tibetan prayer bowl, and Figure 12.15 shows the striking spectra of two actual bowls of this type. The bowls themselves are nearly identical in size, weight, and appearance, but the modal structures (and sounds) are clearly quite different.

Prayer bowls are made from a mixture of many metals. The makers and users believe each metal possesses some particular spiritual power, and the

Figure 12.14. Circular wavepath on a Tibetan prayer bowl.

mixture imparts these and other powers on the bowl. To use for prayer, a bowl is held in the flat of the hand or placed on a pillow, then struck and bowed. Figure 12.16 shows the spectral results of striking one of the bowls three times in the same place, but at different angles. It is clear that the modes are excited very differently, depending on the strike direction, even with the same strike position. This suggests different wavepaths for the different modes. Thus, the Fourier boundary idea of where we hit something determining the sound must be modified to "where and in what direction we hit something determines the sound."

For bowing a prayer bowl, a wooden rod (often wrapped with cowhide) is rubbed in a circular pattern around the outside rim. This circular excitation, tangential to the rim of the bowl, means that the modes that are most likely to be excited by bowing are circular modes (shown around the rim of the bowl in Figure 12.14). This is much like the bowing that we might do by wetting our finger and rubbing it on a wine glass. Figure 12.17 shows the (greatly

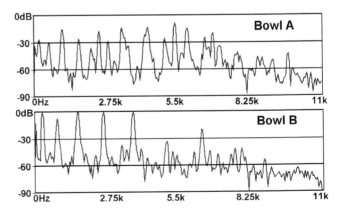

Figure 12.15. Spectra of two different struck prayer bowls.

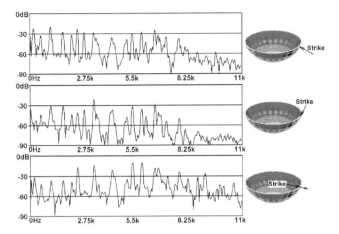

Figure 12.16. Spectra from striking prayer bowl A three times at the same location on the rim, but at three different angles.

exaggerated) first four modes computed from a mesh simulation of a bowl. As would be expected, these exhibit nice symmetries around the rim, and could be candidates for excitation by bowing. We will build and bow a banded waveguide model of the prayer bowl in Chapter 14.

One more topic to briefly discuss relates to objects with very many highly resonant modes. These objects, when struck, can makes sounds that vibrate in odd ways. For example, the struck prayer bowl exhibits *beating*, which is the interference of modes that are close together in frequency. For fun, add $\sin(\pi t)$ and $\sin(1.01\pi t)$ and look at the result. What you actually end up seeing instead of the addition of two sine waves is instead $\sin(1.005\pi t) \cos(0.01\pi t)$, the

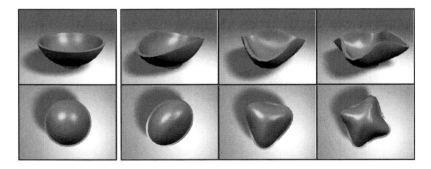

Figure 12.17. First four circular modes of bowl. *(Image courtesy of James O'Brien.)*

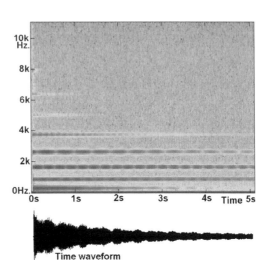

Figure 12.18. Struck prayer bowl B showing beats in upper modes.

product of one sine wave at the average of the frequencies times another slow amplitude modulation (at the difference in tone frequency). Figure 12.18 shows a spectrogram of the struck Tibetan prayer bowl (bowl B). Each of the upper modes seems to exhibit a beating phenomenon at different frequencies! I'll leave it to you to figure out what modes at what frequencies could combine to yield the time domain beat patterns shown.

12.5 Conclusions

The good news from this chapter is that all of the techniques we have used in this book so far are applicable in two and three dimensions. The bad news is that things are generally more complex in higher dimensions. Meshes are the most general way to model the spatial aspects of vibrations, and modes are the most general way to handle the pure spectral behavior. Banded waveguides are applicable in some systems, especially where clear, closed wavepaths can be identified. The next chapter will depart entirely from these types of models, and look instead at the statistical behavior of random type sounds.

Reading:

Claude Cadoz, Annie Luciani and Jean-Loup Florens. "CORDIS-ANIMA: A Modeling and Simulation System for Sound Image Synthesis-The General Formalization." *Computer Music Journal* 17(1): 21–29(1993).

Scott Van Duyne and Julius O. Smith. "Physical Modeling with the Two-Dimensional Digital Waveguide Mesh." In Proceedings of the ICMC, Tokyo: 40–47 (1993).

Philip Morse. *Vibration and Sound,* American Institute of Physics for the Acoustical Society of America (1986).

Thomas Rossing. *Science of Percussion Instruments.* River Edge: World Scientific Press (2000).

James F. O'Brien, Perry Cook, and Georg Essl. "Synthesizing Sounds from Physically Based Motion." *Proceedings of ACM SIGGRAPH*: 529–536 (2001).

Code:

BowedBar.cpp

GUIBowedBar

WGMesh.cpp

Sounds:

[Track 46] Synthesized Square Membrane Modes; Built Up.

[Track 47] Rectangular Waveguide Mesh Sounds (from Scott A. Van Duyne).

[Track 48] Deformable Mesh Bouncing Bowl Sounds (see also Movie).

[Track 49] Struck Tibetan Prayer Bowls.

FOFs, Wavelets, and Particles

13.0 Introduction

Most of physics can be modeled as objects interacting with each other. Lots of little objects are usually called *particles*. Much in life is, or can be, broken into little grains or particles. Are there particles of perception? Aristotle thought so. Some people still think so. But we don't really perceive sound as little bubbles coming into our ears, do we? Let's answer an easier question: Are there particles of sound production? Of course! This chapter will investigate the modeling and synthesis of sound using models based on interacting particles.

13.1 Formants in the Time Domain: FOFs

In prior chapters we looked at subtractive synthesis techniques, such as modal synthesis (Chapter 4) and linear predictive coding (Chapter 8). In these methods a complex source is used to excite resonant filters. The source usually has a flat spectrum, or exhibits a simple roll-off pattern like $1/f$ or $1/f^2$ (6 dB or 12 dB per octave). The filters, possibly time-varying, shape the spectrum to model the desired sound.

The subtractive filter topology which best motivates the topics in this chapter is the parallel resonant form. Referring to Figure 13.1, let's inspect

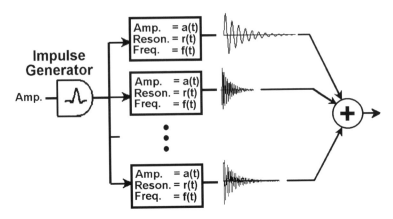

Figure 13.1. Filter view of additive formant synthesis, showing individual impulse responses of parallel formant filters.

the outputs of each individual filter in response to a single impulse. We know from our filter studies that the impulse response of a simple two-pole resonant filter is an exponentially decaying sinusoid. The resonance parameter determines the decay time of the filter, the center frequency parameter sets the frequency of the sinusoidal oscillation, and the phase is determined by the excitation time.

Any individual resonant filter could be replaced by a function generator consisting of an exponential envelope generator multiplied by a sine oscillator (shown in Figure 13.2). The envelope generator would be initialized to the gain of the resonant section at the time the impulse is injected into the replaced filter.

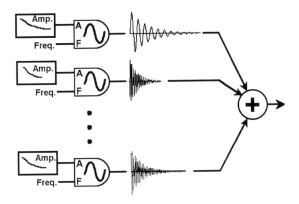

Figure 13.2. Envelope/oscillator view of additive formant synthesis.

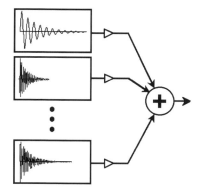

Figure 13.3. Wavetable view of additive formant synthesis.

To continue our manipulations, we can replace the function generator with a simple one-shot table that stores the samples of the exponentially decaying sine wave. By storing each filter impulse response in a table, initializing each table at excitation, and adding the outputs of all tables, the identical impulse response to that of Figure 13.1 could be achieved by the system depicted in Figure 13.3. Further, from the superposition property of linear systems, if we have as many filter impulse response tables as needed (or as many "read" pointers from each filter's corresponding table), we can overlap and add filter impulse table outputs weighted by the excitation impulses (individual input samples in the limit) and implement a resonant filter on a sampled data signal purely by table lookup. Unfortunately the tables might be quite long, depending on the exponential time constants. It is certain that the tables would require much more memory than filter variables, and more memory than the single shared sine table used in Figure 13.2. Worse yet, precomputing the table couples the exponential time constant to the sinusoidal oscillation frequency. Of course, none of this is particularly clever, but it is a good mental picture to visualize convolution with resonators in a different way, and to introduce systems based on tables of impulse responses.

In a source/filter vocal model such as LPC or parallel/cascade formant synthesis, periodic impulses are used to excite resonant filters to produce vowels. We could construct a simple alternative model using three, four, or more tables storing the impulse responses of the individual vowel formants. Note that it isn't necessary for the tables to contain pure exponentially decaying sinusoids. We could include aspects of the voice source, etc., as long as those effects are periodic. FOFs (originally introduced as *Formant Onde Functions* in French, translates to *Formant Wave Functions* in English) were created for

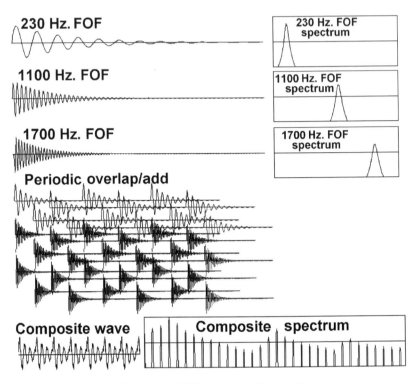

Figure 13.4. FOF synthesis of a vowel.

voice synthesis using such tables, overlapped and added at the voice source pitch. Figure 13.4 depicts FOF synthesis of a vowel. FOFs are composed of a sinusoid at the formant center frequency, with an amplitude that rises rapidly upon excitation, then decays exponentially. The control parameters define the center frequency and bandwidth of the formant being modeled, and the rate at which the FOFs are generated and added determines the fundamental frequency of the voice.

((‹50›))

13.2 Wavelets

In our discussions of subband filters and vocoders (Chapter 7), we looked at using filters to decompose signals into separate frequency bands. Of course, each of these subband filtering operations can be viewed as a convolution of an input signal with the impulse response of each filter. Figure 13.5 is a redrawing of Figure 7.1, showing the time domain impulse responses of the filters rather than the frequency domain responses.

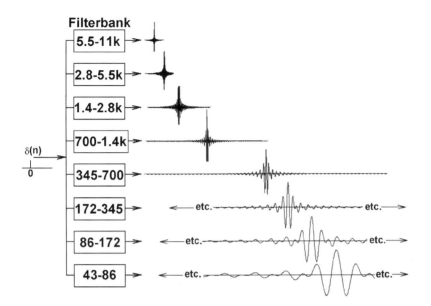

Figure 13.5. Octave band filterbank impulse responses.

We can see from Figure 13.5 that each octave impulse response is simply a halving (doubling) of the time of the adjacent ones. From the similarity theorem of the time/frequency domains (Appendix A), we know that the impulse response must double in length if the bandwidth is halved. This means that the lowest octave filter has an impulse response which is $2^8 = 256$ times longer than the highest octave. We also know that each successive lower octave has one-half the bandwidth of the next higher one, so we really only need to sample the output at one-half the rate of the next higher one.

The similarity and bandwidth properties give rise to a different form of the octave-band filter, shown in Figure 13.6. This filterbank is implemented in cascade rather than parallel form. Each stage consists of complementary high pass and low pass filters that split the signal into two equal bandwidth signals, one containing the top octave and the other containing the lower octave. Each lower octave low-passed signal is decimated by two (throwing out every other sample), and the filtering is repeated. This allows the same low order "top octave" filter to be used at each stage in the filtering chain.

The half band decimation filter structure shown in Figure 13.5 gives rise to a family of filter based frequency transforms known as *wavelet transforms*. Instead of being based on sinusoids like the Fourier transform, wavelet transforms are based on the decomposition of signals into fairly arbitrary

Filterbank

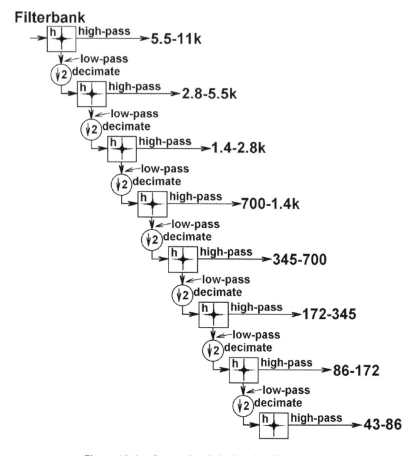

Figure 13.6. Octave band decimation filterbank.

wavelets. These wavelets can be thought of as mathematical sound grains. Some benefits of wavelet transforms over Fourier transforms are that they can be implemented using fairly arbitrary filter criteria on a logarithmic frequency scale rather than a linear scale as in the DFT, and that time resolution can be a function of the frequency range of interest. This latter point means that we can say accurate things about high frequencies as well as low. This contrasts the Fourier transform, which requires the analysis window width to be the same for all frequencies. This means that we must either average out lots of the interesting high frequency time information in favor of being able to resolve low frequency information (large window); or opt for good time resolution (small window) at the expense of low frequency resolution; or perform multiple transforms with different sized windows to catch both time and frequency details.

So you might now ask, is there a fast version of the wavelet transform, like the FFT allows us to compute the DFT rapidly? In fact, there are a number of fast wavelet transform techniques that allow the subband decomposition to be accomplished in essentially $N \log_2(N)$ time just like the FFT. We won't get into that now, for there are lots of books about wavelets and wavelet transforms. Mostly what we're trying to do here is to develop the idea that bandlimited grains might motivate good sound synthesis methods.

13.3 Granular Synthesis

In Chapter 2 we talked about performing time shifting using windowed overlap-add techniques, which is a special case of a synthesis technique called *granular synthesis*. Granular synthesis involves hacking up sound and reassembling it by mixing. The grains usually range in length from 5 to 100 ms. The reassembly can be systematic, as it was in our time-shifting case in Chapter 2. Usually granular synthesis involves significant random components, including randomized grain sizes, locations, and amplitudes. The transformed result usually bears some characteristics of the original sound, just as a mildly blended mixture of fruits still bears some attributes of the original fruits, as well as taking on new attributes due to the mixture. Granular synthesis is mostly used as a compositional and musical effect type of signal processing, but it relates to our current topic of sound particles. The next section will take a physically motivated look at sound grains.

13.4 Particle Models

This section gets back to one of the questions that began this chapter: Are there sound-producing particles? To answer that, we only need to walk around on gravel, shake a glass full of ice cubes, play a game of dice, or reach into our pocket to retrieve change or keys. Each of these acts causes energy to be put into a particle system. The particles move and shift, hitting each other and other objects, causing sound to be made.

The PhISEM (*Physically Informed Stochastic Event Modeling*) algorithm is based on pseudo-random overlapping and adding of small grains of sound. At the heart of PhISEM algorithms are particle models characterized by basic Newtonian equations governing the motion and collisions of point masses as can be found in any introductory physics textbook. Particle systems can be solved numerically using the same discrete differential approximations we used to solve the mass/spring/damper system in Chapter 4 (see development of Equation 4.5). Velocity is approximated by the difference between the current discrete time position and the last, divided by the time step Δt. Similarly, the acceleration is approximated by the first velocity difference.

By selecting a time step that is suitably small, appropriate accuracy and stability can be achieved. In two- and three-Cartesian dimensions, these difference equations are separable in position, velocity, and acceleration. Runge-Kutta methods (or other) can be used for more accuracy at larger time steps. When collisions occur, momentum and center of mass are used for additional solution constraints. To make this all more tangible, we'll look at some specific systems.

13.4.1 A Single Particle Model

As a simple example, a two-dimensional single particle model can be used to model a police/referee whistle. Example 13.1 shows how a collision of a single particle (called a *bean* in the code) with a two-dimensional circular shell would be computed. The collide() function is a distance calculation between the particle and the closest place on the shell, returning TRUE if it's close enough to be considered a collision.

Figure 13.7 shows a side view of a whistle, with a single particle *pea* (bean) suspended in a breath-controlled vector field. The region around the *fipple* (the part that splits the air, like the jet nonlinearity developed in the blown bottle model in Chapter 11) is characterized by a random vector field, modeling the switching airflow, plus turbulence noise. Experiments and spectrograms using real police/referee whistles showed that when the pea is in the immediate region of the jet oscillator, there is a decrease in pitch (about 7%), an increase in amplitude (about 6 dB), and a small increase in the noise component (about 2 dB). The noise component is about −20 dB relative to the first harmonic of the oscillator. The oscillator exhibits three significant harmonics: f_0, $2f_0$, and $3f_0$, at 0 dB, −10 dB, and −25 dB, respectively. Center frequencies of the fundamental frequencies of six test whistles ranged from

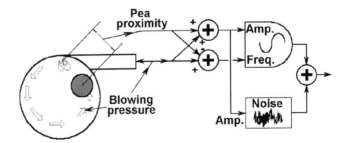

Figure 13.7. Physical control of oscillator/noise synthesis whistle model.

```
/* Check for collision*/
if (collide(bean,shell))
{
   /* Get velocity of particle */
   tempXVel = bean->getXVelocity();
   tempYVel = bean->getYVelocity();

   /* Get position on shell wall */
   tempX = bean->getX();
   tempY = bean->getY();

   /* Compute angle to position */
   phi = -atan2(tempY,tempX);
   cosphi = cos(phi);
   sinphi = sin(phi);

   /* "Rotate" shell particle so that all
   particle velocity is directed in the
   positive x direction. */
   temp1 = (cosphi*tempXVel)- (sinphi*tempYVel);

   temp2 = (sinphi*tempXVel) + (cosphi*tempYVel);

   /* Then we just reverse x vel and
      we can rotate things back again
      and proceed with simulation */
   temp1 = -temp1 * SHELL_LOSS;
   tempXVel = (cosphi*temp1) + (sinphi*temp2);
   tempYVel = (-sinphi*temp1) + (cosphi*temp2);
   beans->setVelocity(tempXVel,tempYVel);
}
```

Example 13.1. C++ Code: Collision of a single particle with the wall of a circular shell in two dimensions.

1800 to 3200 Hz. It would be possible to connect the particle model parameters to a physical model of the air jet fluid dynamics, but the observed effects are easily coupled from the parameters of a physical particle simulation to the control inputs of a simple oscillator/noise synthesis model as shown in Figure 13.7. The figure shows turbulence at the fipple. The pea/fipple proximity modulates both the amplitude and frequency of the oscillator and the noise amplitude.

13.4.2 MultiParticle System Computation

More complex three-dimensional multiple particle model systems, such as maracas, wind chimes, ice cubes in a glass, etc., can also be modeled explicitly

```
for ( i = 0; i < NUM_BEANS; i ++ )
{
   /* Loop over # particles */
   for ( j = i +1; j < NUM_BEANS; j ++)
   {
      /* & over remaining particles
      Check for collision */
      if (collide(beans[ i ], beans[ j ])
      {
         /* Exchange velocities in each direction
            with a little loss */
         temp1 = beans[ i ]->getXVelocity();
         temp2 = beans[ j ]->getXVelocity();
         beans[ i ]->setXVelocity(temp2 * B_LOSS);
         beans[ j ]->setXVelocity(temp1 * B_LOSS);
         temp1 = beans[ i ]->getYVelocity();
         temp2 = beans[ j ]->getYVelocity();
         beans[ i ]->setYVelocity(temp2 * B_LOSS);
         beans[ j ]->setYVelocity(temp1 * B_LOSS);
         temp1 = beans[ i ]->getZVelocity();
         temp2 = beans[ j ]->getZVelocity();
         beans[ i ]->setZVelocity(temp2 * B_LOSS);
         beans[ j ]->setZVelocity(temp1 * B_LOSS);
      }
   }
}
```

Example 13.2. C++ Code: Exchange of energy, with a slight loss, between equal mass colliding particles in three dimensions.

using the idea of particles contained in a shell. Example 13.2 shows a calculation of particle/particle collisions, assuming all particles are of equal mass. It would also be necessary to calculate all particle collisions with the outer shell in three dimensions.

Note how the computational load goes up rapidly (N^2 for bean/bean collisions and N for bean/shell collisions) with increasing numbers of particles, so calculating these models can become quite expensive. The potentially huge number of randomly timed overlapped collisions to be calculated and managed suggests that we should investigate a more economical synthesis algorithm.

13.4.3 Multiparticle System Statistical Analysis

To build a more economical and useful model, we will build a spherical maraca model, and "shake" it with various numbers of beans inside. We'll collect statistics of the waiting time between collisions, and of the collision sound intensity. Only beans hitting the outside shell will be considered significant

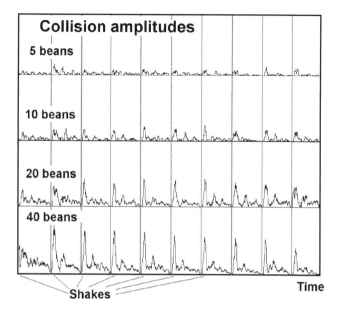

Figure 13.8. Smoothed amplitude responses from ten shakes of simulated maracas containing 5, 10, 20, and 40 beans.

sound-producing collisions, since bean/bean interactions inside the gourd don't couple efficiently to the radiated sound. We'll use the square of the velocity component (kinetic energy) normal (at a right angle) to the maraca surface to calculate the strength of the radiated sound, and we will take corresponding energy out of each wall-colliding bean's velocity. Bean/bean collisions will cause a small decrease in energy of both beans. Figure 13.8 shows the smoothed amplitude responses of simulations calculated using 5, 10, 20, and 40 beans.

As should be expected from all passive physical systems, once energy is put into the maraca, the average intensity of collisions decays exponentially. The oscillation superimposed on the exponential decay is due to the initial bouncing of the beans together in an ensemble, then eventually breaking up into random behavior.

Figure 13.9 shows histograms of waiting times averaged over ten shakes, for simulations calculated using 5, 10, 20, and 40 beans. The likelihood of a significant sound-producing collision occurring is roughly constant for a fixed number of beans, except when all beans are nearly at rest. This points to a Poisson process, common in many natural systems, in which a constant probability of an event at any given time gives rise to an exponential probability of times between events. It is clear that the Poisson process becomes more

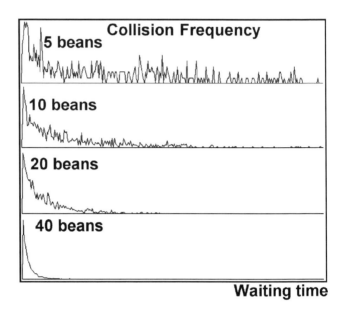

Figure 13.9. Averaged histograms of waiting times between sound-producing events for simulated maracas containing 5, 10, 20, and 40 beans.

like the ideal (smoother exponential probability functions) for larger numbers of beans, and that the waiting time gets progressively shorter for increasing number of beans.

Now we're armed with the statistical results of the simulations, but we still need to know more about the sound(s) made by the collisions. We could drop individual beans on an empty maraca gourd to get a sense of the sound of one collision. The time and frequency domain view of a maraca bean dropped onto an empty maraca gourd is shown in Figure 13.10. Note that the sound is a decaying sinusoidal oscillation, and the spectrum exhibits something close to a single dominant resonance. This makes it much like the FOFs or wavelets discussed before. If we look at the waveform and spectrum of an actual maraca shake (also shown in Figure 13.10), we note that once the maraca shake is complete, the waveform decays exponentially (as our simulation predicted), and the general spectral shape still exhibits the same single dominant resonance as the single bean/gourd collision.

From our experience with subtractive synthesis and LPC (Chapter 8), it might occur to us to fit a filter to the resonant sound and decompose the sound into a source/filter system. Figure 13.11 shows the results of deconvolving the resonance from the maraca sounds of Figure 13.10.

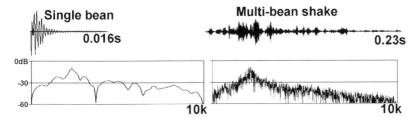

Figure 13.10. Single bean dropped on empty maraca shell (left); multibean maraca shake (right).

As expected, the spectra of the residual signals are generally flat (white), the energy in the residuals is less, and the time length of the single bean excitation is significantly shorter (by nearly a factor of three). Note also that the time envelope of the single bean source residual is a rapidly decaying exponential function. This observation gives us the last piece we need to create our efficient statistically based model of the particle maraca.

13.4.4   Statistical Multiparticle System Synthesis

We will use rapidly decaying, exponentially enveloped noise for the individual collision events, and a single two-pole filter to model the resonance of the maraca gourd. The sum of exponentially decaying random noises is equal to a single noise source multiplied by a decaying value; thus, only a single exponential decay function and a single noise sound source is required to compute the total sound. The sound envelope is increased additively by each new collision, as indicated by the Poisson process calculation. A slower exponential decay models net system energy, and determines how much energy is added with each collision. A linear decay envelope, or some other decreasing sound and system energy decay functions could be used, but the exponential decay requires only one multiply and no comparisons to calculate, and lends

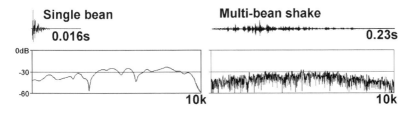

Figure 13.11. Source residuals after removing main resonance for deconvolved maraca bean (left) and multibean shake (right).

```c
#define SOUND_DECAY 0.95
#define SYSTEM_DECAY 0.999
#define SHELL_FREQ 3200.0
#define SHELL_RESO 0.96
#define TWO_PI 6.28318530718
#define SRATE 22050.0

void main(int argc, char *argv[])
{
    FILE *file_out = waveopen("shake.wav");
    double temp = 0, shakeEnergy = 0.0, sndLevel = 0.0, gain;
    double input = 0.0,output[2] = {0.0,0.0}, coeffs[2];
    long i,num_beans = 64;
    short data;
    //  Return random number between -1.0 and 1.0
    extern double noise_tick();

    // open wave file
    extern FILE* waveopen(char* name);
    gain = log(num_beans) / log(4.0) * 40.0 / (double) num_beans;
    if (file_out = fopen(argv[1],"wb")
    {
        // Gourd Resonance
        coeffs[0] = - SHELL_RESO * 2.0 *
                    cos(SHELL_FREQ * TWO_PI / SRATE);

        coeffs[1] = SHELL_RESO * SHELL_RESO;
        // Compute 4 seconds of sound
        for (i=0;i<SRATE * 4;i++)
        {
            if (temp<TWO_PI)
            {
                // Shake over 50 ms. and
                // add cosine shake energy
                Temp += (TWO_PI / SRATE / 0.05);
                shakeEnergy += (1.0 - cos(temp));
            }
            if (i % 5050 == 0) temp = 0;

            // Exponential system decay
            shakeEnergy *= SYSTEM_DECAY;

            // If collision add energy
            if (random(1024) < num_beans)
                sndLevel += gain * shakeEnergy;

            // Actual Sound is Random
            input = sndLevel * noise_tick();
```

```
// Exponential Sound decay
sndLevel *= SOUND_DECAY;

// Do gourd resonance filter calculations
input -= output[0]*coeffs[0];
input -= output[1]*coeffs[1];
output[1] = output[0];
output[0] = input;

// Extra zero for spectral shape
data = output[0] - output[1];
// That's All!! Write it out
waveout(data,file_out);
    }
  }
  waveclose(file_out);
}
```

Example 13.3. C code for synthesizing a maraca.

to efficient implementations. Example 13.3 shows an entire C program for calculating a simple maraca synthesis, and Figure 13.12 shows the block diagram of the simple maraca synthesis.

As can be seen in the code and figure, the PhISEM maraca synthesis algorithm requires only two random number calculations, two exponential decays, and one set of resonant filter calculations per sample. The Poisson

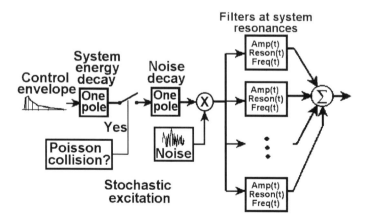

Figure 13.12. Basic PhISEM synthesis algorithm.

process and system exponential decay calculations could be carried out on a multisample basis (although not necessarily at the same granularity), yielding even less computation per sample. This extremely simple model is less complex than synthesis using interpolated PCM wavetables and filtering, and requires no memory for sample storage. The flexibility of real-time manipulation of control statistics, number of particles, and system resonance makes the model much more controllable in an interactive/expressive sense, and makes the model reconfigurable to a large variety of objects of the shaker type. The assumptions of exponential decay of system energy and Poisson probability of sound-producing collisions are more valid with increasing numbers of beans and increasing gourd size, but the model motivated by the simplifying observations has been found to yield plausible synthesis even for small numbers of virtual objects, and many other related sound sources. The next section will add some simple enhancements to the basic model.

Other musical instruments that are quite similar to the maraca include the sekere and the cabasa. The sekere consists of a gourd with beans knitted into a netting suspended over the outside of the gourd. This allows the grains to be manipulated more directly with the hands, and typical playing style includes rubbing while throwing the sekere from one hand to the other. The cabasa (or afuche) is a highly controllable commercially manufactured shaker, consisting of a corrugated metal drum mounted on a handle, and rows of metal beads wound loosely around the drum. The combination of the handle and the symmetric drum allows highly controllable direct manipulation of the beads. Both the sekere and the cabasa exhibit less pronounced resonances than most maracas. Other shaker instruments in this family include various Native American and African rattle drums.

In addition to the realm of multicultural musical instruments, there are many other real-world particle systems that exhibit one or two fixed resonances like the maraca. A bag or box of candy or gum, a salt shaker, a box of wooden matches, and gravel or leaves under walking feet all fit pretty well within this modeling technique. We will look at the analysis and synthesis of walking sounds in Chapter 15.

13.4.5 Stochastic Resonances in PhISEM

In contrast to the maraca and other gourd resonator instruments, which exhibit one or two weak resonances, instruments such as the tambourine (timbrel) and sleighbells use metal cymbals, coins, or bells suspended on a frame or stick. The interactions of the metal objects produce much more pronounced resonances than the maraca-type instruments, but the Poisson event and exponential system energy statistics are similar enough to justify the use of the PhISEM algorithm for synthesis. The tambourine has pairs of

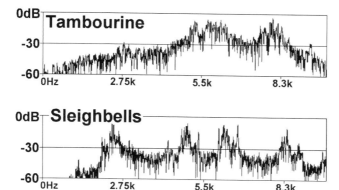

Figure 13.13. Spectra of shaker-type instruments tambourine (upper) and sleighbells (lower). Note the broad flat peaks, caused by a distribution of sharply resonant partials in the different cymbals and bells.

cymbals suspended in spaces in a handheld frame. As a relative of the hand drum, some tambourines have a head stretched over the frame. The individual cymbals are small enough that only one or two sinusoidal modal components are present in the spectrum. There is a random distribution of these partials (due to the difference in manufacture of the individual cymbals) around a set of center resonances, as shown in the tambourine spectrum of Figure 13.13. The sleighbells, as also shown in Figure 13.13, exhibit many more modes, but still show a random distribution around a few main resonant peaks. To implement this in PhISEM, more filters are used to model the individual partials, and at each collision, the resonant frequencies of the filters are randomly set to frequencies around the main resonances. Efficient yet flexible tambourine synthesis is accomplished using two resonances for the cymbals and one weak resonance for the wooden frame. The sleighbell requires five resonant filters. Other related musical instruments from around the world include the African sistrum, and the Turkish/Greek zilli masa. Figure 13.14 shows a more complete block diagram of the PhISEM stochastic modal model.

((‹53›))

Other sounds that can be modeled using stochastic filter resonances include bamboo wind chimes (related to a musical instrument as well in the Javanese anklung). These chimes exhibit weak resonances that are easily modeled by relatively few resonant filters in the PhISEM algorithm. For a set of tuned chimes, the resonances of each chime are fixed, but which chimes collide at any time determines which frequencies get excited. Figure 13.15 shows a spectrogram of bamboo wind chimes. Note that at each collision there are one or two active modes (dark spots occurring on the same vertical

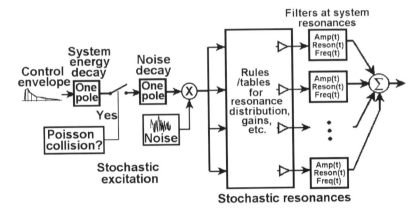

Figure 13.14. Complete PhISEM model showing stochastic resonances.

line), and these modes decay rapidly. The stochastic aspect in this case is not in randomizing the filter frequencies in a continuous range, but selecting one or more sets of fixed resonances from a table and using those frequencies to set the filters. To extend the wooden wind chimes to metal, groups of highly resonant filters may be used, or the filters could be replaced with simple FM pairs in inharmonic frequency ratios.

A final example for this chapter involves modeling the sound of coins in a pocket, box, or other container. Figure 13.16 shows spectrograms of a single strike of a glass coffee mug (our same mug from Chapter 4), a quarter being dropped on a table, a Philippine peso dropped on a table, and both coins being shaken in the coffee mug. If we peer at the rightmost spectrogram for a while, we can make out each of the individual resonances for the coins and cup and note that sometimes they are excited more or less. A simple but convincing PhISEM model of this system excites a fixed set of cup resonances on each collision, randomly picking one or more coin resonance sets on each collision to set the reallocated filters.

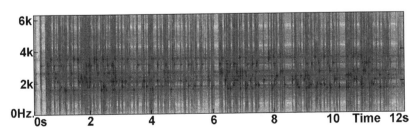

Figure 13.15. Spectrogram of bamboo wind chimes.

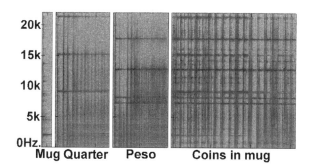

Figure 13.16. Spectrograms of mug, coins, and coins in mug.

13.5 Conclusions

With the techniques of this chapter, we have essentially completed our dictionary of synthesis models, looking at the particle as the basic sonic and physical element. This view of sound is much different from our previous views based on modes, sines, filters, and nonlinear modifications of those linear time-invariant building blocks. We will return to particle models in Chapter 15, where we will build an entire system capable of analyzing and synthesizing the sounds of walking. The next chapter will look at some issues involved with exciting physical models, and various modes and means of controlling and interacting with them.

Reading:

Claude Cadoz, Annie Luciani and Jean-Loup Florens. "CORDIS-ANIMA: A Modeling and Simulation System for Sound Image Synthesis—The General Formalization." *Computer Music Journal* 17(1): 21–29(1993).

Perry Cook. "Physically Informed Sonic Modeling (PhISM): Percussion Instruments." *In Proceedings of the ICMC*:228–231 (1996).

Perry Cook, "Physically Informed Sonic Modeling (PhISM): Synthesis of Percussive Sounds." *Computer Music Journal* 21(3): 38–49 (1997).

Iingrid Daubechies. "Orthonormal Bases of Compactly Supported Wavelets" *Communications on Pure and Applied Math* 41: 909–996 (1988).

Curtis Roads. "Asynchronous Granular Synthesis." In *Representations of Musical Signals*, edited by G. De Poli, A. Piccialli, and C. Roads, pp. 143–185. Cambridge: The MIT Press, 1991.

Xavier Rodet. "Time-Domain Formant-Wave-Function Synthesis." *Computer Music Journal* 8 (3):9–14 (1984).

Nadine Miner. *Creating Wavelet-Based Models for Real-Time Synthesis of Perceptually Convincing Environmental Sounds*. Ph.D. Dissertation, University of New Mexico (1998).

Michael Casey. *Auditory Group Theory with Applications to Statistical Basis Methods for Structured Audio*. Ph.D. Dissertation, MIT Media Lab (1998).

Code:
Shakers.cpp

GUIPhiSM

Sounds:
[Track 50] Building Up FOFs to Synthesize a Voice.

[Track 51] Synthesized Police/Referee Whistles.

[Track 52] PhISEM Synthesis of Maraca, Cabasa, Sehere, etc.

[Track 53] PhISEM Tambourine and Sleighbells Synthesis.

[Track 54] PhISEM Bamboo Wind Chimes and Anklung Synthesis.

[Track 55] PhISEM Coins in Mug Synthesis.

Exciting and Controlling Sound Models

14.0 Introduction

Of course, all of the sound synthesis models that we have talked about so far are exciting. But this chapter is actually about how to excite and interact with those models. We'll begin by analyzing some real-world striking and plucking sounds with varying parameters. We'll use some of those observations to design two computational models of striking/plucking for synthesis. Then we'll look at friction, bowing, rubbing, scraping, etc. Finally, we'll look at a few issues involved with controlling the parameters of our models: In real time for interaction, and off line for production.

14.1 Plucking and Striking

In Chapter 4 we talked some about how the point of excitation of a plucked string determines which harmonics are present, and how strongly, in the spectrum. We also talked about this in Chapter 12 for square membranes. In these cases of systems with simple geometry, we can predict what the modes of the system should be, and then use Fourier methods to compute the amplitude of each of the modes.

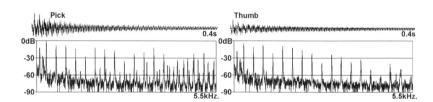

Figure 14.1. Guitar plucked with plastic pick (left) and thumb (right).

As for the excitation function itself, we discussed some of the physical aspects of striking and plucking strings in Chapter 9. Recall also that our filter-based additive modal model included a pulse generator for exciting the filters (Figure 4.5), and we also added a simple low/high pass filter to the impulse generator (Figure 4.6) to control the overall brightness of the synthesis. In the next section we'll look more closely at the plucking interaction.

14.1.1 Plucking a Guitar String

Let's look at plucking a real guitar string. First, we'll pluck it with a guitar pick, then we'll pluck the string in the same place with the fleshy part of our thumb. Figure 14.1 shows the waveforms and spectra of both pick and thumb plucks. Most obvious is the spectral brightness difference, with the pick spectrum exhibiting much more high frequency energy. Another effect is the appearance of high frequency nonharmonic partials in the picked spectrum. These are actually due to torsional (twisting) and longitudinal (compression) waves in the string, which are excited by the sharpness of the pick interaction.

In our next step, let's get rid of the harmonics due to the simple oscillation of the string and look at what's left. We'll do this by harmonic sinusoidal peak picking and removal in the FFT spectrum. Figure 14.2 shows the residuals that remain after removing the harmonics due to the string vibration. We'll zoom in a little on the lower region of the spectrum, ignoring the high frequency components we've already observed. The brightness difference is still pronounced, but many features are the same in the two spectra. For example, the first couple of bumps are nearly identical. These are due to the main

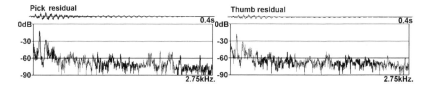

Figure 14.2. Guitar pluck residuals after harmonic mode removal.

resonances of the guitar body. The lower spectral bump is the Helmholtz air resonance (about 96 Hz), and the next higher one is likely due to a wood resonance in the top plate.

We could just use the residuals to excite a simple plucked-string model, and be happy with that. But we'd like to have a more parametric representation of the excitation. We could factor out some of the body resonances using LPC or some other technique. This turns out to be not an easy problem, and in general, it is impossible to know what parts of a signal relate to resonances and which ones relate to the excitation. This is called *blind deconvolution*, and the reason it's blind is that we can't see from outside the signal which parts are which. Remember that (for a given order of predictor) LPC makes this decision for us; whatever is linearly predictable goes in the filter, and the rest goes into the residual. To actually do deconvolution, more experimental data is required. For example, damping all the strings and knocking on the body a number of times to determine the resonances would let us design a filter based on those body resonances.

It is possible, with lots of experimenting and guesswork, to determine from signals the difference between picking excitations. It's also possible to pick something other than a string, such as a force sensor, to gain more insight into the excitaion. Figure 14.3 shows force waveforms of a plastic pick and the fleshy part of the thumb plucking a force sensor.

Note again the clear differences in brightness (spectral rolloff). More importantly, note that the waveforms share important similarities, but at different timescales. That is, force is seen building up gradually in the thumb waveform, as the flesh of the thumb deforms while still in contact with the force sensor. The same force-buildup phenomenon happens in the pick as it bends, but much more rapidly. Then there is a deflection upward, overshooting slightly (this is somewhat an artifact of the sensor, but seems very much related to the speed of the excitation), finally settling back to zero force at rest position. To a gross approximation, the thumb waveform is just a time-stretched version of the pick waveform. We might expect this from the similarity theorem of the time and frequency domains (Appendix A). There are also lots of little wiggles

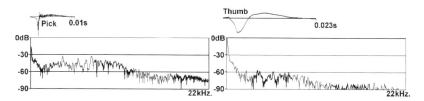

Figure 14.3. Force waveforms from plastic pick (left) and thumb (right).

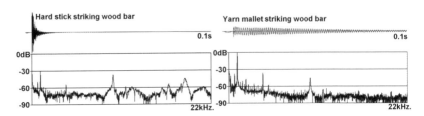

Figure 14.4. Strikes on a wooden bar with a hard stick (left) and soft mallet (right).

in the pick waveform that also add high frequency energy. These appear much like noise imparted on the basic force waveform.

14.1.2 Striking a Wooden Bar

Figure 14.4 compares time waveforms and spectra of a wooden marimba bar being struck with a hard plastic stick and a soft yarn-wrapped mallet. As should be expected, the hard stick spectrum is much brighter. Also note that the fundamental mode is excited more by the soft mallet, since the mallet shape is much closer to the smooth spatial fundamental shape. The hard stick excites higher modes, with much less energy in the fundamental.

Figure 14.5 shows residuals extracted by removing the three lowest modes of the wooden bar strikes of Figure 14.4. The increased high frequency energy is evident in the hard stick, as well as some extra high frequency modes. These modes could be cross-modes (nonlongitudinal) on the bar, or modes of the stick itself. Experimentation by striking the stick on a nonresonant hard surface (marble stone) and recording the sound showed that the two modes at about 17 k and 20 k were indeed modes of the plastic stick itself.

14.1.3 Striking the Prayer Bowl

We could continue plucking and banging on all kinds of objects, with all sorts of striking and plucking devices, for many more pages. Indeed, I encourage you to do so in your own experiments. For now we'll skip plates and

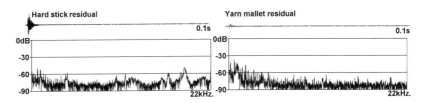

Figure 14.5. Strike residues of a hard (left) and soft (right) mallet on a wooden bar.

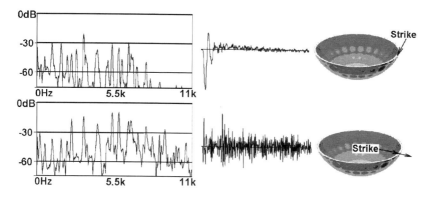

Figure 14.6. Two striking conditions of prayer bowl.

membranes, as well as other simple geometries, and move on to a more interesting system. The Tibetan prayer bowls from Chapter 12 exhibited a number of interesting properties, one being that different spectra resulted from striking in different directions, though on exactly the same point. Let's look at two of those interactions. The top of Figure 14.6 shows the spectrum, waveform, and strike conditions for a pure tangential (parallel to the bowl edge) strike on the rim. The bottom shows a strike normal (right angle) to the edge of the bowl from inside the rim, but in exactly the same location as the other strike. The striking object is a relatively soft wooden stick.

Even though the bowl, the striking position, and the stick are the same, the spectra and waveforms are radically different. By inspecting the initial part of the time domain waveforms, we might assume that the top striking condition makes the wood seem softer, because of the narrow contact area. Therefore, more low frequency modes are excited. The waveform does show a characteristic low frequency pulse, like the thumb excitation in Figure 14.3. The bowl strike inside the rim excites more high frequencies, indicating that the wooden striker appears harder to the bowl, as evidenced in the initial part of the striking waveform as well. Of course, there are other spatial boundary conditions that affect the particular excitation energies of the individual modes. Much more experimentation would be required to really figure out all of the subtleties going on in this wonderfully complex system. This is left to future research.

《 58 》

14.1.4 Models of Plucking and Striking

To conclude our discussion of plucking and striking, two models of impulsive excitation will be introduced. The first model is simple, and fits well within our signal-processing framework of source/filter residual extraction. In general, we know we can inject the residual back into a filter designed using LPC or

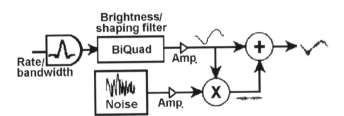

Figure 14.7. Simple parametric pluck/strike model.

other means, and get identity resynthesis. All we need to make the excitation more parametric and useful is to use our knowledge of the general behavior of hard and soft exciting objects, and break it into useful building blocks. Figure 14.7 shows a general pluck/strike excitation model based on a pulse wavetable, a filter, and additive noise. By changing the pulse wavetable playback rate, we exploit the similarity theorem to control bandwidth. We further allow the pulse to be filtered, perhaps by a simple one-pole for brightness, or by a flexible BiQuad allowing at least one resonance and one antiresonance to be controlled. Finally, noise is added to the filtered pulse, scaled by the pulse itself. This model allows us to synthesize many impulsive excitations such as the thumb/pick signals, the soft and hard marimba sticks, and a wide variety of other functions.

The second excitation model fits well within our overall framework of Newtonian physics. It derives from masses, springs, dampers, colliding particles, conservation of energy, etc. This model is based on a nonlinear spring and mass, representing the deformation of the plucking/striking object. It is more physically honest and generic than the pulse/noise model of Figure 14.7, in that it can dynamically deform, chatter, and interact with the object being excited. But it's also more difficult to implement and use because of stability and other computational considerations. Figure 14.8 shows a nonlinear mass/spring/damper system striking a string. Conservation of momentum at the point of impact determines the forces on the string and mass for the entire time of contact. As with the nonlinear spring discussed in Chapter 10 (Nonlinearity), VanDuyne and Smith derived a stable digital filter implementation of what they call the *wave digital hammer*, based on a state-dependent all-pass filter network.

14.2 Friction

To start our frictional discussions, we return to basic physics. The kind of friction we're interested in here acts between two objects, at the point of

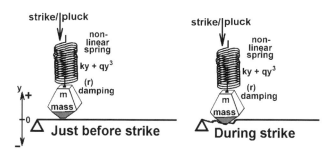

Figure 14.8. Nonlinear mass/spring/damper striking a string.

contact between them, and parallel (tangential if a point contact) to any force acting to slide the two objects along each other while still remaining in contact. Figure 14.9 shows a basic physical diagram of two objects with friction acting between them. The input force (sum of all input forces) acts to pull the object in one direction. The frictional force acts opposite the input forces, and is proportional to the normal force (perpendicular to the frictional force) between the two objects. The constant of proportionality, and friction itself, has two states. The no-motion state is called *static* (or *sticking*) characterized by the coefficient of static friction μ_s. The moving friction state is called "sliding," characterized by the coefficient of sliding friction μ_k (k is for kinetic). Coefficients of friction range from 0.0 (no friction, perfect *slickness*) to 1.0 (really sticky). In the diagram, the only normal force is gravity acting on the mass of the moveable object. If the input forces exceed the frictional force corresponding to the static friction coefficient, then the object moves and the kinetic friction coefficient must be used to compute the acceleration in the standard Newtonian $f = ma$ equation. If the input forces do not exceed the static friction force, the object does not move, and the frictional force is identically equal to the input forces ($f = ma$, and if there's no acceleration

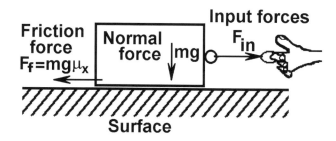

Figure 14.9. Friction between two objects.

then the summary forces must equal zero). One way to view the static friction force is as a force reservoir, always matching the input forces up to a point where it can no longer exert enough force to keep the object still. After this point the kinetic friction force takes over.

14.2.1 Stick/Slip friction

In Chapter 9 (Strings) we developed a simple block diagram of a waveguide bowed string model (Figure 9.9). At that time, however, we left out the critical component of what went into the nonlinear function that modeled the bow/string interaction. Here we will fill that box in and apply it to the bowed-string as well as some nonmusical bowing/rubbing interactions. In bowed strings and other systems that oscillate with a musical or periodic pitch, the frictional interaction is called *stick/slip*. Bowed strings give the best means of visualizing the stick/slip interaction, because string oscillation takes place as a transverse displacement from the equilibrium position. When bowing a string, stick/slip oscillation happens because the bow sticks to the string for a time, dragging it along with velocity equal to the bow velocity. When the tension in the string exceeds a certain point, the tension force pulling the string back toward equilibrium exceeds the static friction force, and the string snaps back (called *slipping*). This motion was theorized by, and named after Helmholtz (yep, the same resonator guy we talked about in Chapter 11 on winds). Helmholtz predicted a sawtooth motion for the bowed string, as shown in Figure 14.10.

The parameters affecting the stick/slip action of the bowed string include the normal force between the bow and the string, the bow velocity, and the two coefficients of friction. To compute the system, the transverse string velocity and bow velocity are compared. The output of a *friction function* (function yielding a number between 0.0 and 1.0) is multiplied by the bow force to compute a frictional force. If the frictional force is greater than the tension force acting to restore the string, then the string sticks and is carried along at the bow velocity. Otherwise the string slips back, at a rate based on the restoring tension force in the string and the kinetic bow/string friction

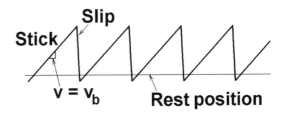

Figure 14.10. Simple Helmholtz bowed-string motion.

force. The stick/slip interaction can be computed literally; or alternatively, there are a number of simplified computational methods to simulate the system.

One popular simple simulation uses the absolute differential velocity between the bow and string $|v_b - v_s|$ (bow velocity - string velocity). This is scaled by dividing by bow force (f_b), and is used as a pointer into a precomputed *friction table*, as shown in Figure 14.11. Of course, we don't divide by the bow force if it is zero, because in that case we're not bowing anyway and the system reverts back to a simple waveguide plucked string. The output of this bow table is used as a scattering coefficient, much as we used the reed table when building our clarinet model in Chapter 11. We use the friction table output coefficient to compute an outgoing string velocity equal to $\mu v_b + (1 - \mu) v_s$. If the delta velocity is small, then $\mu = 1.0$ and the output velocity is equal to the bow velocity. As delta velocity increases (or decreases), the frictional coefficient decreases, allowing more slipping motion. The greater the bow force, the more the differential velocity is pushed toward the sticking region. Except for the possible numerical problems with such simple solutions, this simple scheme works well to simulate the stick/slip mechanism in many systems.

((‹59›))

14.2.2 Bowing Bowls and Opening Spooky Doors

Even though objects such as bars, membranes, bowls, etc., exhibit more complex modal patterns than the simple harmonics of the string, it turns out that the same simple friction table model can work quite well for bowing things other than strings. Modern classical percussionists now frequently bow bars, cymbals, metal plates, wine glasses, and other resonant objects, using a regular violin or bass bow. Objects such as bars, bowls, cymbals, creaking ship's masts, and squeaky doors might have complex geometries and modal structures, but usually only a very few dominant modes will support periodic oscillation due to bowing. Steady state bowing, if it causes a periodic oscillation, will cause vibrations that exhibit a harmonic spectrum, even if the object has no harmonic modes in its natural modal structure. The magic of the nonlinear

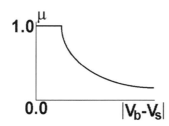

Figure 14.11. Friction table.

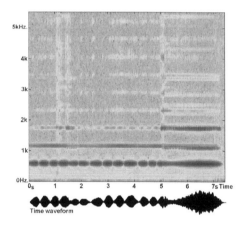

Figure 14.12. Bowed prayer bowl spectrogram and waveform.

bow/object interaction causes the extra harmonics to appear while bowing. Figure 14.12 shows a spectrogram of a bowed Tibetan prayer bowl (bowl A). The amplitude modulation present in the fundamental is not due to beating, but rather, is caused by the circular bowing motion. As the stick moves along the outside rim, the point of maximum vibration follows the wooden stick around. This means that the spatial (circular, around the rim) frequency of the bowed mode is slightly different from the natural standing wave frequency of that same mode, causing slowly beating interference in the standing wave patterns. When bowing ceases at just after five seconds, the extra nonharmonic modes—as well as the rapid beating—return to the oscillation due to closely spaced natural modes (see last section of Chapter 12).

Figure 14.13 shows the time domain waveform and spectrogram of a creaky door hinge. The door sound starts off with some relatively slow pops as initial sticking and slipping takes place (0.0–0.22 s), followed by a silent period, then more rapid pops (0.4–0.6 s) followed by an audio-rate oscillation that sweeps upward in frequency (0.6–0.68 s), settling in a relatively stable oscillation (0.7–1.2 s). A little silence is followed by more quasi-periodic creaky oscillation. This system and vibration is much more complex than the relatively simple oscillation of the bowed prayer bowl, but it is still produced by a stick/slip physical mechanism. The prayer bowl, the door, and many other stick/slip oscillation systems can be simulated using the relatively simple bow table model.

((‹60›))

14.2.3 Friction: Beyond Static and Kinetic?

So you might have already thought to ask, "If the world of friction is split into two simple cases of static and sliding friction, then why is the table shown in Figure 14.11 curvy instead of just having two horizontal lines?" Well, it turns

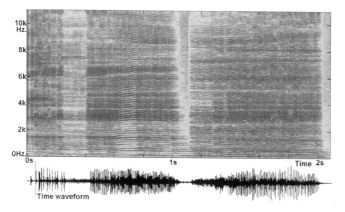

Figure 14.13. Spectrogram and time waveform of squeaking door hinge.

out that friction, like most else in nature, isn't quite so simple. You should know this intuitively from experiences of your own. When you drive really slowly, you feel and hear the friction on your tires. But when you drive really fast the tire friction seems much less (the sound might be louder, but is it proportionally louder? Or is that the wind? anyway…). If you were to drag an object across a rug, you might feel less and less friction as you drag faster and faster. Thus, all of these cases of so-called kinetic friction seem to depend somewhat on the speed of sliding. To get some insight into this, we need to look closer at the region of contact between two objects that are acting on each other by friction. Figure 14.14 refers to our simple system of Figure 14.9, zooming in on the contact surfaces.

The closeup surface views make obvious what we really knew all along, which is that friction between two dry sliding objects is actually caused by little bumps and valleys trying to get by each other. The two surfaces could posses different peak/valley levels, peak/valley shapes, average bump frequencies, etc. Static friction happens when enough peaks nestle into enough

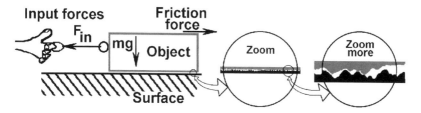

Figure 14.14. Zooming in on the friction thing.

valleys, requiring more force to unseat the objects than the applied force. Once motion between the two surfaces begins, the two surfaces separate some, allowing them to slide. Slow sliding allows more peaks to find valleys, causing resistance, as opposed to fast sliding which would keep the higher peaks bumping into each other, never allowing the surfaces to get close enough to stick. In general, the smoother surface dominates the friction interaction, so a hunk of wood would slide faster on glass than two hunks of wood could on each other. Oil, water, or other lubricants serve to fill in the valleys, separating the average spacing of the surfaces, and also easing the sliding up and down of the peaks and valleys.

Is this all? Nope. There is even more stuff going on with friction between surfaces. For example, two pieces of polished glass will stick to each other vigorously. Certain materials seem to have an affinity for other materials, or themselves. This is due to molecular level interactions, static electricity, and other effects.

But the majority of sound-producing frictional interactions can be thought of in terms of the rough-surface interaction shown in Figure 14.14. So how does this kind of friction produce sound? Basically each of the peak/valley interactions requires a tiny local interaction to take place, and the energy at the point of interaction injects impulsive energy into each object. There is damping (or at least increased local mass) when objects stick, and impulsive excitation when the objects "pluck" each other in their release. The energy injected into each object excites modes depending on where the interaction takes place. This happens at many points, hundreds, possibly thousands or much more for a large contact surface.

In contemplating this from a computational standpoint, and with a developing headache, you might now ask, "Do we have to model all of this explicitly?" We could, but our main purpose has been to find economical yet parametric models for the sounds and objects of interest. Recall from Chapter 14 that we modeled systems of arbitrary numbers of particles banging into each other and other objects, as a simple statistical probability of sound-production. It turns out that the same type of statistical model can work well for frictional interactions as well. We can put the statistics in a computational block representing the frictional peak/valley interactions, and use that to play PCM, fire particle/FOF wavelets, or excite modes. Or, we can use the PhISEM model to take care of all of the integrated statistics and synthesis. Then we would just feed energy and parameter changes into the model based on forces, speeds, texture changes, resonance changes, etc.

Figure 14.15 shows an interactive sliding sound synthesis system. The parameters of object, surface texture, force, and velocity could come from sensors, the parameters of a simulation, etc. These parameters are fed into a

*

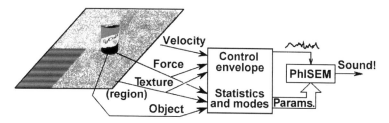

Figure 14.15. Texture/object interaction parameters are used to compute control parameters for parametric PhISEM stochastic modal model.

block that computes the appropriate control parameters for the PhISEM model. For a given texture and object, the *params* being fed into PhISEM might not be updated at all, and the control envelope would be the only dynamic signal. For other textures, varying force, or varying trajectory direction, all PhISEM parameters might need to be updated, but likely at a much lower rate than the final audio synthesis rate. The corrugation for example, would generate different forces depending on the horizontal and vertical components of motion.

(((61)))

14.2.4 Friction: Semi-Deterministic Interactions

There is another class of frictional interaction that we might call *semi-deterministic*. These actually behave like a hybrid between stick/slip oscillations and random peak/valley friction interactions. Most of these semi-deterministic interactions are caused by human-made objects, created through intentional engineering of the surface features of these objects. Essentially any surface that has a deterministic (especially periodic) structure has the potential to slide with a quasi-periodic motion. Some obvious examples of these come from our driving experience, like the "ka-dunk, ka-dunk ..." sound produced by the seams between freeway concrete tiles, or the scored pavement patterns (or Botts dots) placed by the road edges to tell us we're straying from the allowed driving surface.

A fairly ancient interactive example of this engineered semi-deterministic friction is the guiro (a South American fish-shaped corrugated scraper/ musical instrument). The guiro is a hollow resonator whose surface has been modified (by carving) with a sawtooth ratchet pattern. When a wooden stick is scraped over the guiro surface, the quasi-periodic stick/slips cause the gourd resonance to be excited. The waveform resulting from scraping a guiro is shown in Figure 14.16. The quasi-periodic pulsatile nature of the interaction is evident, as well as the resonance of the gourd.

Other examples of ratchet-type semi-deterministic friction include the clinking sound made by a rotating socket wrench, the notches placed in rotary

0s   **12ms**

Figure 14.16. Quasi-periodic guiro ratchet waveform.

volume controls (mainly to give us tactile feedback of volume changes), or a Foley artist/percussionist's sound effects ratchet. Some of the possible semi-deterministic mechanisms are shown in Figure 14.17. The one on the left is like the guiro mechanism. The one shown in the center is a symmetric (rotation either direction is the same) clicking mechanism, as might be found in a stereo volume control. The one on the right is a one-directional mechanism like that found in socket wrenches, hand winches, etc.

To simulate the sounds resulting from these types of interactions, we need simply to craft the appropriate force function as a function of spatial (or rotary) position, and use that force to derive the appropriate excitation for a suitable sound synthesis algorithm. Modal filters, or the PhISEM algorithm, lend themselves well to this kind of synthesis, allowing fixed, stochastic, or table-based pseudo-stochastic resonances to be excited by an excitation envelope or function. The short-time exponentially enveloped noise grains provided by PhISEM give a lively pseudo-random excitation to the resonant filter(s). The longer timescale system energy decay is replaced by the explicit force envelope, which can be any arbitrary function. In a sense, this is like using a wavetable that holds the force profile (random, deterministic etc.), and using a pointer into that table as our surface position/rotation control.

14.2.5 Friction Complete?

Much research remains to be done in the area of friction. Small-scale surfaces and interactions, rolling versus sliding, and other topics remain mysterious.

Figure 14.17. Various semi-deterministic frictional interactions.

How, and in what direction sound energy is transferred and radiated outward from frictional sound sources is also not well understood. Researchers in the field of *haptics* (haptics describes the combined touch senses of tactile, kinesthetic, motion, force, etc.) use robots fixed with force sensors to measure the frictional profiles of various objects and interactions. Recently, Dinesh Pai and others have begun to add sound analysis/synthesis to this work, simultaneously recording forces and sounds, and using the results to calibrate sound synthesis and force-feedback systems.

14.3 Controlling Synthesis Parameters

We've looked at how to excite our sound synthesis models, but there is more to the interactive control of a model than just putting energy into it. Parameters such as damping or position of excitation must also be controlled in many models. Blowing pressure or velocity for wind models is another parameter that must be controlled. Table 14.1 contains a brief list of the many physical parameters we might want to control, depending on the system and interaction.

There are potentially many more physically/gesturally meaningful interactions we might want to control. If our selected synthesis model is truly physical, then these parameters might feed directly into it. If it's pseudo-physical, like parametric modal filters or PhISEM, then the physical parameters might need to be transformed and processed first, as shown in

Pressure	on object, damping, plucking, bowing, etc., strings, plates, solids, surfaces
Breath Pressure	winds
Position	picking, striking, bowing, or damping one-dimensional: string, bar, pipe two-dimensional: membrane, plate three-dimensional: arbitrary objects
Rate, Velocity	picking, striking, bowing, scraping, rotating
What Texture	does it have? scraping/friction/bowing)
What object	is being hit, blown, bowed, struck, etc?
What object	are we hitting, bowing, etc., it with?

Table 14.1. Brief list of physical control parameters.

Figure 14.15. The remainder of this chapter will address some of the available means for controlling sound synthesis models in real time for interaction, or from event lists/score files for production applications.

14.3.1 MIDI

The *Musical Instrument Digital Interface* (MIDI) standard, adopted in 1984, revolutionized electronic music and also profoundly affected the computer industry. A simple two-wire serial electrical connection standard allows interconnection of musical devices and computers over cable distances of up to 15 meters (longer over networks and extensions to the basic MIDI standard). The MIDI software protocol is best described as *musical keyboard gestural*, meaning that the messages carried over MIDI are the gestures that a pianist or organist uses to control a traditional keyboard instrument. There is no time information contained in the basic MIDI messages; they are intended to take effect as soon as they come over the wire. As such it is a real-time gestural protocol, and can be adapted for real-time nonmusical sound synthesis applications. However, there are complaints about MIDI having to do with limited control bandwidth (approximately 1000–1500 continuous messages per second maximum) and the *keyboard-centric* bias of the messages.

Basic MIDI message types include *NoteOn* and *NoteOff, Sustain Pedal Up and Down, Modulation Amount, Pitch Bend, Key Pressure* (also called *AfterTouch*), *Breath Pressure, Volume, Pan, Balance, Reverberation Amount,* and others. NoteOn and NoteOff messages carry a note number corresponding to a particular piano key, and a velocity corresponding to how hard that key is

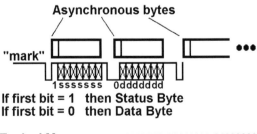

Figure 14.18. MIDI software transmission protocol.

hit. Figure 14.18 shows the software serial format of MIDI, and gives an example of a NoteOn message.

Another MIDI message is *Program Change*, which is used to select the particular sound being controlled in the synthesizer. MIDI provides for 16 channels, and the channel number is encoded into each message. Each channel is capable of one type of sound, but possibly many simultaneous *voices* (a voice is an individual sound) of that same sound. Channels allow instruments and devices to all listen on the same network, and choose to respond to the messages sent on particular channels.

General MIDI and the Standard MIDI File Specifications serve to extend MIDI and make it even more popular. General MIDI helps to assure the performance of MIDI on different synthesizers by specifying that a particular program (algorithm for producing the sound of an instrument) number must call up a program that approximates the same instrument sound on all General MIDI-compliant synthesizers. There are 128 such defined instrument sounds available on MIDI channels 1–9 and 11–16. For example, MIDI program 0 is grand piano, and MIDI program 57 is trumpet. Some of the basic instrument sounds are sound effects. Program 125 is a telephone ring; 126 is a helicopter; 127 is applause; and 128 is a gun shot. On General MIDI channel 10, each note is mapped to a different percussion sound. For example, bass drum is note number 35, and cowbell is note number 56.

The MIDI file formats provide a means for the standardized exchange of musical/sonic information. A MIDI level 0 file carries the basic information that would be carried over a MIDI serial connection, which is the basic bytes in order with added time stamps. Time stamps allow a very simple program to play it back. A MIDI level 1 file is more suited to manipulation by a notation program or MIDI sequencer (a form of multitrack recorder program that records and manipulates MIDI events). Data is arranged by *tracks* (each track transmits on only one MIDI channel), which are the individual instruments in the virtual synthesized orchestra. Meta messages allow for information which is not actually required for a real-time MIDI playback, but might carry information related to score markings, lyrics, composer and copyright information, etc.

Recognizing the limitations of fixed PCM samples in music synthesizers, the *DownLoadable Sounds* (DLS) specification was added to MIDI. This provides a means to load PCM into a synthesizer and use MIDI commands to play it back. Essentially any instrument/percussion sound can be replaced with arbitrary PCM, making it possible to control large amounts of recorded sounds. The emergence of *software synthesizers* on PC platforms has made the use of DLS more feasible than in earlier days when the samples were contained in a static ROM within a hardware synthesizer.

Sadly, one thing that is still missing from MIDI is the ability to download arbitrary synthesis algorithms, and we look forward to this as the next step in parametric synthesis standards. We'll talk more about this in the next section.

It is still possible to co-opt MIDI for the purpose of controlling parametric physical models. The simplicity and ubiquity of MIDI, with thousands of supporting devices and software systems, makes it attractive for us to try to do this. Some of the parameters listed in Table 14.1 already have MIDI controls that map directly to some of our synthesis parameters, or are close enough to suggest a natural use. NoteOn velocity naturally maps to strike/pluck velocity. MIDI Breath Pressure maps directly to wind instrument breath pressure. AfterTouch maps somewhat naturally to damping, as does the Sustain Pedal (also sometimes called the damper pedal). Pitch Bend maps to mode bending in objects that require it. Cheating a little, we could use Pan (left to right location) and Balance (front to back location) to give coordinates for striking a membrane. Beyond this, there are numerous unused controller numbers in MIDI that are left to be *user defined*. Thought not directly compatible with popular music synthesizers, using MIDI for control of synthesis still allows us to use one of the large variety of MIDI control signal generators and processors, all of which emit standard and user programmable MIDI messages. Examples include MIDI sequencers and other programs for general purpose computers, as well as breath controllers, drum controllers, and *fader boxes* with rows of sliders and buttons.

14.3.2 SDIF, Open Sound Control, and SAOL

Beyond MIDI, there are a number of emerging standards for sound and multimedia control. As mentioned in the last section, one of the things MIDI lacks is high bandwidth message capability for handling many streams of gestural/model control data. Another complaint about MIDI relates to the small word sizes, such as semitone quantized pitches (regular musical notes), and only 128 levels of velocity, volume, pan, and other controllers. MIDI does support some extended precision messages, allowing 14 bits rather than seven. Other specifications have proposed floating point representations, or at least larger integer word sizes.

A number of new specifications and systems have arisen recently. Although these have not yet been adopted broadly like MIDI, we would all do well to keep an eye on them, and think about making systems that are or could be compatible within these new frameworks.

One system for describing sounds themselves is called *Sound Description Interchange Format* (SDIF). Originally called Spectral Description Interchange File Format, SDIF is largely intended to encapsulate the parameters arising from spectral analysis, such as spectral modeling sinusoidal/noise tracks, or source/filter model parameters using LPC.

Related to SDIF, but on the control side, is *Open Sound Control* (OSC). Open sound control allows for networked, extended precision, object oriented control of synthesis and processing algorithms over high-bandwidth TCP/IP, FireWire, and other high bandwidth protocols.

As part of the MPEG4 standard, *the Structured Audio Orchestra Language* (SAOL) allows for parametric descriptions of sound algorithms, controls, effects processing, mixing, and essentially all layers of the audio synthesis and processing chain. One fundamental notion of structured audio is that the more understanding we have about how a sound is made, the more flexible we are in compressing, manipulating, and controlling it. Given that this idea is at the basis of this book, SAOL is quite an exciting development. Also, as part of the MPEG standard, it has the capability of being accepted and used widely in the future.

14.4 Controllers

We have developed and learned about many efficient synthesis algorithms with lots of interesting parameters to be manipulated. Faced with the ability to flexibly synthesize sound in real time, we naturally turn to ways to control these processes in real time. Although popularly available, standard MIDI keyboards usually lack the right types of knobs and handles to allow us to really get connected to our parametric synthesis algorithms. Many of the objects being modeled, the models themselves, or the sounds themselves might suggest a natural controller. For example, a suitably constructed electronic guitar controller could control our plucked-string models. Electronic drum controllers might work well for some of our struck objects, but what about bowing, shaking, rubbing, or other interactions we might need for Virtual Reality, gaming, and other applications?

Figure 14.19 shows a set of custom controllers created to control the PhISEM shaker model. These controllers were made by removing the actual sound-producing components (beans, tiny cymbals, etc.) from maracas and tambourines, and replacing them with acceleration sensors. In these *cyber shakers,* accelerometers feed measurements of shaking energy into microcontrollers, which in turn transmit a continuous MIDI AfterTouch signal. Force/squeeze sensors cause the microcontroller to transmit a damping signal via MIDI. Rotary knob controls cause the microprocessor to transmit MIDI controlling system resonances, exponential decay constants, and particle density.

Figure 14.20 shows a number of sound controllers based on common kitchen and dining objects. The table is pressure sensitive, transmitting

Figure 14.19. Shaker controllers for PhISEM model.

frictional information as MIDI AfterTouch. The cup can be struck, transmitting MIDI NoteOn with velocity to control a struck modal model; or shaken, transmitting MIDI AfterTouch to control a PhISEM model. Force sensors in the surface of the table transmit custom MIDI control signals.

Figure 14.21 shows a shoe controller with force sensors placed in the sole and heel, to control the synthesis of walking sounds. In the next chapter on applications, we will also show the Princeton PhOLIEMat (*Physically Inspired Library of Interactive Sound Effects Mat*), which allows the control of walking sounds in Virtual Reality or real-time digital Foley sound production.

Figure 14.20. Kitchen-inspired controllers.

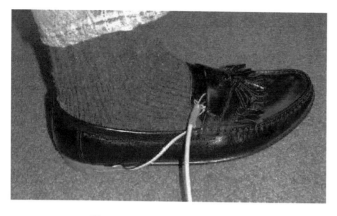

Figure 14.21. Shoe controller.

14.5 Conclusions

To complete our discussions on sonic models, we looked at a variety of excitation mechanisms: By analyzing and understanding these excitation interactions better, we can build a variety of parametric models of them as well. The power of sound synthesis using parametric physical modeling lies in the rich set of parameters that can be dynamically changed to affect the synthesis. But this potential can only be realized if we have suitable mechanisms for controlling these parameters. Real-time demands of interactive systems and the nature of many of our models encourage us to investigate the design and construction of new controllers for interactive sound. In Chapter 16, we will look at a number of applications for parametric sound synthesis, and again see the power of being able to control the parameters in real time.

Reading:

Scott A. Van Duyne, John R. Pierce, and Julius O. Smith. "Traveling-Wave Implementation of a Lossless Mode-Coupling Filter and the Wave Digital Hammer." In *Proceedings of the International Conference on Computer Music*: 411–418 (1994).

Grigore Burdea. *Force and Touch Feedback for Virtual Reality.* New York: John Wiley and Sons, 1996.

Kees van den Doel, Paul G. Kry, and Dinesh K. Pai. "FoleyAutomatic: Physically Based Sound Effects for Interactive Simulation and Animation." In *Computer Graphics (ACM SIGGRAPH 2001 Conference Proceedings)*: 537–544 (August 2001).

Thomas Rossing. *The Science of Percussion Instruments*. River Edge: World Scientific Press, 2000.

The Complete MIDI 1.0 Detailed Specification. La Habra: MIDI Manufacturers Association, 1996.

MIDI: http://www.harmony-central.com/MIDI

S. Jungleib. *General MIDI*, A-R Editions, 1995.

Open Sound Control: http://cnmat.cnmat.berkeley.edu/OSC/

SDIF: http://cnmat.cnmat.berkeley.edu/SDIF/

E. Scheirer and B. Vercoe. "SAOL: The MPEG-4 Structured Audio Orchestra Language," *Computer Music Journal*, 23:2, 1999.

SAOL: www.saol.net

Code:

BowedBar.cpp

GUIBowedBar

Shakers.cpp

GUIPhiSM

Sounds:

[Track 56] Hard and Soft Guitar Picks, Raw Picks.

[Track 57] Hard and Soft Wooden Bar Strikes, Residuals.

[Track 58] Strikes of Prayer Bowl.

[Track 59] Bowed-String Synthesis.

[Track 60] Bowed Prayer Bowl, Wine Glass, Squeaky Door.

[Track 61] Texture-Dependent Granular Scraping-Type Synthesis.

[Track 62] Ratchet-Type Synthesis.

See also movie files of controllers on CDROM Segment.

15 Walking Synthesis: A Complete System

15.0 Introduction

In Chapter 13 we talked about particle models for synthesizing sound. In this chapter, we will develop an entire system for analyzing and synthesizing the sounds of walking. The system is part of a larger sound effects analysis/synthesis effort called PhOLISE (*Physically Oriented Library of Interactive Sound Effects*). This type of system would prove useful for production sound effects (Foley) as well as games. The heart of the parameterization and resynthesis of walking sounds is based on PhISEM (*Physically Inspired Stochastic Event Modeling*). This type of modeling is quite natural, since much of the sound produced by walking on various textures involves particle interactions excited by friction/pressure envelopes from the feet.

15.1 Overall Architecture of the System

Figure 15.1 shows the overall PhOLISE walking system architecture. A sound file is analyzed to determine the individual footfalls and the average gait (tempo plus left/right asymmetries). A control envelope scorefile is written. The sound file is marked and segmented into individual footstep events. The individual envelopes are averaged to yield an average control envelope and a standard envelope deviation. Linear prediction is performed on each footstep sound to determine the overall resonances for a resynthesis filter, and to yield "whitened" (spectrally flat) step sounds. Wavelet extraction of the high frequency band is performed, and the rectified (absolute value) peaks are used to estimate a *particle density*. New files with arbitrary lengths, gaits, materials etc., can be generated automatically, using the extracted average and deviation envelopes. A real-time walking synthesis program can be controlled by parameters from a score file, a *Graphical User Interface* (GUI), data from foot/ground collision detections in a game or simulation, sensors in a virtual reality system, etc.

15.2 Event Analysis

The first stage of signal processing involves extracting and analyzing the overall envelope of a walking sound. Figure 15.2 shows a nonlinear, low pass filter-based envelope signal detector (from Chapter 7). The two signal-dependent pole positions are similar to rise/fall times on audio dynamic range compressors, allowing the output to rise faster when the signal is rising and fall slower when the signal is falling. This helps to ensure that peaks are tracked accurately, while still eliminating high frequency components. Due to the low pass filtering effects of the envelope follower, and the slow nature of walking gestures and steps themselves, the extracted envelope can be stored at a much lower sample rate than the original sound.

An autocorrelation of the envelope signal is performed to get a rough periodicity estimate. Significant peaks (local maxima over a threshold) are marked in the envelope, and then a set of "best peaks" is selected that meets various criteria of periodicity and expected walking tempos. At this point the event-marked envelope can be inspected and peaks can be edited by hand if desired, though the algorithm is quite reliable over a fairly large class of walking sounds. Figure 15.3 shows some envelopes which were automatically marked by the system.

The envelope can be written out as a constant update rate *gestural* scorefile (30 Hz Updates of MIDI AfterTouch, for example). To make the representation parametric, the walking envelope is segmented into individual step events. This is done by finding a set of lowest significant values coming just before the marked step peaks. Again, the same constraints on periodicity used to mark the original peaks are applied to mark the cut points. This set of peak-matched minima form the cut points for the individual footsteps. The original footfall sound segments can be stored as individual soundfiles to allow identity resynthesis later.

Next, the individual envelopes are compared to yield an envelope average and standard deviation, as shown in Figure 15.4. Significant subevents can sometimes be found within the envelopes, such as the Heel/Toe events marked

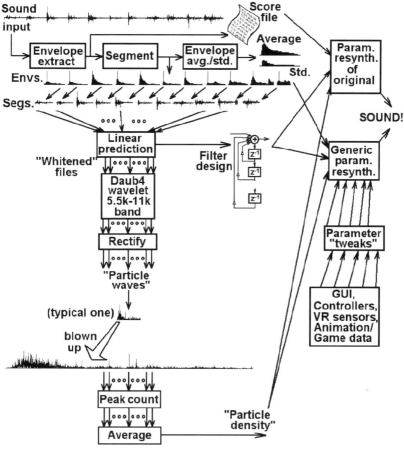

Figure 15.1. PhOLISE walking analysis/synthesis system architecture.

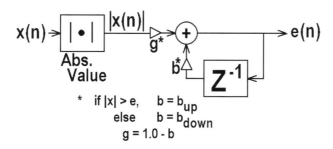

Figure 15.2. Envelope follower for walking sound analysis.

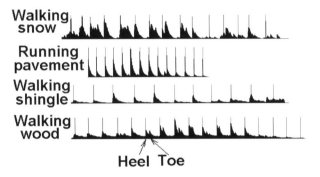

Figure 15.3. Some extracted/marked envelopes.

in Figure 15.3. Events like this have been shown to be important in the perception of identity, age, sex, etc., purely from walking sounds. The parametric prototype envelopes are stored as multiple (6–10) break-point linear envelopes based on ordered triplets of (time, amplitude, deviation), chosen to best fit the peaks, valleys, and slope changes.

15.3 Spectral Analysis

The next stage of signal processing involves identifying and removing the resonant structure using linear prediction (Chapter 8). We keep the "whitened" residuals as the *raw* particle sounds. To determine the proper filter order, the LPC prediction order can be incrementally increased until the residual power does not decrease significantly. Figure 15.5 shows the waveforms and spectra of a particle system before and after second order LPC processing. LPC is performed on a per footstep basis, writing the filter coefficients into the score file along with the excitation envelope. For a given walking material, and for generic resynthesis later, an average LPC filter is also computed and stored.

15.4 Statistical Modeling and Estimation

The PhISEM synthesis algorithm was described in detail in Chapter 13, but we'll briefly recap it here. The basic idea is to model the likelihood that a

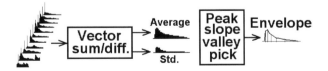

Figure 15.4. Envelope prototyping.

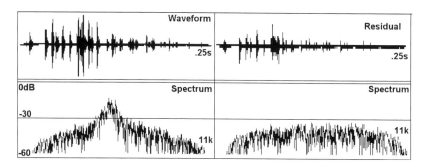

Figure 15.5. Removing resonance by linear prediction.

particle will make a sound at any given time, rather than exhaustively calculating all of the particles themselves. This stochastic parameterization means that we only have to model the probability that particles will make noise. For many particle systems, this is modeled well by a simple Poisson distribution where sound probability is constant at each time step, giving rise to an exponential probability waiting time between events. The sound of each particle is assumed to be a noisy excitation of whatever system resonances are present. The resonances could be those of the actual particles themselves (rocks for instance), or of larger resonating structures (such as planks in the floor excited by scraping of walking feet).

Each particle noise event can be modeled as an impulse, but to "fill in" the events better, a short exponentially decaying (α_c) noise burst is used. To model the total sound, we do not explicitly overlap and add these events, because the sum of exponentially decaying noises (with the same exponential time constant) is just an exponentially decaying noise. On each collision, we simply add energy to the exponential sound state, corresponding to the current system energy (net kinetic energy of all particles in the system). We keep and calculate another exponentially decaying (α_s) state variable representing the system energy, modified (added to) by the control envelope. Both exponential functions are modeled using simple one-pole recursive filters (poles at α_c and α_s). Two random number calculations are required per time step; one for the Poisson collision decision, and one for the excitation noise source. The algorithm is efficient, depending largely on the order of the resonant filter.

So far we have a simple synthesis model, but we still lack complete techniques for actually analyzing walking sounds, specifically to determine N—the Poisson probability constant. N is estimated by inspecting a high frequency band (5.5–11 kHz) of the whitened footstep sounds. A Daubechies four-wavelet filterbank is used to split the signal into subbands, and these subbands are rectified (absolute value). As can be seen by inspecting the top

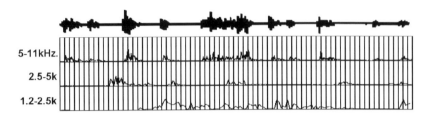

Figure 15.6. Rectified wavelet subbands.

three rectified subband outputs in Figure 15.6, the 5.5–11 kHz band seems to capture the rapid collision events best.

Next, a threshold value is computed from the maximum peak and average values of the rectified subband signal, and the number of peaks per second over the threshold are counted. This one estimate of N (the density of collisions), tends to miss collisions as the probability N increases. To correct for this, the actual N estimate is calculated to be:

$$N_{est} = 2^{avgPeaks/blocks/10},$$ (15.1)

where *blocks* means that the average number of peaks are counted only in blocks where significant peaks occur. In a set of experiments (described next) involving extracting known N values from simulations, we arrived at Equation 15.1 by trial and error.

Using the PhISEM model, 1050 soundfiles were synthesized using a simple raised cosine excitation envelope. System parameters were:

α_c = constant at 0.95 (60 dB decay of 130 samples)

N = 2,4,8,16,64,256,1024

α_s = 0.95,0.99,0.995,0.999,0.9995,0.9999

r = 0.7,0.8,0.9,0.95,0.99

f = 1000,2000,3000,5000,8000 Hz.

where r and f are the pole radius and center frequency of a single second order resonant filter. The steps of envelope extraction; second order linear prediction; rectified high frequency 5.5–11 kHz subband extraction; and N estimations were performed on all 1050 synthesized files. As Figure 15.7 shows, the average frequencies and resonances yielded by linear prediction are more accurate for higher resonances and middle frequencies. Most of the

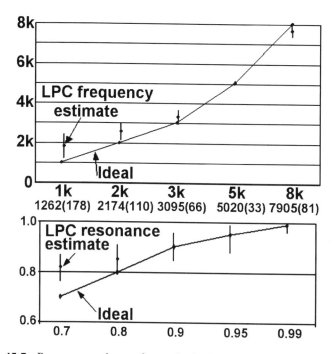

Figure 15.7. Resonance estimates for synthesized data. Numbers below *x*-axis on frequency plot are means and standard deviations.

frequency errors were experienced on files with very low resonance (pole = 0.7 or 0.8), and in those cases we don't much care about frequency misadjustment anyway. The pole estimates were quite accurate, with a slight tendency to underestimate the resonance.

Table 15.1 and Figure 15.8 show the results of calculating estimates of N (using Equation 15.1) for all 1050 files. Given that the synthesis is stochastic, the estimated values of N are fairly good. However, the relatively high standard deviations suggest that we should collect and average as many sound files as possible for any given walking condition. This means that the more individual footsteps we have on a recording, the better the overall estimate of particle density N for the material will be.

15.5 Testing on Real Sounds

To test the analysis techniques on nonsynthesized data, some real-world sounds were collected. The sounds of two types of gravel were analyzed. Large gravel rocks, averaging 1.5 cm in diameter and 14 g in weight; and small gravel

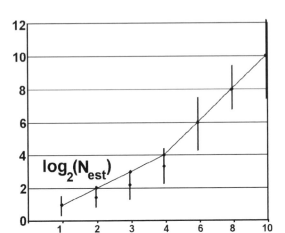

Figure 15.8. Particle density estimates for synthesized data.

rocks, averaging 0.3 cm in diameter and 1 g in weight were analyzed. Ten shaking sounds of different gravel samples were analyzed for each gravel type. For the large rocks, the center frequency and resonance was estimated by LPC to be 6460 +/– 701 Hz, and $r = 0.932$. N was estimated to be 23.22, with a standard deviation of 14.53. For the small rocks, the center frequency and resonance were estimated to be 12670 +/– 3264 Hz and 0.843; and N was

Synth. N	Average Estimate	Standard Deviation
2	2.04	0.82
4	3.06	1.31
8	5.33	2.91
16	13.0	8.26
64	99.1	79.8
256	396	291
1024	699	532

Table 15.1. Particle density estimates for synthesized data.

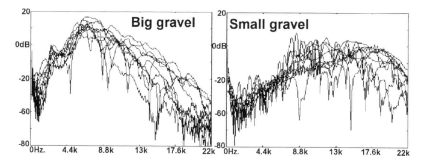

Figure 15.9. Large gravel (left) and small gravel (right) shake spectra.

estimated to be 1068 with a standard deviation of 755. Figure 15.9 shows the superimposed power spectra of the multiple shakes of the two gravels.

15.6 Parametric Resynthesis

Once analysis of a walking sound is complete, the original soundfile can be exactly reassembled by concatenating the stored wave segments. Depending on the amount and nature of the background noise in the original recording, a highly realistic semiparametric resynthesis of arbitrary length and tempo can often be made by randomly overlapping and adding the individual original footstep wave files.

For parametric resynthesis, the extracted envelope parameters can be used to generate new step envelopes using the prototype average multibreakpoint envelope, and perturbing it by the standard deviation parameters. These new envelopes drive the PhISEM model set to the analyzed resonance and particle density, yielding infinite possible new syntheses. In the next chapter on applications we will look at a graphical user interface for controlling PhISEM/ PhOLISE walking synthesis.

((63))

15.7 Conclusion

In this chapter we used a variety of our techniques to build a complete system to analyze and synthesize the sounds of walking. The system was tested on hand crafted, real-world gravel sounds with good results. The system has been applied to a variety of sound effects recordings of walking. One obvious next step would be to connect this system to a motion capture system, automatically lining up the audio footfall sounds with the graphical/ sensor data.

Reading:

Xiaofeng Li, Robert J. Logan, and Richard E. Pastore. "Perception of Acoustic Source Characteristics: Walking Sounds." *Journal of the Acoustical Society of America, America Institute of Physics* 90(6): 3036–3049 (1991).

Perry Cook. "Modeling Bill's Gait: Analysis and Parametric Synthesis of Walking Sounds," *Audio Engineering Society 22nd International Conference on Virtual, Synthetic and Entertainment Audio* (2002).

Code:

GaitLab.cpp

GUIGaitLab

Sounds:

[Track 63] Real/Synthesized Walking Sounds.

See also movie "Seen in Shadow" on CDROM Segment

16 Examples, Systems, and Applications

16.0 Introduction

This final chapter will present a number of applications and scenarios for using parametric sound synthesis. If you're reading this chapter first (recommended) after the book introduction, don't worry if you don't understand all of the acronyms and techniques this first time. Just read to get a quick idea of the possibilities for coupling parametric sound synthesis to user interfaces, animation, Virtual Reality, and games. Then the second time you read it, after reading the whole book, it will all make more sense.

16.1 Auditory Display: Real-Time Multimodal User Interfaces

One exciting area of use for sound synthesis is in augmenting, enhancing, and perhaps reinventing traditional computer/human interfaces. The WIMP (*Windows, Icons, Menus, Pointer*) paradigm, controlled by the computer mouse and keyboard and displayed on a display screen, has had many years of development and success. But there must be more to life than WIMP. Also, the emergence of cell phones and PDAs (personal digital assistants, palmtops, etc.) has made the display, mouse, and keyboard less important, impossible,

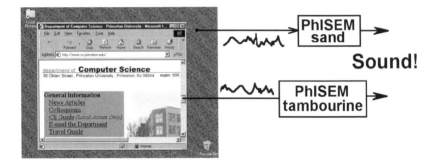

Figure 16.1. Sonically enhanced user interface.

or illegal to use in many circumstances (driving for example). Finally, improving the keyboard or mouse, or enhancing the display with colors or three dimensions might do nothing to make computers accessible to blind and sight-impaired users. Two obvious areas to look when expanding the user interface are the senses of hearing and touch.

A simple example of sonically enhanced two-dimensional pointing is shown in Figure 16.1. Using the PhISEM algorithm, different *audio textures* are associated with different regions of the screen, and different tools on a web browser. Moving on the desktop yields a fine grainy sound, like scraping on sand, increasing in intensity toward the lower right corner of the screen (where the recycle bin is located). The scroll bar of the web browser makes a metallic tambourine shaking sound, with amplitude proportional to the speed of scrolling. A system like this could be used to tell a user roughly where the cursor is located on the desktop, aiding in finding the cursor, and possibly speeding up drag and drop operations. Auditory feedback of the scrolling operation leaves our eyes free to look at other things. It could also aid sight-impaired users in finding the scrollbar or other tools if we mapped sounds to a mouse rollover of these tools.

16.2 Auditory Display: Sonification

Sonification is the use of nonspeech audio to convey information. More specifically, it is the mapping of data relations to sound in order to enable or enhance the finding of patterns and relationships in that data. It can be somewhat viewed as the audio analog to scientific visualization, but not exactly. The human auditory and visual systems evolved with complimentary abilities and acuities. For example, we can't see behind us, yet we are often able to localize the voice of a friend in another room at a party, even when we can't see them. In fact, infants can recognize their mother's voice before they can

Figure 16.2. Stock prices, normalized to a $1 purchase on day 1.

even focus on her face. These different abilities offer the promise that some things might be easier to hear than see, provided the mapping is done correctly. Since there are many possible parameters of data to be mapped, and many ways to map them, having flexible and parametric sound synthesis is critical to sonification experiments and systems.

Figure 16.2 shows the normalized stock prices of Red Hat Linux and Microsoft, for one year, February 2001–2002. It's pretty easy to see the trends in the stocks, but what if we wanted to track other information in addition to these curves? We might be interested in the daily volume of trading, and seemingly unrelated data like our own diastolic blood pressure during this period (to decide if it's really healthy to own these stocks).

Figure 16.3 shows the five normalized curves consisting of two stock prices, two stock volumes, and one daily blood pressure measurement. It clearly becomes more difficult to tell what is going on.

Of course, there are more sophisticated graphical means and techniques we could use to display this data. But some trends or patterns might emerge more quickly if we were to listen to the data. With a suitable auditory mapping of the data, we might be able to hear a lot more than we could see in a single glance. For example, the value of Red Hat could be mapped to the pitch of a plucked mandolin sound in the left speaker, with sound loudness controlled by trading volume (normalized so that even the minimum volume still makes a faint sound). Microsoft could be mapped to the pitch of a struck marimba sound in the right speaker, again with loudness controlled by trading volume. The pitch ranges are normalized so that the beginning prices on the first day of the graphs sound the same pitch. This way, any day on which the pitches are the same, our original (day 1) dollar investment in either stock would be worth the same. Finally, our normalized daily blood pressure could be mapped

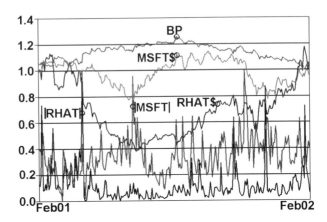

Figure 16.3. Normalized stock prices, plus volumes, plus the blood pressure of someone owning both stocks.

to the volume and pitch of a tuned noise sound, located in the center between the two speakers. Figure 16.4 shows the waveforms of these three signals. Of course, the point here is not to map visual data to visual data (waveforms), but rather to listen to it.

Other motivations for listening to data include situations where our eyes might not be available. For example, if we were driving in our car, a sonification display might be the only way we could get information presented to us quickly (a speech synthesizer would take hours to read the 250 days times 5 streams of information to us, where we might be able to listen to it all play as audio in only 25 seconds). One other important application of using sound for data sonification is that we can listen along as some rapidly changing processes are happening in real time. Tracking network traffic is one application of real-time sonification.

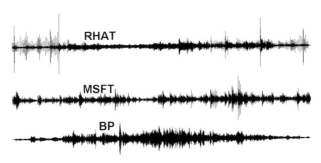

Figure 16.4. Audio waveforms of sonified stock prices, volumes, and blood pressure.

16.3 Digital Foley Production Workstation/Stage

Foley (named after Jack Donovan Foley, who claimed to have walked 5000 miles in the studio doing footstep sounds) is the process of acting the sound effects for movies, television, or other productions. A Foley artist might put shoes on her hands or feet and "walk" in a box of cornstarch (for walking in snow), synchronizing her "steps" to those she sees of an actor on film or videotape. Microphones capture the hand-simulated walking sounds, and the audience is none the wiser. Punching sounds for Kung-fu movies, light sabres for space operas, and countless other sound effects are added to the soundtrack using Foley techniques. This style of production frees the film director from worrying about the sound on the set when the film is being captured, rather concentrating on the visual aspects of location or studio shooting. The Foley artist and sound engineers make everything sonically OK long after shooting, during the final editing phases of production.

In Chapter 14 we developed an entire system for the analysis and synthesis of walking sounds. A prime use of parametric sound computation might be to construct a purely digital Foley stage. For truly flexible parametric walking synthesis, the footstep parameters extracted from walking sounds can be used to generate new step envelopes. Any analyzed parameter can be edited and changed as desired to modify the resynthesis. Figure 16.5 shows "Bill's GaitLab," a TCL/Tk Graphical User Interface for controlling walking sound synthesis/resynthesis in real time.

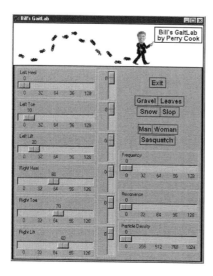

Figure 16.5. Bill's GaitLab walking synthesis controller.

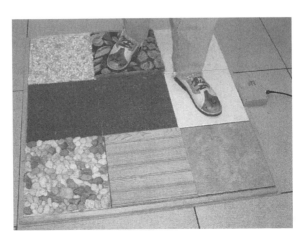

Figure 16.6. Princeton PhOLIEMat pressure sensitive floor.

16.4 Virtual and Augmented Reality

In the final section of Chapter 14, we looked at a few custom devices for controlling real-time sound. Virtual Reality (artificial simulation of a real or imagined environment) and augmented reality (adding computer generated enhancements to an existing, real-life environment) provide a rich area for possible applications of parametric sound synthesis. Figure 16.6 shows the Princeton PhOLIEMat, a pressure-sensitive floor designed for controlling sound effects. The floor can sense the location and pressure of each moveable/removable tile, sending each tile's pressure signal as MIDI AfterTouch on each of nine MIDI channels. Sound synthesis algorithms running on one or more computers provide the real-time sound in response to the sensor signals from the PhOLIEMat. Of course, the PhOLIEMat would be an ideal controller for the digital Foley stage, since walking sounds are an ideal class of sounds to be controlled by the pressure-sensitive floor.

16.5 Computer Music and Interactive Art

Music performance is structured real-time control of sound to achieve an aesthetic goal (hopefully for both the performers and audience). Thus, one obvious application area for real-time parametric sound synthesis is in creating new forms of musical expression. If you've looked at many of the references given in this book so far, you might have noted that the computer music world

Figure 16.7. Cook's DigitalDoo; Trueman's BoSSA; Bahn's "r!g."

was the first to adopt, and actually develop, many of the algorithms we've talked about. Exciting developments in the last few years have emerged in the area of new controllers and systems for using parametric sound in real-time music performance, or in interactive installation art.

Figure 16.7 shows three recent real-time music performance systems, all using parametric digital sound synthesis. The author's DigitalDoo is a sensor/speaker enhanced/augmented digeridoo. Dan Trueman's BoSSA (*Bowed Sensor Speaker Array*) resulted from work in modeling, refining, and redefining the violin player's interface. Curtis Bahn's "r!g" consists of a sensor-enhanced upright (stick) bass, pedalboards, and other controllers. All three of these new "instruments" use spherical speakers to allow flexible control of the sound radiation into the performance space. These instruments have been used with computers to control percussion sounds, animal noises, string models, flute models, and a large variety of other sample-based and parametric synthesis algorithms.

16.6 Animation and Gaming

With the sophisticated computational modeling that is becoming more and more commonplace every day, it seems inevitable that computational sound will begin to take its place in the areas of animation production and computer gaming. Having a fully articulated model of a dinosaur, slinky-dog toy, or warrior robot allows the computed animated motion to look more natural. Many of the same parameters that are required for the animation could also provide controls for sound synthesis. Even if the computed motion is not fully parametric, things such as collisions, positions, or contact forces might be available and could be used to control sound synthesis.

As an example, Figure 16.8 shows a few frames from an animation produced using hand-drawn figures composited onto a background, but with

Figure 16.8. Two scenes showing automatic shadow generation. *(Image courtesy Grady Klein (artist), Lena Petrovic, Brian Fujito, Adam Finkelstein, and Lance Williams.)*

the shadows generated automatically by computer. This automatic shadow generation was accomplished by generating a simple *blob* model of the character, and tracking that to the hand-drawn figure coordinates. Having the shadows generated automatically frees the animator from having to draw them, but more importantly it allows the changing of lighting at any phase of the production. One set of automatically computed shadows are *contact shadows*, which animators use to show that feet are in contact with the ground. The automatic contact shadow appears when the foot is within a small distance of the ground. This time-varying contact information was used in the final production of the animation "Seen in Shadow" to generate control envelopes for automatic PhISEM synthesis of walking sounds. Other sound effects in the animation were also parametrically generated.

The techniques used for production and animation aren't necessarily real-time, but the recent trend has been that these techniques find their way into real-time game computation quickly after (or even before) being perfected in the animation/ production communities. I look forward to a typical game computation scenario of the (hopefully near) future, where parametric computational sound plays a critical role, comparable to graphics.

As just one example, a networked multiuser game could use LPC or the vocoder to morph players' voices in real time, depending on the characters they are playing. Modal synthesis would be used for the sounds of objects (swords and shields are just one possibility). Physically modeled musical instruments could be manipulated, and bows/crossbows could be simulated using the string model. Particle models would model the walking and scraping sounds. Changing objects, interactions, or scenes would involve simply changing parameters. Essentially every technique talked about in this book could be employed to make the game more expressive, reactive, real, and fun.

16.7 The Future

The most compelling aspects of the techniques, concepts, and research presented in this book are that they are essentially infinitely open ended. There will always be interesting new sounds, new physical discoveries, and new sound synthesis techniques developed which can bring expression and realism to sound effects synthesis. Our physical understanding is not yet complete in the areas of friction, nonlinear fluid dynamics, and countless other phenomena which cannot be easily observed or measured. Even if this knowledge were complete, systematic studies of the sound generation and radiation of such systems have not yet been carried out.

As with much of physical and pseudo-physical nonlinear systems for sound generation, there exist no closed-form analysis techniques capable of automatically extracting the correct synthesis parameters from recorded sounds. Combinations of linear filter design, nonlinear system identification, and human guidance can be used to arrive at new models and parameters, as has been done for most of the objects described in this book. With more complete and sophisticated tools for machine classification of sounds, the computer might eventually be trusted to select a synthesis technique based on, a target sound. Then optimal parameters could be derived for matching the model to the target.

The "Virtual Kitchen" and "Virtual Woodshop" have not yet been completed, and the day when the fully digital Foley workstation is available might be far in the future. I look forward to more interesting research in this area. I also encourage you the reader to take a role in moving forward our understanding of the physics of sound production, our interactions with sound-producing objects, new algorithms for sound analysis/synthesis, and an abundance of new uses and applications of parametric digital sound synthesis.

Reading:

Auditory Display and Sonification: www.icad.org

Lena Petrovic, Brian Fujito, Adam Finkelstein, and Lance Williams. "Shadows for Cel Animation." In *Proceedings of ACM SIGGRAPH*: 511–516 (2000).

Perry Cook. "Toward Physically Informed Parametric Synthesis of Sound Effects." *IEEE Workshop on Applications of Signal Processing to Audio and Acoustics*: 1–5 (October 1999).

Perry Cook and Daniel Trueman. "Spherical Radiation from Stringed Instruments: Measured, Modeled, and Reproduced." *Journal of the Catgut Acoustical Society*: 3–15 (November 1999).

Daniel Trueman and Perry Cook. "*BoSSA: The Deconstructed Violin Reconstructed*." *Journal of New Music Research* 29(2): 121–130 (2000).

Daniel Trueman, Curtis Bahn, Perry Cook. "Alternative Voices for Electronic Sound: Spherical Speakers and Sensor-Speaker Arrays (SenSAs)." *International Computer Music Conference*: 248–251(August 2000).

Code:

scrub.c

Shakers.cpp

GUIPhiSM

GaitLab.cpp

GUIGaitLab

Sounds:

[Track 64] Sonification of Stock/Blood Pressure Data.

See also Movie Files of PholieMat, DigitalDoo, BoSSA, and R!g, and Animation "Seen in Shadow"

A DFT, Convolution, and Transform Properties

A.1 Orthogonality of the Fourier Transform Kernel

In simple geometric terms, *orthogonal* means that two directions lie at right angles, or there is no *projection* (shadow) of one direction onto the other. Linear algebra gives us our definition of orthogonality, saying that the inner product of two orthogonal vectors is equal to zero. For functions, it means that their integral (or discrete sum) over some interval is zero. For sinusoids in the DFT, orthogonality is shown pictorially in Figure A.1.

To state the orthogonality of harmonically related sinusoids in words: Any two harmonically related sines (or cosines), when multiplied by each other and integrated (summed) over the fundamental interval, yield a zero result if the sinusoids are not of the same harmonic frequency. Further, any harmonically related sine, when multiplied by any harmonically related cosine and integrated over the fundamental interval, always yields zero.

To state the orthogonality of harmonic sinusoids mathematically:

$$\Sigma_{n = 0 \text{ to } N - 1}\sin(2\pi pn/N)\sin(2\pi qn/N) = 0 \qquad \text{if } q \neq p$$
$$= N \qquad \text{if } q = p. \qquad (A.1)$$

$$\sum_{n = 0 \text{ to } N - 1} \cos(2\pi pn/N)\cos(2\pi qn/N) = 0 \quad \text{if } q \neq p$$
$$= N \quad \text{if } q = p. \quad (A.2)$$

$$\sum_{n = 0 \text{ to } N - 1} \sin(2\pi pn/N)\cos(2\pi qn/N) = 0 \quad \text{for all } q \text{ and } p. \quad (A.3)$$

Orthogonality means that we can extract the individual sinusoidal Fourier terms of $f(n)$ by multiplying each, one at a time, and obtain the projection of each sinusoidal component of $f(n)$ individually.

A.2   Uniqueness of the Fourier Transform

The best way to prove the uniqueness of the Fourier transform is to exploit the orthogonality property of sinusoids, combined with some basic linear algebra. We can express the DFT as a matrix multiplication:

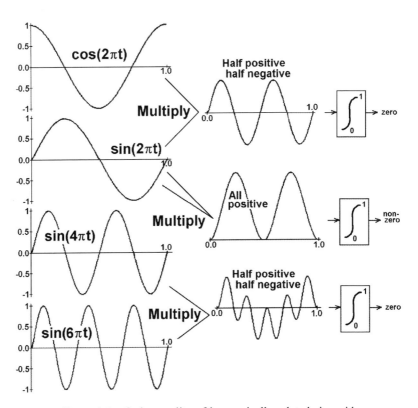

Figure A.1. Orthogonality of harmonically related sinusoids.

$$F(m) = [f(0) \ldots f(N-1)] \begin{bmatrix} 1 & 1 & \ldots & 1 \\ 1 & e^{-j2\pi m/N} & \ldots & e^{-j2(N-1)\pi m/N} \\ \ldots & \ldots & \ldots & \ldots \\ 1 & e^{-j2(N-1)\pi m/N} & \ldots & e^{-j(N-1)(N-1)\pi m/N} \end{bmatrix}$$

or $\qquad F(m) = [f] \; [D]$ $\hspace{3cm}$ (A.4)

It's easy to show that each column of the matrix is orthogonal to all others, which is just another proof of sinusoidal orthogonality. From linear algebra, a matrix with all orthogonal columns has a unique inverse. That means that the operation of multiplying $f(n)$ by the DFT matrix is uniquely invertible by multiplying $F(m)$ by D^{-1}. The matrix D^{-1} is the inverse DFT operation. Seem too simple to be true? Let's step through it with a real example, using a length 4 data signal and DFT.

$$F(m) = [f(0) \; f(1) \; f(2) \; f(3)] \begin{vmatrix} 1 & 1 & 1 & 1 \\ 1 & -j & -1 & j \\ 1 & -1 & 1 & -1 \\ 1 & j & -1 & -j \end{vmatrix}$$

$$D^{-1} = 1/4 \begin{vmatrix} 1 & 1 & 1 & 1 \\ 1 & j & -1 & -j \\ 1 & -1 & 1 & -1 \\ 1 & -j & -1 & j \end{vmatrix}$$

$$f(n) = f(n) * D * D^{-1} = 0.25 * f(n) * \begin{vmatrix} 1 & 1 & 1 & 1 \\ 1 & -j & -1 & j \\ 1 & -1 & 1 & -1 \\ 1 & j & -1 & -j \end{vmatrix} \begin{vmatrix} 1 & 1 & 1 & 1 \\ 1 & j & -1 & -j \\ 1 & -1 & 1 & -1 \\ 1 & -j & -1 & j \end{vmatrix}$$

$$= 0.25 * f(n) * \begin{vmatrix} 4 & 0 & 0 & 0 \\ 0 & 4 & 0 & 0 \\ 0 & 0 & 4 & 0 \\ 0 & 0 & 0 & 4 \end{vmatrix} = f(n)$$

So the DFT matrix is the inverse of the IDFT matrix. Cool huh?

A.3 Convolution

Convolution of the signal x with the signal h is defined as:

$$y(n) = \Sigma_i x(i)h(n-i)$$ $\hspace{3cm}$ (A.5)

Usually, $h(n)$ is an impulse response of a linear time-invariant system, and $x(n)$ is the input signal to that (see Chapter 3). Also, $h(n)$ and $x(n)$ are usually assumed to start at time = 0; that is, their value is zero for negative values of n. This property is called *causality*. So for causal signals x and h, Equation A.5 can be rewritten as:

$$y(n) = \Sigma_{i=0 \text{ to } \infty} \, x(i)h(n-i). \tag{A.6}$$

If $x(n)$ has finite length P, and $h(n)$ has finite length M, then we can further limit the convolution summation to:

$$y(n) = \Sigma_{i=0 \text{ to } P+M-1} x(i)h(n-i). \tag{A.7}$$

This is because computing any points beyond those boundaries would result in a zero result. Note that x and h can be swapped and the equation result is the same (this is called *commuting*, and the property is called *commutativity*). This means that it makes no difference which signal corresponds to the system or which is the input. Thus, singing in a room (convolution of a voice with the room impulse response) is mathematically identical to a room impulse response singing through the voice.

If we let $n - i = k$, then $i = n - k$. We can now sum over k, and because of the causality of $h(n)$, the summation range is still from 0 to n. We can then rewrite Equation A.3 to:

$$y(n) = \Sigma_{k=0 \text{ to } n} x(n-k)h(k). \tag{A.8}$$

The fact that we only need to sum from 0 to $P + M - 1$ means that convolution of one signal of length P with another signal of length M yields a result signal which has length $P + M - 1$. Figure 3.1 shows this; an input signal of length 7 is convolved with an impulse response of length 3 to yield an output of length 9. Figure A.2 shows the convolution of a trumpet tone with a room impulse response.

A.4 Convolution and the DFT

We can take the Fourier transform of the convolution of two causal signals— $x(n)$ of length P, and $h(n)$ of length M—by noting that the length of the final output signal is of length $P + M$. Let's define $N = P + M$ and write the equation for this Fourier transform:

$$Y(M) = \Sigma_{n=0 \text{ to } N-1}[\Sigma_{i=0 \text{ to } N-1} x(i)h(n-i)]e^{-j2\pi mn/N} \tag{A.9}$$

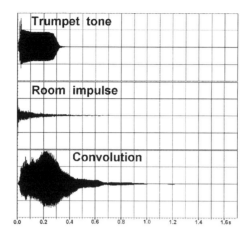

Figure A.2. Convolution of trumpet tone (top) with room impulse response (center).

Define $k = n - i$, thus $n = k + i$.
Note that when $n = 0$, $k = -i$; and when $n = N - 1$, $k = N - i - 1$.

Then: $Y(M) = \Sigma_{k = -i \text{ to } N - i - 1}[\Sigma_{i = 0 \text{ to } N - 1} x(i)h(k)]e^{-j2\pi m(k + i)/N}$.   (A.10)

Swapping the summation order and factoring the complex exponential into a product of two exponentials yields:

$$Y(M) = \Sigma_{i = 0 \text{ to } N - 1} x(i)e^{-j2\pi mi/N} \Sigma_{k = -i \text{ to } N - i - 1} h(k)\, e^{-j2\pi mk/N}.$$ (A.11)

Note that from causality and the length of $h(k)$, we know that the sum over k will have only nonzero terms for k ranging from 0 to $M - 1$. Noting also that $M - 1$ is less than $N - 1$ (by exactly P, in fact), we can change the summation boundaries on k to $[0, N - 1]$ (we're doing this to make it look like an N-length DFT). Our Fourier transform of a convolution now looks like:

$$Y(M) = \Sigma_{i = 0 \text{ to } N - 1} x(i)e^{-j2\pi mi/N} \Sigma_{k = 0 \text{ to } N - 1} h(k)\, e^{-j2\pi mk/N}$$ (A.12)

$$= [\Sigma_{i = 0 \text{ to } N - 1} x(i)e^{-j2\pi mi/N}][\Sigma_{k = 0 \text{ to } N - 1} h(k)\, e^{-j2\pi mk/N}]$$ (A.13)

$$= \quad X(M) \qquad H(M),$$

which is the product of the individual N-length Fourier transforms of the x and h signals. Since multiplication is commutative, this is another proof that either $x(n)$ or $h(n)$ can serve as the source or the system without changing the convolution result.

A.5 A Few Useful DFT Properties and Theorems

These are useful as practical tools, and for gaining intuition about the time and frequency domains. I'll prove some of them, and leave the rest for you.

A.5.1 Duality of Time and Frequency Domains:

The only difference between the forward (time to frequency) and inverse (frequency to time) DFT is a negative sign in the sinusoidal exponent, and the $1/N$ normalization factor that is applied in one direction. This implies that any transform property can apply in either direction, sometimes with the appropriate correction for the minus sign and normalization.

For example, we know from Chapter 3 and Section A.4 that convolution in the time domain corresponds to multiplication in the frequency domain. Similarly, multiplication in the time domain corresponds to convolution in the frequency domain. The place where this is perhaps most important is in the common practice of time domain *windowing*. Figure A.3 shows a sinusoid being multiplied by a simple window (a raised cosine), and the resulting change in the transform. The pure sinusoid exhibits a single spike in the spectrum, while the windowed sinusoid shows the transform of the window function convolved with the sinusoidal spike.

A.5.2 Shift Theorem:

$$\text{If } f(n) \to F(m) \quad \text{then} \quad f(n-P) \to e(j2\pi Pm/N) \, F(m) \qquad (A.14)$$

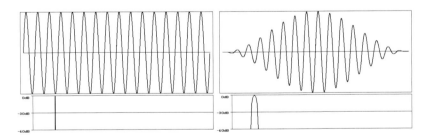

Figure A.3. Multiplication in the time domain is convolution in the frequency domain. Pure sinusoid shows a single narrow peak (left). Windowed sinusoid shows a widened peak (right).

Proof: $\sum_{n=0 \text{ to } N-1} f(n-P)e^{-j2\pi mn/N} = \sum_{n=0 \text{ to } N-1} f(n-P)e^{-j2\pi mn/N}$

$= \sum_{n=P \text{ to } P+N-1} f(n)e^{-j2\pi m(n-P)/N} = \sum_{n=P \text{ to } P+N-1} f(n) \, e^{j2\pi mP/N} \, e^{-j2\pi mn/N}$

$= e^{j2\pi mP/N} \sum_{n=P \text{ to } P+N-1} f(n) \, e^{-j2\pi mn/N} = e^{j2\pi mP/N} \, F(m)$

This proof assumes that either the signal buffer is zero-padded by at least P samples in the direction of the shift, so that we don't lose any samples when we perform the shift. Alternatively, the shift could take place circularly within the buffer (negative P wraps to $N-P$ in the buffer, etc.). The trick in doing the proof is to exploit the properties of exponents where addition within the exponent is equivalent to multiplication of two exponents with a common base ($e^a \, e^b = e^{a+b}$).

The implication of the shift theorem is that all that happens to the transform of a time-shifted signal is a phase shift in the frequency domain, linear in m with slope equal to the amount of shift, represented by the $e^{j2\pi mP/N}$ term. Nothing happens to the spectral magnitude of the shifted signal.

To understand the shift theorem in the frequency domain, we can invoke the duality of the time and frequency domains as discussed in Section A.5.1. Instead of saying that we multiplied the sine wave by the window, we could say that we multiplied the window by the sine wave. Doing this shifted the transform of the window from zero frequency up to the frequency of the sinusoid. This is sometimes called heterodyning, or shifting a spectrum by multiplication by a sinusoid in the time domain.

A.5.3 Similarity (Stretch) Theorem:

If $f(n) \rightarrow F(m)$ then $f(\alpha n) \rightarrow F(m/\alpha)$ (A.15)

Proof: $\sum_{n=0 \text{ to } N-1} f(\alpha n) \, e^{-j2\pi mn/N} = \sum_{n=0 \text{ to } N-1} f(\alpha n) \, e^{-j2\pi mn/N \, (\alpha/\alpha)}$

$= \sum_{n=0 \text{ to } N-1} f(\alpha n)e^{-j2\pi m(n\alpha)/N/\alpha} = F(m/\alpha)$

This property states that stretching a time domain signal causes its spectrum to become narrower, and shortening a time domain signal causes its bandwidth to spread. Of course, care must be taken to properly bandlimit and interpolate the resampled signal.

The similarity theorem is a specific statement of a more general law of signal processing, the *uncertainty principle*:

$$\Delta x(n) \, \Delta X(m) > K, \qquad\qquad (A.16)$$

where K is a constant related to the units of x and X. This equation states that the product of the uncertainties in the time and frequency domain must always be greater than a computable nonzero constant.

Practically speaking, this means that if we want fine frequency resolution in our spectra, we must use a large time window, and thus we cannot say as much about what goes on instantly in time. Similarly, if we want to say much about small time events, we will be less able to say anything about the frequency content of short events.

As an example, a window size of 4096 samples at a sampling rate of 22,050 Hz would give us a resolution of 5 Hz between adjacent frequency samples in the DFT, but would also act to average all events that happen within 0.2 seconds of each other. In contrast, a window size of 100 samples would allow us to inspect an event that takes place in 4.5 milliseconds, but our spectral frequency resolution (space between DFT frequency bins) would be 220 Hz per bin.

A.5.4 Evenness, Oddness, and Symmetries:

Even signals ($f(n) = f(-n)$) require only cosine components of the DFT.

Odd signals ($f(n) = -f(-n)$) require only sine components.

The DFT of any real valued signal will exhibit Hermitian symmetry (real spectral components are even, and imaginary components are odd).

$$\text{if } f(n) \text{ is real, } F(m) = \text{Re}(F(m)) + j \, \text{Im}(F(m))$$

$$\text{Re}(F(m)) = \text{Re}(F(N - m)) \qquad (A.17)$$

$$\text{Im}(F(m)) = -\text{Im}(F(N - m)) \qquad (A.18)$$

A.5.5 Time Reversal:

$$\text{If } f(n) \to F(m)$$

$$\text{then } f(-n) = f(N-n) \to \text{Re}(F(m)) - j \, \text{Im}(F(m)) \qquad (A.19)$$

This says that conjugating the spectrum (negating the imaginary components) causes the signal to be reversed in time. This might be more easily seen as changing the minus sign in the Fourier exponential:

$$e^{-j2\pi mn/N} \text{ becomes } e^{j2\pi mn/N},$$

which is the same as replacing Z^{-1} with Z. Since Z^{-1} is a sample of delay, then Z must be a sample of "look-ahead"; thus, time is reversed.

A.5.6 Zero Padding:

Given $f(n) \to F(m)$ form a new signal $g(n) = f(n)$ for $0 < n \le N$

$$= 0 \quad \text{for } N \le n < PN$$

P is the "zero padding factor"

Then:

$$\Sigma_{n = 0 \text{ to } PN - 1} \, g(n) e^{-j2\pi mn/PN} = \Sigma_{n = 0 \text{ to } N - 1} \, f(n) e^{-j2\pi mn/PN} + 0$$

$$= F(m/P), \, 0 \le m < NP \quad \text{(A.20)}$$

This states that zero padding a time domain signal causes *spectral interpolation*, yielding a spectrum that is sampled more finely (and with more total samples) than the nonzero padded version. Technically, there is no new information in the interpolated spectrum, but zero padding is often used to make aspects of the spectrum more apparent. Figure A.4 shows spectral interpolation by zero padding. Here the windowed sinusoid transform shows even more detail of the window transform. Before, in Figure A.3, the window transform was sampled on the main lobe and exactly in the sidelobe valleys, thus not showing the sidelobe structure at all.

Zero padding is also used to avoid *time-aliasing* when the spectrum is manipulated by convolution (multiplication in the frequency domain). This is necessary because convolving two signals results in a signal whose length is equal to the sum of the lengths of the two original signals. Thus, if we convolve

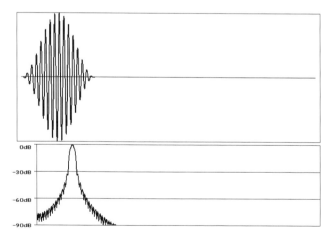

Figure A.4. Zero padding shows more spectral detail (compare to right side of Figure A.3).

two 1024 sample signals, we must zero pad them both to 2048 samples, transform them, multiply their transforms, then inverse transform to yield a 2048 length signal.

A.5.6 Power Theorem:

If $f(n) \rightarrow F(m)$

The power in signal f(n) can be computed by:

$$\Sigma_{n = 0 \text{ to } N - 1} |f(n)|^2 \qquad\qquad (A.21)$$

or by:

$$1/N \, \Sigma_{m = 0 \text{ to } N - 1} |F(m)|^2 \qquad\qquad (A.22)$$

This turns out to have important implications for many algorithms. For example, linear predictive coding (Chapter 8) minimizes the least-squared error in both the time and frequency domains, because the sum of squares of the time error signal is equal to the sum of squares of the spectral magnitude error.

Reading:

Ronald Bracewell. *The Fourier Transform and its Applications.* New York: McGraw Hill, 1999.

B

The Ideal String

B.1 The Ideal String

Start with a segment of string under tension T with length density ρ grams per meter. We will perturb the shape by a small amount y from its rest position ($y = 0$). We want to compute the force, in the y direction only, on each little segment of the string so that the motion of each little string section can be determined. The string, and a blowup of a little segment of it, is shown in Figure B.1.

We will ignore gravity, assuming that the tension force in the string is much greater than any gravitational force. As an example, there is a tension

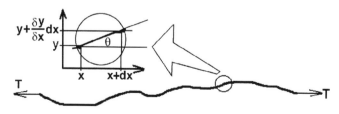

Figure B.1. Ideal string under tension T.

force of approximately 70 Newtons in a low E classical guitar string, compared to only 0.04 Newtons of gravitational force acting on the entire length of such a string. The displacement angle θ must be smaller than .0006 radians, or .001 degrees, for the gravitational force to exceed the tension force. Thus, the force on the string in the y direction that we care about will be due to the tension component acting upward or downward. This component is equal to $T \sin \theta$, where θ is the angle between the horizontal and the string segment (see Figure A.1). The difference in force between two adjacent points (x and $x + dx$) along the string is then:

$$df_y = (T \sin \theta)_{x+dx} - T \sin(\theta)_x. \tag{B.1}$$

The Taylor's series for expressing the force at point $x + dx$ as a function of the force at point x on the string, is:

$$f(x + dx) = f(x) + (\delta f/\delta x)\, dx + \tfrac{1}{2}\, (\delta^2 f/\delta x^2)\, dx^2 + \dots \tag{B.2}$$

Assuming dx is very small, we will keep only the first two terms of the Taylor's series of Equation B.2. Rewriting this simpler form, we get:

$$f(x + dx) - f(x) = (\delta f/\delta x)\, dx \tag{B.3}$$

$$\text{or } df_y = (\delta f/\delta x)\, dx. \tag{B.4}$$

Combining Equations B.1 and B.4 yields:

$$df_y = (\delta(T \sin \theta)/\delta x)\, dx = T\, (\delta(\sin \theta)/\delta x)\, dx. \tag{B.5}$$

If θ is small, we can replace it with an approximation, $\delta y/\delta x$ (opposite divided by hypoteneuse, or change in y divided by length in x direction (see Figure B.1).

$$df_y = T\, (\delta^2 y/\delta x^2) \tag{B.6}$$

To relate this all to physics, we invoke Newton's second law:

$$F = ma \quad \text{or} \quad df_y = (\rho\, dx)\, d^2y/dt^2. \tag{B.7}$$

Noting that Equations B.6 and B.7 are both expressions for df_y, we set their right sides equal, yielding:

$$d^2y/dx^2 = (1/c^2)\, (d^2y/dt^2). \tag{B.8}$$

Equation B.8 is called *the wave equation in one dimension*. Note that we have defined $c = (T / \rho)^{1/2}$, where c is the speed of wave motion along the string (proportional to the square root of tension and inversely proportional to the square root of linear string mass density).

B.1.2 D'Alembert Solution Proof

In linear differential equations, if a solution works, then it's a solution. The D'Alembert solution to Equation B.8 is:

$$y_{\text{D'Al}} = y(x, t) = y_1(t + x/c) + y_r(t - x/c). \qquad (B.9)$$

To check this, we need to take the derivative with respect to x twice:

$$d(y_{\text{D'Al}})/dx = (1/c)\, y_1(t + x/c) - (1/c)\, y_r(t - x/c)$$

$$d^2(y_{\text{D'Al}})/dx^2 = (1/c^2)\, y_1(t + x/c) + (1/c^2)\, y_r(t - x/c)$$

$$= (1/c^2)\, [y_1(t + x/c) + y_r(t - x/c)]$$

$$= y_{\text{D'Al}} / c^2, \qquad (B.10)$$

and the derivative with respect to t twice:

$$d(y_{\text{D'Al}})/dt = y_1(t + x/c) + y_r(t - x/c)$$

$$d^2(y_{\text{D'Al}})/dt^2 = y_1(t + x/c) + y_r(t - x/c)$$

$$= y_{\text{D'Al}}. \qquad (B.11)$$

Substituting Equation B.11 into B.10 yields:

$$d^2(y_{\text{D'Al}})/dx^2 = d^2(y_{\text{D'Al}})/dt^2 / c^2, \qquad (B.12)$$

which is identical to Equation B.8. ∎

B.1.3 Fourier Series Boundary Solution and Proof

In a string under tension, the ends are restricted from moving (that's how we make the tension). The conditions of non-movement at the ends are called *boundary conditions*. The boundary condition solution to an ideal string of length L terminated at both ends is:

$$y(t, x) = \Sigma_{n = 1 \text{ to } \infty} \, a_n \sin(\pi nx/L)\cos(\pi nct/L) \qquad\qquad \text{(B.13)}$$

This is called the *Fourier series boundary solution*, which must satisfy the wave equation at all points, including the boundaries. As with the D'Alembert solution given in Section B1.2, a solution must simply satisfy the differential wave equation (Equation B.8):

$$d^2y \,/\, dx^2 = (1 \,/\, c^2) \, (d^2y \,/\, dt^2) \,.$$

Since the differential wave equation is linear, the derivative (and second derivative) of the infinite sum of Equation B.13 is the sum of the derivatives of the individual terms. Plugging Equation B.13 into the second derivatives of each side of Equation B.8, we get:

$$d^2[\Sigma_{n = 1 \text{ to } \infty} \, a_n \sin(\pi nx/L)\cos(\pi nct/L)] \,/\, dx^2 =$$
$$- (\pi/L)^2 \, \Sigma_{n = 1 \text{ to } \infty} \, a_n \sin(\pi nx/L)\cos(\pi nct/L)$$

$$d^2[\Sigma_{n = 1 \text{ to } \infty} \, a_n \sin(\pi nx/L)\cos(\pi nct/L)] \,/\, dt^2 =$$
$$- (c\pi/L)^2 \, \Sigma_{n = 1 \text{ to } \infty} \, a_n \sin(\pi nx/L)\cos(\pi nct/L)$$

$$= c^2 \, d^2y \,/\, dx^2 \qquad \blacksquare$$

Note that Equation B.13 easily satisfies the boundary conditions at $x = 0$ and L because all the sine terms are identically zero at those points in space. The coefficients a_n can be found from any initial condition (displacement shape) by Fourier analysis as discussed in Chapter 5. After the coefficients are determined from the initial shape, any observation point x can be chosen, and the resulting vibration at that point can be calculated for all time thereafter. For example, if $x = L/2$ is chosen, no even harmonics will ever be observed in the vibration. Alternatively, any time t can be chosen, and the displacement of the string can be calculated at each point on the string. In a real string with damping, each sinusoidal harmonic would also have an exponential damping term. These damping exponentials will usually be different for each sinusoidal oscillation harmonic, and generally they will damp more quickly for increasing frequency.

Reading:

Philip Morse. "Vibration and Sound." *Acoustical Society of America, American Institute of Physics* (1986).

C Acoustic Tubes

C.1 The Ideal Acoustic Tube

We analyze a segment of cylindrical tubing of cross-sectional area a, as shown in Figure C.1. We assume that flow is in the x (longitudinal) direction only.

We can start with the physical property of conservation of momentum (conservation of energy):

$$p = m \times v \qquad\qquad (C.1)$$

momentum = mass × velocity,

and we can take the derivative of momentum with respect to time:

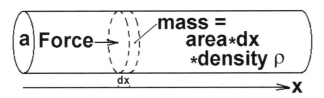

Figure C.1. Acoustic tube with area a.

$$dp \: / \: dt = d(mv) \: / \: dt, \tag{C.2}$$

which gives us a different form of Newton's second law ($F = m \times a$). We can rewrite Newton's second law in differential form:

$$\frac{dF(x)}{dx} = m\frac{dv}{dt}. \tag{C.3}$$

Then we can multiply both sides by $a \: / \: a$ (area divided by area = 1),

$$\frac{a}{a}\frac{dF(x)}{dx} = \frac{a}{a}\,m\frac{dv}{dt}, \tag{C.4}$$

which would be silly, since that's just multiplying by one, except if we group the terms—then things take on interesting physical meanings:

$$a\,\frac{dF(x)}{a\:dx} = \frac{m}{a}\,\frac{dv}{dt}\frac{a}{} \tag{C.5}$$

$$\Delta \text{ Pressure } \quad [\text{density}] \: [\text{volume flow}].$$

Looking at each term, a is area as defined. Force per unit area is pressure, which we will denote as P. Differential force per unit area is the change in pressure with spatial position, also called *pressure gradient*. Pressure gradient is important, because that's what causes flow. Mass per unit area, which we will denote as ρ (Greek letter rho), is a measure of air density. A gas area density might seem odd, but we will always be able to multiply it by particle flow rate to get mass flow. Air velocity multiplied by area is volume flow, which we denote as U. Pressure and volume flow are time varying (otherwise there's nothing worth writing all these equations for), so we get:

$$a\,\frac{dP(x,t)}{dx} = -\rho\,\frac{dU(x,t)}{dt}. \tag{C.6}$$

Now we use the physical equation for Conservation of Mass:

$$\frac{dU(x,t)}{dx} = -K\,\frac{dP(x,t)}{dt}, \tag{C.7}$$

where $K = a \: / \: c^2$, and c is the speed of sound in air. Putting equations C.6 and C.7 together, we get:

$$\frac{d^2U(x,t)}{dx^2} = \frac{1}{c^2}\frac{d^2U(x,t)}{dt^2} \tag{C.8}$$

or

$$\frac{d^2P(x,t)}{dx^2} = \frac{1}{c^2}\frac{d^2P(x,t)}{dt^2}. \tag{C.9}$$

Do Equations C.8 and C.9 look familiar? They should, because the form is exactly the same traveling wave equation we derived for the plucked string in Appendix B. Note that the area term has cancelled out in both traveling wave equations.

C.2 D'Alembert Solution to the Acoustic Tube Equation

Just as we proved the D'Alembert solution to the ideal string (Section B.1.2), we know that a solution to Equation C.9 for the acoustic tube is:

$$P_{\text{D'Al}} = P(x, t) = P_1(t + x/c) + P_r(t - x/c), \tag{C.10}$$

a sum of left- and right-going traveling wave components in the tube.

C.3 Relating Pressure and Velocity in Acoustic Tubes

We can relate pressure and velocity in the acoustic tube by going back to Equation C.5:

$$a\,\frac{dF(x)}{a\,dx} = \frac{m}{a}\frac{dv\,a}{dt} \tag{C.5}$$

$$\Delta\,\text{Pressure}\quad[\text{density}]\;[\text{volume flow}]$$

or

$$\frac{dP(x,t)}{dx} = \frac{\rho c}{a}\frac{dU(x,t)}{dt}. \tag{C.11}$$

We can also express this using the D'Alembert solution form:

$$\frac{dP^+(x,t)}{dx} + \frac{dP^-(x,t)}{dx} = \frac{\rho c}{a}\left(\frac{dU^+(x,t)}{dt} + \frac{dU^-(x,t)}{dt}\right). \tag{C.12}$$

These state that the spatial derivative of pressure is equal to a constant multiplied by the time derivative of flow. The constant $\rho c/a$ is called the *characteristic impedance*, which we will use in the next section.

C.4 The Acoustic Tube With Varying Cross-Sectional Area

We can rewrite Equation C.12 to account for the fact that area might change (abruptly) within the tube:

$$\frac{dP_m^+(x,t) + dP_m^-(x,t)}{dx} = \frac{\rho c}{a_m} \frac{dU_m^+(x,t) + dU_m^-(x,t)}{dt} \quad (C.13)$$

where m is the index of a particular section of the tube with constant area a_m. Figure C.2 shows a junction between two cylindrical acoustic tubes of different areas.

We can define a new term to encapsulate the density, speed of sound, and area terms:

$$\text{Characteristic impedance} = R_m = \frac{\rho c}{a_m}$$

and invoke once again some physical conservation and continuity constraints. First, at the boundary between two sections of tubing, volume flow must be conserved (conservation of mass). Also, pressure must be continuous at the precise point of the boundary (pressure is an energy term, and cannot change instantaneously in time or space without an infinite source of energy at that point). For the acoustic tube, the pressure continuity and flow conservation constraints dictate that:

$$P1 = P2 \qquad U1 = U2.$$

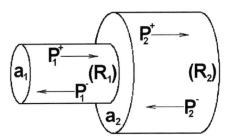

Figure C.2. Junction of two acoustic tubes with different areas.

If the areas of the two segments are different, and thus the characteristic impedances are also different, we can solve for the out-going pressures and velocities, as functions of the incoming ones:

$$P_1^- = \frac{R_2 - R_1}{R_2 + R_1}P_1^+ + \left(1 - \frac{R_2 - R_1}{R_2 + R_1}\right)P_2^- \tag{C.14}$$

$$P_2^+ = \left(1 + \frac{R_2 - R_1}{R_2 + R_1}\right)P_1^+ - \frac{R_2 - R_1}{R_2 + R_1}P_2^- \tag{C.15}$$

$$U_1^- = -\frac{R_2 - R_1}{R_2 + R_1}U_1^+ + \left(1 + \frac{R_2 - R_1}{R_2 + R_1}\right)U_2^- \tag{C.16}$$

$$U_2^+ = \left(1 - \frac{R_2 - R_1}{R_2 + R_1}\right)U_1^+ + \frac{R_2 - R_1}{R_2 + R_1}U_2^-. \tag{C.17}$$

To simplify things, we can define a new variable k to encapsulate the $R2 - R1 \, / \, R2 + R1$ relationship,

$$k = \frac{R_2 - R_1}{R_2 + R_1} = \frac{a_1 - a_2}{a_1 - a_2},$$

and rewrite the expressions of Equations C.14–C.17 as:

$$P_1^- = kP_1^+ + (1 - k)P_2^- \tag{C.18}$$

$$P_2^+ = (1 + k)P_1^+ - kP_2^- \tag{C.19}$$

$$U_1^- = -kU_1^+ + (1 + k)U_2^- \tag{C.20}$$

$$U_2^+ = (1 - k)U_1^+ + kU_2^-. \tag{C.21}$$

The variable k is called the *scattering coefficient,* (from wave scattering theory) and the equations are called *scattering equations.* They express the behavior of the wave equation at the boundary between acoustic tube segments of different characteristic impedances, where part of the incoming wave is transmitted to the next tube segment, and the remainder is reflected back into the other tube segment.

Note that if $k = 0$ (same area in both segments, no discontinuity, same characteristic impedance), the equations degenerate into simple waveguide transmission expressions:

$$P_1^- = P_2^- \qquad P_2^+ = P_1^+$$
$$U_1^- = U_2^- \qquad U_2^+ = U_1^+,$$

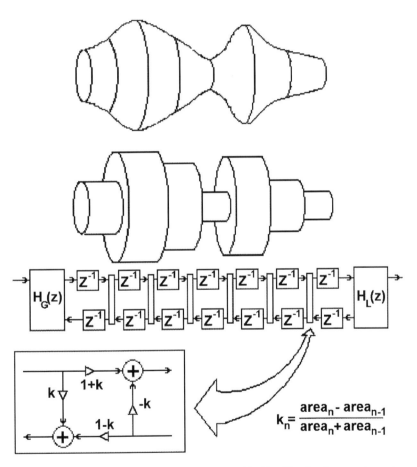

Figure C.3. Network of acoustic tube segments, and ladder filter implementation using chain of scattering junctions.

showing that the waves just continue on their one-directional ways. If $k = 1$ (area of segment 2 is zero), U_2 and P_2 must be zero because the area of that segment is zero. Plugging this into the equations indicate pure reflections at a closed tube end:

$$P_1^- = P_1^+$$
$$U_1^- = -U_1^+.$$

If $k = -1$, we get inverted reflection results for a right-going wave:

$$P_1^- = -P_1^+$$
$$U_1^- = U_1^+.$$

C.5 An Acoustic Tube Network

We can build a network of tube sections as shown in Figure C.3. The filter structure shown below which implements the chain of scattering relationships at the tube junctions is called a *ladder filter*. This is the basis of many models of the human voice. The reflection filters at each end represent the acoustic activity at the glottis (vocal folds) and at the lips.

Reading:

Philip Morse. "Vibration and Sound." *American Institute of Physics, for Acoustical Society of America* (1981).

D Sound Examples and Code

D.1 Sound Examples
Available at http://www.akpeters.com/rss/

Chapter 1

Chapter 2

Chapter 3
[Track 11] One-Pole Filtered Speech, $r = 0.9, 0.95, 0.99,-0.9,-0.95, -0.99$.
[Track 12] BiQuad Filtered Noise and Music.
[Track 13] Noise Filtered Through Topologies of Figures 3.15 and 3.16.

Chapter 4
[Track 14] Direct and Discrete Mass/Spring/Damper Oscillations.
[Track 15] Guitar Pluck Edge Versus Center, "Playing Overtones."
[Track 16] Coffee Mug Strike and Residual.
[Track 17] A Variety of Metallic/Glass Modal Sounds.
[Track 18] A Variety of Wooden Modal Sounds.

Chapter 5
[Track 19] Building a Square Wave from Sine Waves (Bottom Up/Top Down).
[Track 20] Convolving an "ahh" Impulse with a Pulse Train to Make "ahh."
[Track 21] "Synthesize" and Individual Frames.

Chapter 6
[Track 22] Harmonic Sounds: Trumpet, "ahh," and "eee."
[Track 23] Inharmonic Sounds: Synth Bell, Stone Tile, Djembe Drum.
[Track 24] White Noise, Pink Noise, Whispered "ahh" and "eee."
[Track 25] Marimba Strike and Residue, Voice Original, Periodic, and Residue.
[Track 26] Transient Extraction/Modeling (From Verma and Meng).

Chapter 7
[Track 27] Original "Synthesize" and Separate Octave Subbands.
[Track 28] Cross-Synthesis Examples.
[Track 29] Phase Vocoder Pitch and Time Shifting Examples.

Chapter 8
[Track 30] Impulse Train Filtered through "ahh" Filter Yields Subtractive "ahh."
[Track 31] Speech Original, LPC Residual, Resynthesis, Pulse Resynthesis.
[Track 32] Guitar Pluck, LPC Residual, Resynthesis, Pulse Resynthesis.
[Track 33] Hammer Nail, LPC Parametric Resynthesis.

Chapter 9
[Track 34] Simple Plucked String.
[Track 35] More Complete Plucked String.
[Track 36] Bowed-String Model.
[Track 37] Weak All-Pass Stiffness in a String Model.
[Track 38] Banded Waveguide Bar.

Chapter 10

[Track 39] Nonlinear Mass/Spring/Damper System.
[Track 40] Plucked String and Drum Displacement-Modulated Pitch.
[Track 41] Guitar Chatter Nonlinearity.
[Track 42] Simulated Sitar/Dobro Model.
[Track 43] Various FM Sounds.

Chapter 11

[Track 44] Synthesized Clarinet.
[Track 45] Real and Synthesized Blown Bottles.

Chapter 12

[Track 46] Synthesized Square Membrane Modes, Built Up.
[Track 47] Rectangular Waveguide Mesh sounds, from Scott Van Duyne
[Track 48] Deformable Mesh Bouncing Bowl Sound (see also Movie).
[Track 49] Struck Tibetan Prayer Bowls.

Chapter 13

[Track 50] Building Up FOFS to Synthesize a Voice.
[Track 51] Synthesized Police/Referee Whistles.
[Track 52] PhISEM Synthesis of Maraca, Cabasa, Sekere.
[Track 53] PhISEM Tambourine and Sleighbells Sythesis.
[Track 54] PhISEM Bamboo Wind Chimes and Anklung Synthesis.
[Track 55] PhISEM Coins in Mug Synthesis.

Chapter 14

[Track 56] Hard and Soft Guitar Picks, Raw Picks.
[Track 57] Hard and Soft Wooden Bar Strikes, Residuals.
[Track 58] Strikes of Prayer Bowl.
[Track 59] Bowed-String Synthesis.
[Track 60] Bowed Prayer Bowl, Wine Glass, Squeaky Door.
[Track 61] Texture-Dependent Granular Scraping-Type Synthesis.
[Track 62] Ratchet-Type Synthesis.

See also movie files of controllers.

Chapter 15

[Track 63] Real/Synthesized Walking Sounds.

Chapter 16

[Track 64] Sonification of Stock/Blood Pressure Data.

See also movie files of PholieMat, DigitalDoo, BoSSA, r!g, and animation "Seen in Shadow."

D.2 Source Code and Other Materials Available in Online Data Segment

All .c files operate on 16-bit, mono only sound files. The type of sound file depends on the byte-ordering of your machine. For Intel or other Little Endian machines, use .wav format. For Big Endian machines use .snd files. Edit waveio.h to select your architecture before compiling any .c file. Typing any .c executable without arguments gives the useage. Please also consult Appendix E for information on the .cpp files, which are part of the Synthesis Toolkit in C++. See also documentation (individual README files, etc.) availble at http://www.akpeters.com/rss/.

waveio.h	Wave header management.
quantize.c	Quantize a sound file to N bits.
srconvrt.c	Pitch shift a sound file using linear, sinc, or no interp.
mulaw.c	Compress a sound file using mu law, write .mu file.
demulaw.c	Decompress a Mu law file to a sound file.
adpcmcod.c	Compress a sound file using ADPCM, write .adp file.
adpcmdec.c	Decompress an ADPCM file to a sound file.
timeshif.c	Overlap-add time shifting of a sound file.
filter.c	Filter a sound file using coefficients from a .spc file.
ResoLab.cpp	TCL/TK GUI control of filtered pulse/noise waveforms.
masprdmp.c	Mass/spring/damper simulation writes a sound file.
GUIModal	TCL/TK GUI control of struck modal synthesis.
fft.c	Calculate FFT of sound file; write .fft file (or back).
peaksfft.c	Print N peaks in .fft file, optional sinusoidal synthesis.
notchfft.c	Remove (or leave) peaks of .fft file; write new .fft file.
pitch.c	FFT peak and Autocorrelation pitch estimation of sound file.
convolve.c	Convolve two sound files.
reverse.c	Reverse a sound file.
subband.c	Write out (as fft files) octave subbands of fft file.
vocod.c	Implement vocoder cross-synthesis using two fft files.
fitlpc.c	Calculate and write lpc analysis of sound file.
lpcresyn.c	Resynthesize sound file from .lpc file, with options.
wv2float.c	Convert soundfile to floating point file.
float2wv.c	Convert floating point sample file to soundfile.
STKDemo	GUI Controller for all STK instruments.
Plucked.cpp	Program with TCL/TK GUI for plucked string synthesis.
Mandolin.cpp	Program with TCL/TK GUI for mandolin synthesis.
Bowed.cpp	Program with TCL/TK GUI for bowed-string synthesis.
StifKarp.cpp	Program with TCL/TK GUI for all-pass stiff string synthesis.
GUIBowedBar.cpp	Program with TCL/TK GUI for bowed-bar synthesis.
GUIPlukStruck	Program with TCL/TK GUI for plucked-string synthesis.
nlmsprdm.c	Nonlinear mass/spring/damper simulation, write sound file.
Sitar.cpp	Program with TCL/TK GUI for nonlinear sitar synthesis.

Clarinet.cpp	Program with TCL/TK GUI for clarinet synthesis.
BotlBlow.cpp	Program with TCL/TK GUI for blown bottle synthesis.
WGMesh.cpp	Program with TCL/TK GUI for waveguide mesh synthesis.
Shakers.cpp	Program with TCL/TK GUI for PhISEM synthesis.
GaitLab.cpp	Program with TCL/TK GUI for walking synthesis.
scrub.c	Mouse drag program for controlling PhISEM synthesis.

Synthesis Toolkit (see Appendix E).

Movie Files:

Various shaker/other controllers

PhOLIEMat

DigitalDoo, Perry Cook

BoSSA, Dan Trueman

R!g, Curtis Bahn

"Seen in Shadow," Grady Klein, Lena Petrovic, Adam Finkelstein, Brian Fujito, music by TrollStilt (Dan Trueman and Monica Mugan), sound Effects software by Perry Cook

Other files:

Various MIDI files for generating synthesis examples.

Other source files for examples in the book and online.

The Synthesis Toolkit
in C++

Many thanks to Gary Scavone of McGill University (formerly of Stanford's Center for Computer Research in Music and Acoustics) for writing large amounts of this documentation, and for supporting and expanding the Synthesis ToolKit over the years. Thanks also to those on the STK mailist and other STK users for giving us great feedback and code improvements.

E.1 What is the Synthesis Toolkit?

The *Synthesis ToolKit in C++* (STK) is a set of audio signal processing and synthesis C++ classes and algorithms. You can use these classes to create programs that make sounds with a variety of synthesis techniques. This is not a terribly novel concept, except that the Synthesis Toolkit is extremely portable (it's mostly platform-independent C and C++ code), and it is completely user-extensible (no libraries, no hidden drivers, all source code is included). This means that the code you write today (and the code we've written over the last 10 years) will still work in another 10 years. It currently runs with real-time support (audio and MIDI) on SGI (Irix), Linux, Windows, and Mac (OSX) computer platforms. Non-real-time support has been tested under NeXTStep, SunOS, and other platforms, and should work for soundfile creation with any standard C++ compiler.

The Synthesis Toolkit is free for noncommercial use. The only parts of the Synthesis Toolkit that are platform-dependent concern real-time sound and MIDI input and output, and all of that is taken care of in a few special classes. The communications interface for both MIDI and the simple Tcl/Tk *Graphical User Interfaces* (GUIs) is the same. This makes it easy to experiment in real time using either the GUIs, or MIDI, or both. The Synthesis ToolKit can generate simultaneous .snd, .wav, .aif, and .mat output soundfile formats (as well as realtime sound output); thus, you can view your results using one of a large variety of sound/signal analysis tools already available (e.g., Snd, Cool Edit, Goldwave, Matlab).

The Synthesis Toolkit isn't one particular program. Rather, it is a set of C++ classes that you can use to create your own programs. A few example applications are provided to demonstrate some of the ways to use the classes. If you have specific needs, you will probably have to either modify the example programs or write a new program altogether. Further, the example programs don't have a fancy GUI wrapper. If you feel the need to have a "drag and drop" graphical patching GUI, you probably don't want to use the ToolKit. Spending hundreds of hours making platform-dependent graphics code would go against one of the fundamental design goals of the ToolKit—platform independence.

For those instances where a simple GUI with sliders and buttons is helpful, we use Tcl/Tk (which is freely distributed for all the supported ToolKit platforms). A number of Tcl/Tk GUI scripts are distributed with the ToolKit release. For control, the Synthesis Toolkit uses raw MIDI (on supported platforms), and SKINI (*Synthesis ToolKit Instrument Network Interface*, a MIDI-like text message synthesis control format). See the ToolKit documentation at http://www.akpeters.com/rss/ for more information on SKINI.

This software was created to be made publicly available for free, primarily for academic and research purposes, so if you use it, pass it on with this documentation, and for free. If you make a million dollars with it, you have to promise to seek out Perry and Gary and buy us a sandwich if we're poor. Better yet, give us some real money. If you make music compositions with it, put us in the program notes. If you make movie sound effects with it, put us in the credits. Some of the concepts are covered by various patents, some are known to us, and others that are likely unknown. Many of the ones known to us are administered by the Stanford Office of Technology and Licensing. The good news is that large hunks of the techniques used here are public domain. To avoid subtle legal issues, we will not state what's freely useable here in terms of algorithms, but we will try to note within the various classes where certain things are likely to be protected by patents.

The Synthesis Toolkit is free. Thus, we don't have to guarantee anything. We've been hacking on this code for a long time now and most of it seems to work pretty well. But there are certainly some bugs floating around. Sometimes things work fine on one computer platform but not so fine on another. FPU overflows and underflows cause very weird behavior that also depends on the particular CPU and OS. Let us know about bugs you find and we'll do our best to correct them.

E.2 A Brief History of the Development of The Synthesis ToolKit

In the early 1990s, Perry Cook began developing a precursor to the Synthesis ToolKit (also called STK) in Objective C under NeXTStep at the Center for Computer Research in Music and Acoustics (CCRMA) at Stanford University. With his move to Princeton University in 1996, he ported everything to C++ on SGI hardware, added real-time capabilities, and greatly expanded the synthesis techniques available. With the help of Bill Putnam, Perry also made a port of the ToolKit to Windows95. Gary Scavone began using it extensively in the summer of 1997 and completed a full port to Linux early in 1998. He finished the fully compatible Windows port (using Direct Sound API) in June 1998. Numerous improvements and extensions have been made since then. The C++ Toolkit has been distributed continuously since 1996 via the Princeton Sound Kitchen (http://www.music.princeton.edu/psk), Perry Cook's home page at Princeton (http://www.cs.princeton.edu/~prc), Gary Scavone's Homepage at CCRMA (http://www-ccrma.stanford.edu/~gary), and the main ToolKit home page at CCRMA (http://www-ccrma.stanford.edu/software/stk). The ToolKit has been included in various collections of software over the time of distribution. Much of it has also been ported to MAX/MSP on Macintosh computers by Dan Trueman and Luke Dubois of Columbia University, and is distributed as PeRColate (http://music.columbia.edu/PeRColate). Help on real-time sound and MIDI has been provided by Tim Stilson, Bill Putnam, Gabriel Maldonado, Ge Wang, and Ari Lazier.

E.3 Synthesizing Sound in Real Time

Synthesis Toolkit real-time support is provided for Linux, SGI, and Windows95/ 98/2000/XP operating systems. Real-time functions include audio and MIDI input/output, and SKINI control input via sockets and/or pipes. Real-time SKINI control input via pipes is possible under Linux, SGI, and Windows2k/ XP only. Control input and audio output options are typically specified as command-line arguments to ToolKit programs. For example, the demo (basic synthesis) program is invoked as:

demo instrument flags,

where instruments can be any of:

Clarinet: Pretty good physical model of the clarinet
BlowHole: Clarinet physical model with tonehole and register vent
Saxophony: Pretty good physical model of the saxophone
Flute: Pretty good physical model of the flute
Brass: Simple physical model of a brass instrument
Bowed: Simple physical model of a bowed-string instrument
BotlBlow: Simple Helmholtz model of blown bottle
Plucked: Basic plucked-string physical model
Stiff: Basic plucked-string with added all-pass stiffness
Mandolin: Two-string commuted mandolin physical model
Sitar: Nonlinear string model
Rhodey: Rhodes-like electric piano FM synthesis model
Wurley: Wurlitzer-like electric piano FM synthesis model
TubeBell: FM synthesis model
HeavyMtl: Distorted synthesizer FM synthesis model
PercFlut: Percussive flute-like FM synthesis model
BeeThree: Cheezy organ FM synthesis model
Moog: Swept filter sampler
FMVoices: Three-formant FM voice synthesis
VoicForm: Source/Filter voice synthesis
Resonate: Four formants excited by noise/pulse
Drummer: Drum sample synthesis
Shakers: Various stochastic event models
BandedWB: Banded waveguide model, bar, bowl, wine glass
ModalBar: Four struck resonances, marimba, vibraphone, much more
Mesh2D: Simple 10 × 10 waveguide mesh
Whistle: Physical model of referee/police whistle

and flags can be any or all of:

-or for real-time audio output
-ow for .wav soundfile output
-os for .snd soundfile output

-om for .mat MAT-file output
-oa for .aif soundfile output
-if for reading SKINI file
-ip for real-time SKINI control input via piping
-is for real-time SKINI control input via socketing
-im for MIDI control input
-s use other than default sample rate
-n to specify the number of voices to allocate (default 1).

The <-ip> and <-is> flags are used when piping or socketing real-time SKINI control data to a Synthesis ToolKit program. The <-im> flag is used to read MIDI control input from your MIDI port. Note that you can use all three input types simultaneously under SGI, Linux, and Windows2K/XP. Assuming a successful compilation of the demo program, typing:

demo BeeThree -or if scores/bookert.ski

from the demo directory will play the scorefile bookert.ski using the BeeThree additive organ instrument and stream the resulting audio data in real time to the audio output channel of your computer. Typing demo without any arguments will provide a full program usage description.

E.4 Non-Real-Time Soundfile Synthesis

Non-real-time operation of Synthesis ToolKit programs is possible under all supported operating systems. In theory, it should be possible to compile the source code for non-real-time use on any computer platform with a C++ compiler. Complications will sometimes arise with regard to random number generators, or byte ordering. In non-real-time mode, it is assumed that input control messages are provided from a SKINI scorefile, and that audio output is written to a soundfile (.snd, .wav, .aif, .mat, .raw). A number of SKINI scorefiles are provided in the scores directory of the demo project. Assuming a successful compilation of the demo program, typing:

demo BeeThree -ow myfile.wav -if scores/bookert.ski

from the demo directory will use the scorefile bookert.ski to control the BeeThree additive organ instrument and writing the resulting audio data to a .wav soundfile called "myfile.wav." Typing demo without any arguments will provide a full program usage description.

E.5 An Example Instrument: Blown Bottle

To see how a sound synthesis algorithm would be implemented in the Synthesis ToolKit, we will refer back to the blown bottle model developed in Chapter 11 (Figure 11.8). Example E.1 below shows the basic calculations performed in the tick( ) function of the BotlBlow.cpp instrument. Almost every object in the Synthesis ToolKit implements a tick function. Calling tick causes the object to calculate a single time step, yielding an output sample. All tick functions return a floating point numeric value that is the result of the calculation. Tick functions for objects that require an input take a floating point argument. Examples of these would include filters, delay lines, wave output objects, etc. Thus, calling something like

$$OUT = filter \rightarrow tick(IN)$$

would cause the filter to do all of its internal calculations using IN as input, and would set OUT equal to the output value calculated by the filter.

The blown bottle instrument has an ADSR envelope generator that models the blowing across the bottle neck, thus the tick function of the blown bottle does not accept any input. After the ADSR is ticked, noise is added proportionately to the envelope output value, and also modulated by the differential blowing and bottle pressure. Next, the current differential pressure is calculated, and used as an input to the jet reflection coefficient table. The net pressure input to the bottle resonator is calculated to be the noise-modulated breath pressure, minus the jet-table coefficient multiplied by the delta pressure. This might not look exactly like the block diagram of Figure 11.8, but algebra ensures that calculating

$$BottleInput = (1-\alpha)*BlowPressure + \alpha*BottlePressure,$$

is exactly the same as calculating

$$BottleInput = BlowPressure - \alpha*(BlowPressure - BottlePressure)$$

$$= BlowPressure - \alpha*DeltaPressure.$$

The bottle resonance is calculated by ticking the BiQuad resonator filter with the bottle input, and the result is conditioned for output by removing the constant (ambient) pressure. This constant pressure is important for the behavior of the model, but is not acoustically important for us hearing the oscillation, so we remove it.

```
MY_FLOAT BotlBlow :: tick()
{
    StkFLOAT temp;
    StkFLOAT randPressure;
    static StkFLOAT dPressure;
    static StkFLOAT reflPressure;
    StkFLOAT breathPressure;

    /* Breath Pressure */
    breathPressure = adsr->tick();
    /* Random Deviation */
    randPressure = noiseGain * noise->tick();
    /* Scale by Breath Pressure and delta pressure */
    randPressure *= breathPressure;
    randPressure *= (1.0 + dPressure);
    /* New delta pressure */
    dPressure = breathPressure - reflPressure;
    /*  Evaluate jet function */
    temp = jetTable->lookup(dPressure) ;
    /* Non-Lin Jet + reflected */
    reflPressure = breathPressure + randPressure -
        (temp * dPressure);
    /* Apply bottle resonance */
    reflPressure = resonator->tick(reflPressure);
    /* Normalize wave and remove constant pressure */
    lastOutput = 0.1 * outputGain *
    dcBlock->tick(dPressure);
    return lastOutput;
}
```

Example E.1. C++ Code for Blown Bottle.

Other C++ methods in the BotlBlow class allow setting the noise level, adjusting the resonant frequency, and controlling the blowing amount.

E.6 Real-Time Synthesis Control

There are a number of Tcl/Tk GUIs supplied with the Synthesis ToolKit projects. These scripts require Tcl/Tk version 8.0 or later, which can be downloaded for free over the internet. On Unix and Windows2k/XP platforms, you can run the various GUI executable scripts (e.g., GUIPhysical) provided with each project to start everything up (you may need to symbolically link the wishXX executable to the name wish). The Physical (physical.bat) script implements the following command-line sequence:

wish < tcl/Physical.tcl | demo Clarinet -or −ip.

The following operations are necessary to establish a socket connection between the Tcl/Tk GUI and the synthesis program:

1. Open a DOS shell and start the syntmono program with the -is flag

syntmono Clarinet -or -is.

2. Double-click the Tcl/Tk GUI (e.g., tcl/TCLPhys.tcl), or type in another DOS shell:

wish < tcl/TCLPhys.tcl.

3. Establish the socket connection by selecting "Socket" under the Communications menu item in the Tcl/Tk GUI.

Note that it is possible to specify a hostname when establishing the socket connection from the socket client. Thus, the Synthesis ToolKit socket server program and the Tcl/Tk GUI need not necessarily reside on the same computer. This can be a powerful capability, allowing controllers, sensors, or simulations on one machine to control sound synthesis on another.

On all supported real-time platforms, you can direct real-time MIDI input to a Synthesis Toolkit instrument by using the <-im> flag

demo Clarinet -or –im.

E.7 Classes and Instruments

Here we'll highlight the main applications and sound producing algorithms. See the documentation (available from http://www.akpeters.com/rss/ or with any Synthesis ToolKit release) for much more information on the Synthesis ToolKit, and also check the websites for breaking updates and new algorithms/ instruments.

Stand Alone Synthesis Programs and Other Example Programs:

demo.cpp—Demonstration program for most synthesis algorithms
effects.cpp—Demonstration program for the effects algorithms
ragamatic.cpp—Nirvana just waiting to happen
examples/—Directory with a number of examples and utility programs

Synthesis Classes:

Clarinet: Pretty good physical model of the clarinet
Flute: Pretty good physical model of the flute
Brass: Simple physical model of a brass instrument
Bowed: Simple physical model of a bowed-string instrument
BlowHole: Clarinet physical model with tonehole and register vent
BotlBlow: Simple Helmholtz model of blown bottle
Saxophony: Pretty good physical model of the saxophone
Plucked: Basic plucked-string physical model
StifKarp: Basic plucked-string with added all-pass stiffness
Mandolin: Two-string commuted mandolin physical model
Sitar: Nonlinear string model
BandedWG: Banded waveguide model, bar, bowl, wine glass
ModalBar: Four struck resonances, marimba, vibraphone, much more
Mesh2D: Simple waveguide mesh
Rhodey: Rhodes-like electric piano FM synthesis model
Wurley: Wurlitzer-like electric piano FM synthesis model
TubeBell: FM synthesis model
HeavyMtl: Distorted synthesizer FM synthesis model
PercFlut: Percussive flute-like FM synthesis model
BeeThree: Cheezy organ FM synthesis model
Moog1: Swept-filter sampler
FMVoices: Three-formant FM voice synthesis
VoicForm: Four-formant source/filter voice
Sampler: Simple sampling synthesizer
Moog: Wavetable/filter synthesizer
Simple: Simple wavetable/noise instrument
Resonate: Wavetable, noise, and 3 resonances
Drummer: Drum synthesizer
Tabla: Sample-based tabla drums
VoicDrums: Indian tabla vocalize sample instrument
Whistle: Physical model of referee/police whistle
Shakers: stochastic granular model,
    Maraca
    Sekere
    Cabasa
    Bamboo
    Water Drops
    Tambourine
    Sleigh Bells

Guiro
Wrench
Coke Can
Sticks
Crunch
Sand Paper
Snow
Grass
BigRocks
LittleRocks
CupCoins
Ice Cubes

Various reverberators and audio effects are also available.

E.8 The ChucK Audio/Music Programming Language

ChucK is a new programming language for music and audio signal processing that emphasizes ease of use, accurate control of timing, concurrency (multiple small programs running in parallel), and on-the-fly programming (add/delete/modify code while the audio engine continues to run). The entirety of STK is compiled into ChucK as native unit generators (UGs), along with many more UGs for added functionality. ChucK accepts control input from MIDI, Open Sound Control, mice, joysticks, the computer keyboard, and a variety of other devices.

ChucK is open source and available for free from http://chuck.cs.princeton.edu

E.9 Conclusions

Consult the documentation at http://www.akpeters.com/rss/ for more information on the Synthesis ToolKit in C++. Also watch the main Synthesis ToolKit website for updates and late breaking news at http://www-ccrma.stanford.edu/software/stk/.

Index

Printed and bound by CPI Group (UK) Ltd, Croydon, CR0 4YY

22/10/2024

01777624-0004